Dawn of the End-Time Remnant

While every precaution has been taken in the preparation of this book, the publisher assumes no responsibility for errors or omissions, or for damages resulting from the use of the information contained herein.

DAWN OF THE END-TIME REMNANT

First edition. October 27, 2022.

ISBN: 979-8215199459

Written by Riaan Engelbrecht.

Table of Contents

To God be the glory. And to my wife, Lynette, thank you for all your motivation, inspiration and strength.

Paul never glamorised the gospel! It is not success, but sacrifice! It's not a glamorous gospel , but a bloody gospel, a gory gospel, and a sacrificial gospel! 5 minutes inside eternity and we will wish that we had sacrificed more! Wept more, bled more, grieved more, loved more, prayed more, gave more!

Leonard Ravenhill

The rise of the end-time remnant

What is this end-time remnant? It is the true Bride on the earth; therefore, the sons and daughters who seek God, who follow Him, and who uphold God's values, ways, and will as established in the eternal Kingdom. Yes, the dawn rises of God's end-time remnant, those who are humble, pure in spirit, and who are called to free the lost from the clutches of darkness through the Blood of Jesus.

They are born for a time like this. Born to fight. Born to worship. Born to usher in the last and greatest reformation, which will see a return to the truth of God! God is seeking His true worshippers who walk in love, truth and honesty, seeking no glory but only His will. The Lord is raising those who have a heart and a voice for the Kingdom. He is raising an army that refuses to be silent, who will not flinch in times of trial or tribulation, will not shy away when faced with evil and who will not compromise His Truth. They are rising in the earth because the King is coming; there is a harvest to be collected.

Such an army is right now being formed on the earth, the remnant that will arise out of the ruins of religiosity and carnality. They are like the 7000 faithful who God said to Elijah refused to bow the knee before Baal. Yes, this is a dangerous remnant, filled by the Spirit of God, for they will be like the first apostles and disciples. They are dangerous because they are not unsettled by Baal, do not fear man, and laugh along with God, who loves His enemies. They are dangerous because they love the truth, and they know the battle belongs to God.

These are indeed glorious days of the movement of the Lord. These are the days to arise, to awake and heed the Lord's call. Come all from the valleys, from the mountains, over the rivers, out of the dark, out of slavery, to heed the Lord and to praise Him. Praise the Lord, oh my soul; praise Him, for the Lord establishes His Kingdom to reign eternal and true. Let the watchmen, the obedient and the faithful and the true arise with a song and a hope in the strength of the Spirit. For this is the remnant who loves the Lord above all else!

The Lord is calling, establishing foundations, restoring order, calming the waves of fearful notions and setting the spiritual captive free. Come one and come all, for the harvest is here – shall we reap the lost or shall we weep for lack of gain? These are the days for the spiritual fire to fall as in the days of Elijah, when the Lord sifts and refines His Bride while declaring Himself Lord and King. Yet by fire and Spirit, He will shake all things, every foundation and stronghold and every altar and every word and every deed that stands against Him.

These are the days of the outpouring to birth rivers of life – spiritual rivers within the darkened soul and the caged mind. These are days of purification, refinement and revival for a time and a season. This is a time for the birth of His glory within His Bride. A time and a season have been granted to gather the Harvest until the one of lawlessness comes. This is the time and season for His power and might to flow for His manifested glory, for His manifested presence and for Him to turn us back to His heart in an intimate embrace.

These are such days where He is reminding His people who He is – He is the only and true Living God, and He should be our only hope, strength, life and joy. There is no other, and only in Him can we trust, for He is faithful and true. He reminds us that we exist for He exists, and He is the essence and the existence of all. Why then shall we doubt or fear the terrors of the night or the burdens of the world? For in Him is the liberty and glorious eternal promise of freedom.

The Lord remains active and seated on the Throne. He is moving, seeking those who will follow Him and not merely a religion. What more can we say except that all toil and labour and effort and achievements in this world fade to dust and pass into a distant memory, for all that remains and is of worth and effort is that we are remembered by the Lord eternal. We may conquer lands, invade empires, build bridges, be glorious in thought and deeds, yet it fades with the passing of summer to winter, over time and age, over blossom and harvest time, from springs to ice caps, yet all that is important is when we lay down to sleep the deep sleep that out of the darkness, a waking occurs where we hear our name being whispered to awaken unto His presence. Shall we not, through humility and a sound resolve of being a servant, strive to please the Master and make a contribution to the eternal empire where the sun never fades, instead of striving to impress our vanity and ego upon this world?

What then can we say except that we are made in spirit to return unto spirit, to strive to be rid of the temporary, to rise above the mundane, to soar in the liberty of the Spirit so that we may seize the eternal magnitude of being given life – a life bound by a deep sense of belonging to divinity and a paradise prepared unto us. After all the striving and toil, all that remains is the truth that we have been created by divinity, destined to be returned unto divinity, where all earthly striving for knowledge, understanding, and wisdom collapses like a soldier weary from the battle.

What then can be said that we must work in faith and in the Spirit to be free, to be liberated, to be reborn, to rise, to awake from our slumber and to embrace the Lord? Shall we then not all seek His glory and majesty, for is He not enough? Shall we then not let go of the chains that bind and together arise in the splendour of the freedom that was paid for by Blood? For in Him, and His glorious

Son and the glorious Spirit, there abides a rest and the abounding and ever eternal peace and joy – a joy and peace beyond human comprehension or beyond human understanding.

He is the Living God who holds man in His right hand. There is none like Him, for there is no other. Only those who seek Him and yearn and long for Him as their hope and delight, and only those who take refuge in Him and who seek Him as their strength, shall see the Promised Land.

For this will be a remnant of 'dark horses', those who have been deemed to be nobodies, who have been judged as we judge a book by the cover, those who have been ridiculed, mocked, dismissed, laughed at and who apparently will amount to nothing. Watch out for these 'dark horses'. Those who shake the gates of hell are those who burn for God, who yearn for His Presence and who will not relent in serving God. They will be like the two witnesses of Revelation 11 for they have the power to shut heaven, so that no rain falls in the days of their prophecy, and they have power over waters to turn them to blood, and to strike the earth with all plagues, as often as they desire.

They will be those without fancy degrees, titles or even 'impressive' credentials. God is not interested in that, for He is interested in our hearts, our minds, and our willingness to serve, to yield, submit, surrender and seek His beauty and glory of His splendour above all else. It is they who agree with Paul, who wrote in "Galatians 1:11 But I make known to you, brethren, that the gospel which was preached by me is not according to man. 12 For I neither received it from man, nor was I taught it, but it came through the revelation of Jesus Christ." Some will say as Paul did in 2 Corinthians 11 that "even though I am untrained in speech, yet I am not in knowledge" (verse six). They will speak as God leads, for their words are anointed just as when a lump of hot coal touched and purified the lips of Isaiah.

These are the young and the old, for what matters is boldness and faithfulness. They are relentless, fearless and devoted to God, like a young Timothy. Paul spoke of being filled with joy because of Timothy's genuine faith (verses 4, 5). He also encouraged Timothy to "13 Hold fast the pattern of sound words which you have heard from me, in faith and love which are in Christ Jesus," and "1 Timothy 4:12 Let no one despise your youth, but be an example to the believers in word, in conduct, in love, in spirit, in faith, in purity." God is calling for a remnant who holds onto the faith, who seeks purity, and who shall not be moved by the opinions or the narratives of this world!

Romans 8 says, "19 For the earnest expectation of the creation eagerly waits for the revealing of the sons of God. 20 For the creation was subjected to futility, not willingly, but because of Him who subjected it in hope; 21 because the creation itself also will be delivered from the bondage of corruption into the glorious liberty of the children of God." Watch out for the true Bride, for this is the royal priesthood of 1 Peter 2!

The remnant will rebuild the ruins of God's watchtowers and the walls of his Kingdom as they declare liberty to the captive and freedom for the broken-hearted. They move in the power of the Spirit to declare the Gospel of the Kingdom! They are rising for the Lord calls them to become lions in the spirit to move in the power of God. For the power of God does not move because of man's supposed intellect, wisdom, status or fortune. It moves where the disciples yield in submission to the divine touch of God, abiding in His holy presence to be a vessel for His glory.

God knows the true remnant. He sees and He alone empowers and equips as He did with Paul, Joseph, Moses and many others. God is looking for the brave, the courageous, the bold, and those who seek Him as the true and only king. Watch out for the dangerous remnant, says God, for they will be the greatest messengers and servants for God in these last and perilous days.

For the Spirit of the Lord is moving across the world, interrupting lives, uprooting, shaking, breathing life for the time of the great harvest is here and the great separation of the weed and the wheat. This is the time of the great outpouring, of the fire of revival, but also the fire of judgment. For look, the Lord who holds the winnowing fork in His hands, He who baptises in fire, stands by the door and He knocks! For the heavens declare His Glory, and He calls His sons and daughters to arise. For such a time is upon us now, for those who look at the cross and behold Him shall surely be washed by the Blood, sealed by the Spirit and redeemed!

David Wilkerson, in his 1973 prophecy, saw the rise of the apostate church and the rise of the remnant. Regarding the apostate church, he saw it as a union that would start as a cooperative charity program, and it would end in a political union. This visible super world church, he said, would be spiritual in name only, freely using the name of Jesus Christ, but would in fact be antichrist and political in many of its activities.

Praise the Lord, he also saw the rise of another 'super church' during the end-times. Instead of being political like the first church, this one would have almost no political power. Instead, they would be filled with supernatural power. Instead of speaking out openly and visibly like the first church, the second church would be silent on social issues and would operate invisibly to the world, even going underground to avoid severe persecution. Wilkerson saw great persecution against this church; however, the same persecution that forces them to go underground would also cause them to unite and draw closer to the Lord. The prophecy declared that in God's supernatural power, they would boldly proclaim the gospel throughout the world.

According to Wilkerson, the supernatural, invisible church would be a union of deeply spiritual followers of Jesus Christ, bound together through the Holy Spirit and mutual confidence in Christ and His word.

This supernatural church of true believers will include Catholics and Protestants of all denominations, young and old, black and white, and people of all nations. Glory to God, it was shown to Wilkerson how these believers will be less concerned about denominational ties and more concerned with an emphasis on the coming of Jesus Christ. The Holy Spirit will bring them together as one people in all walks of life.

Wilkerson mentioned that while this visible super church (apostate) gains political power this invisible body of believers will grow tremendously in spiritual power.

Glory to God, this is the remnant! This is the tribe of warriors who remain to be quiet! For this army surely walks in the steps of the Shepherd – He who is the Lamb slain before the foundation of the world was laid. It is He who is the Lion of Judah that returns with the hose of heaven. He calls for the 'dangerous' and the 'fearless' to come forth, for they will shake even the foundations of the earth. God is calling forth the faithful remnant, liberating them from religious systems, programmes and agendas to be true worshippers in spirit and truth. For in the process of liberation – a release of bondages and yokes - they will again know who God is and serve with a pure heart.

Indeed, the Lord is calling for sons and daughters who seek no recognition, award, reward, praise or applause. For they are like John the Baptist, eager, hungry, willing and ready to serve. These are the ones who have a true heart of the Kingdom and will cry repent, for indeed the coming of the Lord is upon us! For such sons and daughters of the Kingdom will prepare the way of the Lord. They shall make straight the paths of the Lord! They shall declare His holiness, His righteousness, and they shall not shy away from the cross, mock the Blood, for they are sold out, they are ready, they are willing, and they have bent their knee to the true Lord and King. They shall remain standing in the storm, they shall remain standing when the mountains shake, and they shall remain standing when the world flees to hide from the majesty of the Lord! For those who speak in His Voice know it is not about them, but about the Lord! It is not about their pleasure, gain, truth, plans, or dreams, but it is about the plan, purpose and truth of the everlasting Kingdom!

Understand says the Lord, there are many like John the Baptist who for a while and a season have been in the wilderness, crying out, struggling, suffering, sacrificing and hoping for a better day. But take heart, says the Lord, for the remnant is untamed by religion or traditions. They are wild for God, and they are ready to gallop. For out of the wilderness they will come, no more hidden but revealed, but unveiled, for as Lazarus came out of the tomb, so the Lord cries to His manifested sons and daughters to embrace the light of His Glory! Yes, they will run and not grow weary, and they shall walk and not grow faint.

How they love the Lord, His Word and His Kingdom! Yes, they yearn for God day and night, for they have been revived. The Lord says I will lead them as I led Israel by a pillar of fire and cloud. The Lord shall separate the light from the dark, and He will reveal the glory of His majesty and divinity. God will let their voices be heard! Yes, servants of God who are burning with the Spirit and who rejoice that the Word is like a fire in their bones. I will let their hearts burn for Me, says the Lord! Watch out for the remnant, for soon they gallop and run free to shine the light of the eternal hope of glory.

The Lord seeks those who, like John, sacrificed it all, who lost themselves for the sake of His Glory and laid it all down to gain the great honour of beholding the Lord in His Glory. For John's obedience, toiling for years in the wilderness, he was allowed to baptise Jesus Himself! Yes, there is a great reward for those who seek the Lord above all, no matter the cost or the price. The Lord calls for dedication, perseverance and endurance in faith.

For the Lord says many people have for a time been walking in the wilderness, crying out for the Kingdom is at hand, their hearts burning with truth and with holy fire, yet their voices have gone unnoticed. For many will feel this wilderness is too harsh, the journey too long, and it too difficult to tread, all the while your voice is not being heard, but take heart, for a time will come that those who speak in His Spirit shall be heard. Yes says the Lord, they shall be heard. My true sons and daughters say the Lord shall be heard, and their voices will not go unnoticed!

Many voices are crying out in the wilderness – crying out God's Truth in Spirit – yet many are not listening, but the time shall come. Yes, it will come says the Lord! Like in the days of John, now is the time to remain steadfast, to remain true to the Lord and true to His message and His Truth. For out of the wilderness they will come, no more hidden but revealed, but unveiled, for as Lazarus came out of the tomb, so the Lord says Come forth, His sons and daughters, come out of your wilderness and embrace the light of His Glory!

John came proclaiming the truth of the Kingdom – not the truth of any church or of man. It was the message from the King Himself. The Lord is raising those who speak with the heart of the Kingdom and who speak the message of the King. This is not a message that will glorify any church group or denomination, but a message that glorifies God and that will raise the Bride out of the ashes of religion and man-made mediocrity, tradition and culture. It is they who walk in His glory, and who seek not glory. It is they who seek the treasures of heaven, not the riches of the earth. It is they who move in the Spirit, who are led by the Spirit and who fear not man but fear God.

John was not a rich man. He was not adorned. He did not live in a luxury house. His ministry was only for a short while, but during all the trials, he remained faithful. For he understands the Kingdom is not of wealth, prosperity, riches, fame, popularity, self-enrichment, or self-glorification, but the Kingdom is about the Lamb who died for all to be saved, and he knew this was a Kingdom of power that will set free those who believe from the tyranny of darkness here on earth and forever more! The Gospel is the truth of the eternal King, who has laid down His life so that all who believe will be saved.

This is the Kingdom! This is the Gospel for which John died and he defended. The Gospel of the Kingdom that Jesus preached. A Kingdom Gospel of life. Not a gospel of buildings, status, appraisal, religion, or agendas. It was the Gospel of a King who would shed His Blood so that mankind may be free from its fallen ways and from the ways of the devil. For this Gospel, John braved the wilderness – alone and for a long time. He lived in solitude, and he lived by eating locusts and honey because he was consumed by the Gospel of the Kingdom. He knew his purpose and was driven by nothing else.

What does the Kingdom mean to us? Is it a Gospel that we will die for, no matter the cost or the sacrifice, or is this a mere Gospel of self-gratification, of self-accumulation and self-worth? Listen to the Lord. He is raising men like John the Baptist, who lived for nothing else but the King of Heaven, and he lived for nothing else than the truth of such a Gospel. Listen. God is raising men and women with the singular vision and determination of John. They will not back down. They do not seek to be pampered. They realise this is not about fortune, fame or riches. They can only speak to a few, and their ministry may be short-lived, but they know it is about faithfulness, obedience and their love for the King!

And the Lord says I will lead them out of the wilderness! I will lead them and I will let their voices be heard! I will them their words burn with fire! I will let their hearts burn for me! Seek not the ways of the world, but seek only the Lord. Seek Him only! For John lived a humble life, so the Lord calls for humility, He calls for sacrifice, He calls for utmost dedication, for our God is an all-consuming fire and He is a jealous God!

For look says the Lord, they are coming out of the wilderness! They are coming – the ignored, the trodden, the dismissed, the scared, the bruised and the broken – they are coming to speak and to speak the word of God. Repent cries the Lord, repent, for the Kingdom of God is in hand!

The remnant is coming says the Lord. They are coming. They are not adorned with riches, with fame or splendour, but look, they wear the mantle of God, and listen, for their words will shake the very foundations of God and their words will shake the very foundations of the heart of man. They come to profess the Kingdom, to profess the truth of the king and they come in the power of the Spirit for the Kingdom of God is one of power!

Ignore their voice says the Lord if you wish, but what they speak shall come to pass and there shall be no delay! And My power says the Lord shall be with them and all shall know these are my servants who have chosen Me, no matter the cost. For they know the voice of their King, for they have turned their ears to His calling, and they have obeyed and they have followed. Hallelujah! For they come in the power of God. Men, women and yes says the Lord, even children will speak with His voice. They are coming, and every rock shall shake and mountains shall quake and the heavens will declare God's Word will split the foundations.

A quickening! A quickening! There is a quickening of the Spirit as the Lord will birth His Bride in Glory and by the Blood of the Lamb. For those who come with His voice shall be quickened by the Spirit, burning with holy fire, for they seek not the mantle of the world or the mantle placed on them by man, but the hand of God and God alone. For even now says the Lord, many are burdened by the mantles of this world, and there are many mantles of burden in the churches, so it is time to cast away these mantles, to cast away one's crown of self-glory to seek the glory of the King.

Praise the Lord. Praise the Lord. He is raising up an army that speaks of the Kingdom. With them comes great baptism. In water. In Spirit. In divine fire. For they come, for whom have they but God? They serve no other, they seek no other god or riches, but they seek only His Kingdom.

God is calling for a relentless remnant. Those devoted to prayer, and to see god's light shine in the darkness! What is right must be upheld. What is wrong must be exposed. Idolatry should have no place in our lives or homes. We must not flinch in the face of danger, even though around every corner we may face monstrous darkness, lurking predators and wolves in sheep's clothing. Be relentless says God! Keep the faith, stay on the path, walk by faith and burn in His holy fire. How we need to yield and submit to God! How we need to surrender more than ever to the Spirit of God so that we are overwhelmed by His holy presence. For then we shall remain standing, strong in His might, and strong in His glory.

The hymn, Sent the Fire by William Booth, is my prayer in such a time where God is calling for His sons and daughters to arise for truth, to stand up for the liberty of Christ and to again share the whole counsel of God as intended and taught by Jesus our Lord and only true Saviour of a world hell-bent of destruction. We must seek the fire so that we may burn for Him and so that we may truly become relentless to His Glory!

The prophet Jeremiah often did not want to speak the word of God because it was hard and difficult. But then we read the following in Jeremiah 20, at the same time while he is lamenting his calling: It says the following: "Then I said, "I will not make mention of Him, nor speak anymore in His name." But His word was in my heart like a burning fire Shut up in my bones; I was weary of holding it back, And I could not." Praise God! No matter what Jeremiah was going though, he could NOT keep silent because the Word of God burned in his heart and burned in his bones. After all, our Lord is an all-consuming fire. Jeremiah 23:29 says: "Is not my word like fire," declares the LORD, "and like a hammer that breaks a rock in pieces?

God's Word is like fire. And God wants His Word to burn like fire in us! Yes, the remnant in the end times will burn for God! They will only speak His truth, and they will not relent! They will not back down! For those in the prophetic, they will know it is impossible to keep silent when God speaks for such is the power of conviction. Yet this applies not only to the prophetic. Is the Word of the Lord burning like a fire in your heart and bones? Such will be the remnant, for the remnant shall burn with the spirit and with the Word of God. For the Scriptures speaks about what the heart is full of will overflow out of the mouth. If we are full of the Lord, and the Lord is a consuming fire, and His Word like a fire, then surely the fire of His Word must rest upon our lips and burn within us! It is time for the fire of His Presence, the fire of His Truth, the fire of His Words and the fire of the Spirit to again burn in our hearts and bones! Glory to God! Yes, Lord, let there be a cry, LIGHT THE FIRE AGAIN!

This is a remnant that will resist fear, self-pity, self-righteousness and carnality. God wants us, the true sons and daughters, to BURN for Him so that the world may see our God as a God who is alive and who is powerful and true! It is time for the fire of God to burn again in our bones UNTIL WE ARE LIKE JEREMIAH WHO CRIES 'BUT EVEN IF I WANT TO BE SILENT AND I CAN NOT BE SILENT BECAUSE OF THE FIRE OF THE LORD THAT BURNS WITHIN!' We are living in times of great idolatry, falseness, deception, compromise, apostasy and rebellion. The question is, do we remain silent or is the fire of God burning so that we cannot remain silent? Do we burn for Him even if we run the risk of being ridiculed, mocked and persecuted? Do we seek to be popular or to be a vessel of honour for the Lord?

Lord, let it burn. Lord, let Your Word burn in our bones. Let it burn. Let us be ablaze for You. Let us be on fire for you. No compromise. No stepping back, but we shall stare in the cold gaze of the enemy and not flinch. We shall stare into the eyes of the Goliaths and not back down. For we are redeemed and the Lord is an all-consuming fire!

We can no longer be silent, no matter the cost or the price. We can no longer be silent as this world burns with rage, hate, rebellion and iniquity. We can no longer be silent as the world burns with the fire of hell, slipping deeper into damnation. It is time to speak up, speak out and declare God's Word, God's Truth and God's love in the midst of the furnace and in the den of lions. We can no longer be silent ... we can no longer compromise, or bow the knee to a world that is crippled with anxiety, fear, stress and carnality. We need to rise up, let His light shine, and declare His truth even when the world defies the Great I AM. For even in the times of storms, or in the times of captivity, or in the times of blessings, or in the times of calamity, let us speak out, and let the fire burn in our bones to the glory of God!

This is indeed the end-time season of threshing and of sifting, says the Lord. The Lord will expose all and bring all things wicked and deceitful into the light. There is a mighty move of the Spirit for God's people to operate in glory, but so many will find themselves on sand that will turn to mud as the flood of the Lord cleanses and purifies. Alas, some believe they are on the unmovable Rock of Jesus, who will find this is a false reality - it is the time to stand in Spirit and Truth on the true Rock that smashes the dominion of the devil. For a fire burns from heaven, purging the barren branches. A fire burns to raise up the warriors of the Lord, BUT this calls for abandonment unto God and a yearning to lay it all down. So many will fall for they stand on clay and dirt as the Lord roars and shakes, bringing Babylon to its knees.

Repentance and humility are key. Seek Him and seek His Truth for the devil deceives the whole world. Stand, stand and fight the good fight in His Glory! O, such a move from the Lord to shatter the darkness. Walk in His Glory to see strongholds fold.

This is indeed the time for the true disciples to arise. Those who are bold and mighty in the Lord, those who are baptised and led by the Spirit. Disciples burning with Shekinah fire, and who walk in the truth of Acts 5 (verse 29) that one ought to obey God rather than men. Indeed, these are disciples who speak not like the scribes, but in the authority of God. They speak by God's wisdom, knowledge and understanding and foolishness is not found on their lips. Glory to God, they shall fight for the soul of the church, glorifying and praising Jesus for they shall have no other king but Jesus! They seek only the will of God on earth as in heaven.

Jan Hus, the Reformer, once said: "Therefore faithful Christian, seek the truth, listen to the truth, learn the truth, love the truth, speak the truth, adhere to truth and defend truth to the death. For the truth will set you free from sin, the devil and the destruction of the soul, and ultimately from eternal death, which is eternal separation from God's grace and the joy of salvation." Indeed, we can stand for the truth and defend it when God's fire of conviction burns within us! A fire that will not yield to the ways of the fallen world, the seductions of the devil.

Believers of the Lord, we must seek the fire of God's Spirit! We must yearn for it! We must desire the presence of God. How hungry are you to dwell with God, to move in His glory? The fire of God is a fire of love, purity and power. We need His fire every day of our lives. We need it to overcome, to endure, to stand strong and to prosper in spirit, soul and body to the glory of God.

We need to remember that there is a fire, a fire of love that also burns for us. Did you know that God's heart burns with a blazing love for you? This is the reality of John 3:16, of the cross and the empty tomb! Everything God did from the beginning of time to the end of all things as we know it is for His creation to be reconciled unto Him. That is an awesome and amazing love! It is love that never changes, for God is constant, consistent and unfailing. A love that remains as so clearly spelt out in Romans 8. A love that is waiting to turn your life upside down. Ask God for His fire. Ask Him for this blaze of His love. Make it the most important prayer of your life: "Father, give me Your blazing fire of love. Let me be filled with that fire. Let me be on fire with you by the Spirit of God. Yes, Lord, sent the fire to burn in me!"

Yet, we need to be hungry for such a fire. We need to hunger and yearn to receive this fire in our hearts, the burning love of God, His burning presence, and His burning holy touch so that we shall be ignited by love to love more and to walk in holiness. By such fire, we will be changed to reach the world. This fire is stronger than death. This fire is more beautiful than life itself. This fire is more intense than anything that exists. Ask God for His fire to burn by the Spirit, for it is the baptism by the Spirit. Such fire comes from complete yielding and submission unto God.

Without the fire of God, you live without true life, without passion. Without the fire of God you have religion, human wisdom derived from the Bible and insights that appear to be godly but which do not result in the power of God. It is empty. It sounds nice, but it doesn't change lives. It doesn't heal the sick. It doesn't set the possessed free. It doesn't help the suffering. We need the fire to be changed and to change lives! It is the fire of Pentecost that birthed the Church! Yes, the fire of God changed Jerusalem into a place of fire on the day of Pentecost, when the Holy Spirit was poured out. How the Pentecost fire has been setting hearts aflame for God for hundreds of years! We need the presence of God! How we need the fire of God to burn intensely. The fire of God still lights up the hearts of people worldwide, and it changes them more than anything else.

The reality is that the blazing fire of God's love captures your heart and sets you on fire for the salvation of other people. For the fire that burns in God's heart should burn in us. How we need to be so on fire with love that consumes what is evil, love that moves like a whirlwind of compassion and commitment. Fire also cleanses. It purifies, for it burns away your self-fabricated image. Fire humbles you. Fire strips away the ragged garments, consumes the dirt, and leaves you cleansed and free, so Jesus can clothe you with His humble garments. Fire is what we need. Ask for the fire of God.

With words alone, you will never reach the people who are lost. You can caress the carnal mind and intellectual, religious, hypocrisy of the sinful man, but that will not help anyone. We need the power of God. We need His Presence. We need His fire to shatter strongholds and set the captives free!

Think about the parable of the virgins who had their beautifully polished Christian oil lamps with them, but only a few of them also had the oil that could make the FIRE burn. Scriptures say that at that time the kingdom of heaven will be like ten virgins who took their lamps and went out to meet the Bridegroom. Five of them were foolish and five were wise. The foolish ones took their lamps but did not take any oil with them. The wise, however, took oil in jars along with their lamps." (Matthew 25:1-4). Some were ready, on fire, and some had grown cold. Is your oil lamp empty? Or are you on fire for God? Ask for the oil so your fire can burn. Seek the Lord, yearn for Him, for only you can fellowship with Him! How the Lord desires true intimacy.

How easily do we not quench the fire because of our carnality, because we are so busy and we are so preoccupied with our lives and problems? Yet when we lay it all down, deny ourselves and carry the cross, we shall learn true yielding and submitting unto God. For then, the fire shall come, the fire shall burn, for the fire destroys our pride and ego. For God is in the fire of humility, in gentleness and kindness. For God is a loving God. His love is fire. God is pure fire, real fire. How we need to be changed by that fire! Yes, Lord, burn through our pride and defences with your consuming fire. Make us real, Lord. Make us blaze with Your fire, Lord. Fill us, Lord, in the eternal fire of your love.

How we need to constantly seek God's fire. We need to hunger and thirst for the word of God. We need to pray earnestly and all the time. We need to live a life of holiness and complete obedience to God. Yes, how we need to have a great desire for the return of the Lord. How we need a true, real and steadfast faith in God. To burn for God we need to love sacrificially. We cannot merely submit today and not tomorrow, for it will be like a flame that flickers for a while but is quenched or put out by the dust of life. Every day we need a new fire. The world is seeking fire. The world is seeking love and authenticity. The world is seeking passion, answers, and hope. The world is seeking the power that frees and heals and delivers from the swamps of darkness. So seek Him.

Of the Lord we read in "Ezekiel 1: 27 Also from the appearance of His waist and upward I saw, as it were, the color of amber with the appearance of fire all around within it; and from the appearance of His waist and downward I saw, as it were, the appearance of fire with brightness all around. 28 Like the appearance of a rainbow in a cloud on a rainy day, so was the appearance of the brightness all around it. This was the appearance of the likeness of the glory of the Lord." This description shows that God consists of fire! His body is fire. That is why fire is so important. The fire is His presence. So seek the fire. Yearn for His presence. And from sunrise to sunset, burn for God! Such will be the hunger in the remnant.

1 Peter 5:10: But may the God of all grace, who called us to His eternal glory by Christ Jesus, after you have suffered a while, perfect, establish, strengthen, and settle you.

It is only by God's might, glory and presence that we are settled, established and perfected to walk in His ways, His will and glory.

Thus, this calls for the Lord our God to lead us ultimately, daily, according to His good and perfect will. Thus we are taught to pray in Matthew 6 for the Lord's will to be done on earth as it is heaven. We are urged to first seek His Kingdom, for our story should be Kingdom-focused, driven and inspired. As we do so when God pens our last chapter and our last word, we shall be found in the Book of Life (Revelation 20:12, 21:27). If we completely yield to the Lord, submitted unto His divinity, He shall indeed grant us the grace and the mercy to run the course and finish our race as God designed and ordained.

God's intention is for us to grow into the fullness of His glory, the fullness of His majesty and nature, and thus to come to the perfection of His will. Such will be the nature of the remnant. Ephesians 4 speaks of the saints coming to the unity of the faith and of the knowledge of the Son of God, to a perfect man, to the measure of the stature of the fullness of Christ (verse 13), and that "by speaking the truth in love, may grow up in all things into Him who is the head—Christ— from whom the whole body, joined and knit together by what every joint supplies, according to the effective working by which every part does its share, causes growth of the body for the edifying of itself in love (verse 15, 16). We can only know the fullness of God, His love, His truth and glory when we allow God to be the author and finisher (perfector) of our faith. For then we grow to the measure of the stature of the fullness of Christ, all to the honour of God.

In 2 Timothy 3, Apostle Paul writes about the last days that will be perilous. And we should sit up and take note, because perilous denotes something which holds danger, thus some things will happen that will pose a danger unto believers, but at the same time, believers must also avoid such pitfalls lest they become perilous (a danger) to others. Perilous also speaks of great stress and trouble.

Such times have been with us for some time, and the remnant that walks in His glory and power will stand strong in such apostasy and bring many into the harvest of salvation.

1 John 2 speaks of the antidote to guard against such perilous times: "15 Do not love the world or the things in the world. If anyone loves the world, the love of the Father is not in him. 16 For all that is in the world—the lust of the flesh, the lust of the eyes, and the pride of life—is not of the Father but is of the world. 17 And the world is passing away, and the lust of it; but he who does the will of God abides forever."

If one looks at the world today, we are already living in such perilous times. We are certainly in the times of 1 Timothy 6:10, which says, "For the love of money is a root of all kinds of evil, for which some have strayed from the faith in their greediness, and pierced themselves through with many sorrows." We are certainly in the times of the Book of Jude, where it says, "4 For certain men have crept in unnoticed, who long ago were marked out for this condemnation, ungodly men, who turn the grace of our God into lewdness and deny the only Lord God and our Lord Jesus Christ." In the same passage of Scripture, it says, "3 Beloved, while I was very diligent to write to you concerning our common salvation, I found it necessary to write to you exhorting you to contend earnestly for the faith which was once for all delivered to the saints."

Yes, people in this world have become unthankful, greedy, covetous and unholy. Jesus taught in Mark 7 the following: 20 He went on: "What comes out of a person is what defiles them. 21 For it is from within, out of a person's heart, that evil thoughts come—sexual immorality, theft, murder, 22 adultery, greed, malice, deceit, lewdness, envy, slander, arrogance and folly. 23 All these evils come from inside and defile a person." Thus, perilous times are marked by rising immorality, the corruption of character and the heart that continues to be deceitful above all things (Jeremiah 17:9).

We read in "Ephesians 4:31-5:2: Get rid of all bitterness, rage and anger, brawling and slander, along with every form of malice. Be kind and compassionate to one another, forgiving each other, just as in Christ God forgave you. Follow God's example, therefore, as dearly loved children and walk in the way of love, just as Christ loved us and gave himself up for us as a fragrant offering and sacrifice to God." We are called to glorify God and His Kingdom; therefore, to live not as the world lives. May we continue to walk in the ways of God, always thankful, always praising and always loving, for indeed let us give thanks in all circumstances (1 Thessalonians 5:18).

Because of such perilous times, we read in "1 Peter 1: 13 Therefore gird up the loins of your mind, be sober, and rest your hope fully upon the grace that is to be brought to you at the revelation of Jesus Christ; 14 as obedient children, not conforming yourselves to the former lusts, as in your ignorance; 15 but as He who called you is holy, you also be holy in all your conduct, 16 because it is written, "Be holy, for I am holy." 22 Since you have purified your souls in obeying the truth through the Spirit in [j]sincere love of the brethren, love one another fervently with a pure heart, 23 having been born again, not of corruptible seed but incorruptible, through the word of God which lives and abides [m]forever, 24 because "all flesh is as grass, and all [n]the glory of man as the flower of the grass. The grass withers, and its flower falls away, 25 but the word of the Lord endures forever."

So why then is the perilous time so dangerous? Because we then walk no longer in the light, but in darkness. We no longer walk in truth, but in deception. We no longer walk in freedom, but in slavery. And yes, our soul, spirit and body suffer damage. And we become subject to the mandate of John 10, where the enemy steals, kills and destroys. Perilous times mean we face danger in regard to our health, mental stability, the wholeness of the spirit and our redemption/salvation. The entire New Testament, from Jesus to the apostles, thus warns of the wicked actions of man, within and without the church, that will contribute to the perilous times. Why? Because it puts man in danger for himself and others! Jesus said in "Revelation 22: 11 He who is unjust, let him be unjust still; he who is filthy, let him be filthy still; he who is righteous, let him be righteous still; he who is holy, let him be holy still." Such times are indeed upon us.

These are days of great depravity, evil and wickedness. In 2 Timothy 2, King James uses the Greek word "Anemeros" which speaks of not tame, savage, thus fierce. And we are indeed living in such a time of fierceness, of savagery, where men are not tame. It is a time of excesses, of depravity, or carnality and where man does all kinds of wickedness, just as in the days of Noah. One can only survive such perilous times when you abide in God (John 15), for then you shall walk in God's power and grace to survive the perilous times. Indeed, God gives us self-control to walk in His Spirit, and not in the carnality and excesses of this world. One of the characteristics of the perilous times is a lack of self-control, evident if you look at all the sexual immorality, debauchery, substance abuse, levels of violence and general wickedness in societies.

The fact that believers will be hated, not just in the great tribulation but even now, is because people will more than ever hate the Truth of God, for the Truth has become offensive to mankind. And we are seeing the world truly rebelling against God's morality and holiness, choosing a path of lawlessness, lewdness and where love has grown cold. Thus, Paul writes in 2 Timothy 4 that the time will come when people will not put up with sound doctrine (v 3). Yes, people will turn to all kinds of blasphemies, deceptions, and lies instead of being governed by the truth of God.

Indeed, everything Jesus said and as spoken by the apostles warned about the perilous days, and of its signs, and of the perilous behaviour of man. Paul spoke a lot about the nature of man and how believers should behave because truly a child of God must glorify God in spirit, soul and body. He wrote in "Romans 8: 5 For those who live according to the flesh set their minds on the things of the flesh, but those who live according to the Spirit, the things of the Spirit. 6 For to be carnally minded is death, but to be spiritually minded is life and peace. 7 Because the carnal mind is enmity against God; for it is not subject to the law of God, nor indeed can be. 8 So then, those who are in the flesh cannot please God." Thus, perilous times are the times of the flesh. It is the times of carnality, and where we seek to turn away from the truth and purity of God.

We need to understand the devil wants us to abandon the path of God to walk the path of the wide gate, thus abandoning the Truth, the Way and the Path of Life. He wants us to step out into disobedience, rebellion and onto the path of iniquity. Why? For then we move into a state of no control, of immorality, of darkened minds, the bewilderment of heart and even spiritual blindness. Again, we need to remember John 10:10, which speaks about the enemy/thief (the devil) coming to steal, destroy and kill. The enemy, therefore, wants us to engage in perilous times and act upon such peril to cause division, strife, confusion, death and destruction. He is the serpent - deceiving, sly, manipulative and arrogant. We are called to resist the devil, for if we don't, he shall make his presence known to destroy us.

For Paul, to live is Christ and to die is gain (Philippians 1:21). For Paul, it was all about leading holy and pure lives, in proper conduct, seeking the Truth, seeking the Way of God and building structured lives and families and the Church on the solid foundation of Jesus.

The apostles constantly taught, encouraged, and admonished on leading pure and undefiled lives in the Spirit of God, for this is the only way to make sure that we walk in a manner that counters perilous days. Only in God can we truly walk in the fruit of the Spirit – love, kindness, meekness, gentleness, faith – which ensures that we do not step into the pitfalls of perils and dangers. For the remnant, it should all be dying to the Self to gain Christ!

On an end-time mission

What is the mission of this Spirit-filled, relentless and fearless remnant? To fulfil the Great Commission! The mission has always remained the same, and so has God. The end-time remnant will be truly active and mobilised, not just the so-called clergy, but all the disciples who follow Christ! For these disciples walk in the reality of "Mark 16: 16 Whoever believes and is baptized will be saved, but whoever does not believe will be condemned. 17 And these signs will accompany those who believe: In my name they will drive out demons; they will speak in new tongues; 18 they will pick up snakes with their hands; and when they drink deadly poison, it will not hurt them at all; they will place their hands on sick people, and they will get well."

In the last several decades, we have seen how the Church has systematically wandered away from the Great Commission. While it is great to feed the hungry and clothe the poor, as Jesus highlighted as being of great importance in Matthew 25, the primary and most important mission of the remnant (the Bride of God) remains to save lives and to make disciples! What does it help to feed a person bread, yet he never receives the Bread of Heaven? The church has definitely become caught up in tackling all kinds of social injustices to the point that we have forgotten our main purpose is to bring the lost to Christ. While the Church has played its part over the centuries to help make the world a better place, such as playing a pivotal role in abolishing the slave trade in England (Wilberforce), we are ultimately called to raid hell to populate heaven!

We will say that the Great Commission has always been the mission. What is so different now? Firstly, the church has not really been fulfilling the commission of Matthew 28, meaning making active and mobilised disciples. So the error of our ways we need to correct, and we have to do it fast. We need to return to the Great Commission RIGHT NOW, meaning a return to what it means to be a disciple and how to make disciples. We have been too busy the last 2000 years creating a pseudo-religion saturated with pagan ideas, man-made traditions and legalisms. We have created a religion called Christianity that at times feels like the real thing, but it is only a whitewashed tomb where the so-called clergy rule and reign over the so-called laity. There is no such thing as the clergy and laity. In fact, Ephesians 4 makes it clear that those who equip and train the Body of Christ are not even supposed to be doing the work of the Lord among the lost!

Matthew 12 says, "37 Then he said to his disciples, "The harvest is plentiful but the workers are few. 38 Ask the Lord of the harvest, therefore, to send out workers into his harvest field." Right now, the harvest remains plentiful, but because we have not truly made disciples who are trained, activated and mobilised, we struggle to bring in the harvest. The end-time remnant will be ready to labour, and also be prepared to prepare and equip others to labour in the fields to bring in the harvest!

Secondly, the mission is of utmost importance because of the time and season we are living in. It is becoming increasingly difficult to stand for God's truth (note, not the truth as proclaimed by man in so many churches). It is becoming harder to keep shining the light, to be the salt, and to be sold out to the eternal Kingdom. Never before has there been so much darkness in this world, and because of the pseudo-religion, many "Christians" are finding it harder and harder to keep the faith and endure to the end. The end-time remnant will be a people purged, refined, purified, tested, sifted and prepared specifically for such perilous times where the truth has been forsaken and where deception crawls in every street.

Even more importantly, and for some this is controversial, the remnant has been specifically trained and prepared to not only endure and 'overcome' the tribulation but to share the Gospel in God's power. This is why the remnant needs to be filled with the Spirit of God and planted upon the Rock of Ages. Yes, many do believe the church will be raptured at the start of the tribulation, but the Scriptures speak otherwise. It also doesn't make sense for God to prepare the remnant for such a weighty task only for the remnant to be taken out of the fight at the start!

The great spiritual 'fight', or battle as one may say, for the lost will take place smack in the middle of the tribulation. This is when the spiritual warfare will reach its zenith, and the climax of intensity will shake one's bones. In his vision of heaven, John sees a vast number of these tribulation saints who have been martyred by the Antichrist: "There before me was a great multitude that no one could count, from every nation, tribe, people and language, standing before the throne and in front of the Lamb. They were wearing white robes and were holding palm branches in their hands" (Revelation 7:9). When John asks who they are, he is told, "These are they who have come out of the great tribulation; they have washed their robes and made them white in the blood of the Lamb" (verse 14).

The tribulation saints are, quite simply, saints living during the tribulation. It will be a time of trouble upon the world and the great persecution for the believers—or saints—because of the Antichrist's persecution (Revelation 13:7). Daniel saw the Antichrist "waging war against the saints and defeating them" (Daniel 7:21). Of course, the saints' eternal salvation is secure:

Daniel also saw that "the Ancient of Days came and pronounced judgment in favour of the saints of the Most High, and the time came when they possessed the kingdom" (Daniel 7:22; cf. Revelation 14:12–13). So there will be a great harvest produced during troubled and difficult times.

We live in a time when it seems more and more people are losing their faith, turning away from the truth, ignoring God, or even mocking Him. The church is becoming less and less effective, mainly because it functions as a pseudo-religion more interested in personal gain and gratification. Just look around you. How many are sold out for God, meaning they choose not to follow a religion but God Himself? In western countries, we sit with thousands upon thousands of churches, yet lawlessness, immorality, spiritual corruption and rebellion are increasing on the earth. It is also intensifying within the church! So if the church is making little progress in such times, even though times are very tough, how on earth will the tribulation saints find God within the remnant? After all, it speaks of a great multitude that no one could count!

Some will say the tribulation saints will be able to hear the gospel from several possible sources once the Bride has been raptured. The first is the Bible; there will be many copies of the Bible left in the world, and when God's judgments begin to fall, many people will likely react by finding a Bible to see if prophecies are being fulfilled. It is also said that many of the tribulation saints will also have heard the gospel from the two witnesses (Revelation 11:1–13), who will prophesy for 1,260 days [three and a half years] and perform great miracles (verse 6).

Let us be honest, this world is saturated with the Word of God. You find it on every app store, on TV, and on the radio. Yet, how many people are even reading the Bible, and I'm talking about believers? Why will they be grabbing a bible during the tribulation if they are not doing so now? The work of the two witnesses will be great, but will it truly move people to repentance? Thousands and thousands of sermons are being preached week in and week out, and we are seeing God's power moving, but so many are not really following God. The harvest field remains unploughed because of the ineffectiveness of the church, which holds onto religion rather than God. Why would they, in times of trouble, suddenly turn to God? The reality is that the remnant is being prepared to bring in a great harvest during the time of trouble. They will be able to endure the 'trouble', but also lead many to Christ. God is raising up such a remnant right now to already sow the seeds and raise up disciples who will make an impact.

Remember, the tribulation saints will serve their Lord Jesus Christ in the midst of desperate surroundings. Faithful to the end, many of these believers will die for their faith. But in their death, they overcome; "They overcame [Satan] by the blood of the Lamb and by the word of their testimony; they did not love their lives so much as to shrink from death" (Revelation 12:11). And God will reward them: "He who sits on the throne will spread his tent over them. Never again will they hunger; never again will they thirst. The sun will not beat upon them, nor any scorching heat. For the Lamb at the centre of the throne will be their shepherd; he will lead them to springs of living water. And God will wipe away every tear from their eyes" (Revelation 7:15–17).

Revelation 20 says, "4 And I saw thrones, and they sat on them, and judgment was committed to them. Then I saw the souls of those who had been beheaded for their witness to Jesus and for the word of God, who had not worshipped the beast or his image and had not received his mark on their foreheads or their hands. And they lived and reigned with Christ for a thousand years. 5 But the rest of the dead did not live again until the thousand years were finished. This is the first resurrection. 6 Blessed and holy is he who has part in the first resurrection. Over such the second death has no power, but they shall be priests of God and of Christ, and shall reign with Him a thousand years."

Let us then address the debate regarding the rapture and the second coming of Christ. The tribulation is a future seven-year period of time when God will finish His discipline of Israel and finalise His judgment of the unbelieving world. Throughout Scripture, the tribulation is referred to by other names such as the Day of the Lord (Isaiah 2:12; 13:6-9; Joel 1:15; 2:1-31; 3:14; 1 Thessalonians 5:2); trouble or tribulation (Deuteronomy 4:30; Zephaniah 1:1); the great tribulation, which refers to the more intense second half of the seven-year period (Matthew 24:21); time or day of trouble (Daniel 12:1; Zephaniah 1:15); time of Jacob's trouble (Jeremiah 30:7).

Daniel 9:24-27 speaks of 70 weeks that have been declared against "your people". God declares that "seventy sevens" will fulfil all these things. With 483 years having passed from the decree to rebuild Jerusalem to the cutting off of the Messiah, this leaves one seven-year period to be fulfilled in terms of Daniel 9:24: "to finish transgression, to put an end to sin, to atone for wickedness, to bring in everlasting righteousness, to seal up vision and prophecy and to anoint the most holy." This final seven-year period is known as the tribulation period—it is a time when God finishes judging Israel for its sin.

Daniel 9:27 says that the beast (antichrist) will make a covenant for seven years, but in the middle of this week (3 1/2 years into the tribulation), he will break the covenant, putting a stop to sacrifice. Revelation 13 explains that the beast will place an image of himself in the temple and require the world to worship him. In summary, the Tribulation is the 7-year time period in the end times in which humanity's decadence and depravity will reach their fullness, with God judging accordingly.

From the start, most believers agree that there will be tribulation with the coming of the antichrist, a false prophet, and a false teacher. We can also agree there is a second coming of Jesus Christ, and yes, there will be some sort of rapture of believers where the believers will be caught up to meet the Lord. Many Christians, however, disagree on when the rapture will happen. Some believe a rapture is a separate event from the second coming. It is important to discuss this because if the church is not going to go through the tribulation, then what is the purpose of the end-time remnant? There will also be no need to really prepare for the remnant to endure in such times.

A Scripture used to support the rapture as a second event is "1 Thessalonians 4: 16 For the Lord Himself will descend from heaven with a shout, with the voice of an archangel, and with the trumpet of God. And the dead in Christ will rise first. 17 Then we who are alive and remain shall be caught up together with them in the clouds to meet the Lord in the air. And thus we shall always be with the Lord." Some also quote 1 Thessalonians 5:9 as evidence we will not endure hardship or tribulation. It says, "9 For God did not appoint us to wrath, but to obtain salvation through our Lord Jesus Christ." Yet, this is talking about the eternal outpouring of God's wrath, which is poured out on those who continually reject God!

Jesus speaks of His second coming in "Matthew 24: 29 Immediately after the tribulation of those days, the sun will be darkened, and the moon will not give its light; the stars will fall from heaven, and the powers of the heavens will be shaken. 30 Then the sign of the Son of Man will appear in heaven, and then all the tribes of the earth will mourn, and they will see the Son of Man coming on the clouds of heaven with power and great glory. 31 And He will send His angels with a great sound of a trumpet, and they will gather together His elect from the four winds, from one end of heaven to the other."

Jesus also talks of His coming in Matthew 25, "31 "When the Son of Man comes in his glory, and all the angels with him, he will sit on his glorious throne. 32 All the nations will be gathered before him, and he will separate the people one from another as a shepherd separates the sheep from the goats. 33 He will put the sheep on his right and the goats on his left." There is only a SEPARATION of the sheep and the goats when He comes, not before the time. The sheep will be with God, and the goats will be judged on earth.

If you study these Scriptures, they actually agree and tell the same event! The Church will indeed be raptured, but according to Christ, this is during His second coming. And according to Matthew 24, it will be during the great tribulation (towards the end of it). If we take what Jesus said, Christ returns to save Israel and also gather the elect from across the world. Matthew 24 also says, "22 If those days had not been cut short, no one would survive, but for the sake of the elect those days will be shortened." So Israel and God's Bride will not endure the full timespan of the great tribulation, for the period will be cut short. After the coming of Christ, we find God's judgment on the earth, which we read about in the Book of Revelation. By this time, the Church will no longer be on earth but will wait for the 1000 years of peace and the coming of the New Jerusalem.

The coming of the Lord is described as a period when the sun will be darkened, and the moon will not give its light. We also read that the stars will fall from the sky, and the heavenly bodies will be shaken. This period of time was prophesied in Zachariah 14 when the Lord will go out and fight against those nations, as he fights on a day of battle. The day of the Lord and the battle were also vividly described in Joel 3.

While we may be hoping and praying for pre-tribulation, we'd better prepare for mid or post-tribulation! The reality is that the

Bible talks about only one second coming of Jesus Christ. If the rapture were to happen seven years before the second coming of Jesus, and the Bible clearly states that during the rapture we will meet the Lord in the air (signifying the Lord is coming), this would mean that His second coming will happen twice. The Bible makes it clear there is only one second coming - the first coming, to die, and the second coming, to reign. If we will meet Him in the air while He is coming down, this is describing the second coming of Jesus when the rapture will take place.

Yes, the rapture to the Lord and His coming is the same event. There will be a shout, a trumpet sounding, and the voice of an archangel when He comes. This verse also does not specify that we are going to heaven, but just that we will be with Jesus. 1 Corinthians 15, "51 Behold, I tell you a mystery: We shall not all sleep, but we shall all be changed— 52 in a moment, in the twinkling of an eye, at the last trumpet. For the trumpet will sound, and the dead will be raised incorruptible, and we shall be changed." In these verses, we see the sound of the trumpet mentioned to describe His descent from heaven and our meeting Him halfway. There is also no clear Scripture that indicates that the Church will skip the tribulation.

We wish to believe in pre-tribulation because of the fear of hardship and suffering, even though Christ has told us to take heart because He has already overcome the world! Revelation 3:10 says, "Because you have kept My command to persevere, I also will keep you from the hour of trial which shall come upon the whole world, to test those who dwell on the earth" God can keep Christians from His full wrath as we go through the tribulation! This could mean two things: either Christ will protect believers amid the trials, or He will deliver believers out of the trials. This is similar to how God did not take Noah out of His wrath but took the bad away from Noah. Noah had to endure the flood. God did not take the Israelites out of Egypt during the 10 plagues; God protected Israel in Egypt as the plagues intensified.

During the tribulation, people will be saved, but people will also die for Christ—those who refuse to worship the beast and receive his mark. This is the reality and the cost of serving Christ for some. If the church has already been raptured, the Holy Spirit will also be removed with the Church. How, then, can new believers be saved without the Holy Spirit on earth? We also read that the people who die and didn't worship the beast or take his mark will rise again and reign with Christ for 1000 years. This is the first resurrection. If there is a resurrection happening with the rapture seven years before that, when we are changed, and the dead will rise, then which resurrection is that?

Let us remember, Daniel's entire prophecy of the seventy-sevens (Daniel 9:20-27) is speaking of the nation of Israel. It is a time period in which God focuses His attention, especially on Israel. Zachariah 12 speaks also of the coming of Christ and how it will impact Israel as a people: 10 "And I will pour out on the house of David and the inhabitants of Jerusalem a spirit of grace and supplication. They will look on me, the one they have pierced, and they will mourn for him as one mourns for an only child, and grieve bitterly for him as one grieves for a firstborn son." Yes, the great harvest includes the redemption of Israel! This is confirmed by Revelation 7, which speaks of the 144,000 who are sealed from all the tribes of Israel. All the tribes are mentioned to indicate God's restorative plan for the ENTIRE nation of Israel. The number 12 can be seen symbolically to speak of the perfection of government or rule. There were 12 tribes and 12 apostles, for example. The number 144 is made up of 12 x 12, meaning God will completely and perfectly save Israel as part of His perfect governance.

Yes, Jesus returns to save Israel, but this does not necessarily indicate that the church could not also be present. By all accounts, as Jesus returns, the Gentile believers will also be saved. And so Israel again becomes the blessing to all nations. If we think about it, what makes the believers so special in the last days that they will be spared from persecution? Nothing makes believers special to be exempt from the tribulation. Believers for the past 2000 years have undergone great suffering, death, and persecution for the cause of Christ. Just because the Western Church enjoys freedom, for many believers around the world, tribulation is a normal experience (see 2 Timothy 3:12, John 16:33). So we will meet Him regardless of when it happens. We need to prepare for persecution and for tribulation, but we pray that we escape it.

The work of the Church has always been about bringing people back to God and making disciples of them. This mission will only become harder the closer the time draws for the coming of Christ.

Already we are living in very troubling times of violence, hatred, evil and suffering. The end-time remnant is called RIGHT NOW in already perilous times to be very active to bring in a mighty harvest. This mission will spill over to the great tribulation to produce a great harvest! Yes, in troubled times, the remnant will stand in the power of God, while God will also be restoring Israel to faith and extending grace to all who believe, both Jew and Gentile. God has always been in the business of saving people, and that salvation will still be available during the tribulation. This, however, doesn't mean God is not moving already. Now is the time for all to receive Christ (John 1:12).

Committed to God as end-time apostasy intensifies

More than ever, we live in the reality of 2 Thessalonians 2, which refers to the great falling away or rebellion. The Greek word translated "rebellion" or "falling away" in verse 3 of the Scripture is apostasia, from which we get the English word apostasy. It refers to a general defection from the true God, the Bible, and the Christian faith. Every age has its defectors, but the falling away at the end times will be complete and worldwide within the church first. The apostasy is also referred to in the KJV as the "falling away," while the NIV and ESV call it "the rebellion." And that's what an apostasy is: a rebellion, an abandonment of the truth. The end times will include a wholesale rejection of God's revelation, a further "falling away" of an already fallen world.

Apostasy means "a defiance of an established system or authority; a rebellion; an abandonment or breach of faith." In the context of 2 Thessalonians, this refers to the rebellion within the church, for the simple reason that the world cannot fall away from faith when you are not in the position of faith.

Who can argue that we have not already seen an abandonment of the Truth of the Lord? Doctrines on Jesus Only, Universalism, and Hyper-Grace, along with the Word and Faith Movement, abound, leading people further down a path of spiritual darkness and confusion. The Holy Spirit has been shunned, and so has sound doctrine. The church has been engulfed by moral relativism, humanism and secularism as it continues to be also moulded, influenced and shaped by religious and traditional perspectives and outlooks.

We are living in the time of the Emerging Church movement, where it is about adapting to the times and the culture to be relevant. Yet adapting has become nothing more than the practice of conforming and compromising. And so many of the 'faiths' have opted for tolerance and acceptance in the name of love, yet at the same time, we violate God's Truth and eternal principles. For this reason, same-sex marriages, abortions, and tattoos are all condoned. Church worship looks like a rock concert, as we sway to the music, caught up in the hypnotic hype, left confused and dazed as if we were truly in the presence of God or just caught up by our own emotions.

This is a time where we opt for openness and transparency without repentance, tolerance at the cost of dismissing holiness and acceptance of all at the cost of mocking the Lord. Yes, we are all sinners, and we are called to reach out to the broken and the lost, yet sin cannot be tolerated, condoned or even promoted.

We forget God never changes, and His truth and eternal laws never change. And so we continue to fall into the trap of humanism, secularism, and condoning the ways of the world. This movement of love is not about placing God at the centre, but man takes the centre stage. It is similar to the Flower Power movement of the 1960s, where acceptance and tolerance covered up all sin. Yes, love does cover up all sins, but this speaks of a love we have for the Lord, whose love for us shone brightly on the cross when He shed His Blood for our redemption. And such a show of love we cannot mock, yet we do so if we condone the sin that was covered by the Blood.

Only the Truth of Jesus will set people free. Therefore, not the diluted, changed or altered Gospel. We may continue to be seeker-friendly, never rocking the boat or never offending, but as we continue on this path, we also become seeker-friendly, therefore friendly to the devil. The devil still roams like a lion, and he shall still devour those who open the door to his malicious intent. Yes, we shall seek and we shall find the Lord, but in our mockery, in our rebellion and our abandonment of sound doctrine, we shall also find the serpent waiting and lurking.

We read in "2 Thessalonians 2: 3 Let no man deceive you by any means: for that day shall not come, except there come a falling away first, and that man of sin be revealed, the son of perdition; 4 Who opposeth and exalteth himself above all that is called God, or that is worshipped; so that he as God sitteth in the temple of God, shewing himself that he is God. 5 Remember ye not, that, when I was yet with you, I told you these things? 6 And now ye know what withholdeth that he might be revealed in his time. 7 For the mystery of iniquity doth already work: only he who now letteth will let, until he be taken out of the way.8 And then shall that Wicked be revealed, whom the Lord shall consume with the spirit of his mouth, and shall destroy with the brightness of his coming: 9 Even him, whose coming is after the working of Satan with all power and signs and lying wonders, 10 And with all deceivableness of unrighteousness in them that perish; because they received not the love of the truth, that they might be saved. 11 And for this cause God shall send them strong delusion, that they should believe a lie: 12 That they all might be damned who believed not the truth, but had pleasure in unrighteousness."

Paul reminds us that the coming of the Lord will only follow the great falling away, which will pave the way for the coming of the last Antichrist. And we are reminded that such a worker of the devil comes after the working of Satan with all power and signs and lying wonders. We are also left with the following sobering truth: 11 And for this cause God shall send them strong delusion, that they should believe a lie: 12 That they all might be damned who believed not the truth, but had pleasure in unrighteousness.

The word heresy comes from a Greek word meaning a self-chosen opinion, or a choice. We live in a time where we can all decide and choose. Ignorance is no longer an excuse. Verse 11 speaks of those who choose to believe a lie instead of the truth. And this is the mark of the apostasy. Many within the church will CHOOSE to believe a lie instead of the truth. And no, we cannot blame the pastor or anyone else if we walk in deception. We are all called to test all things or all spirits, to test the word and to walk in Truth by being led by the Spirit. Yes, we all have a choice, just as the false prophets on Mount Carmel had a choice.

Paul's writing to the church in Thessalonica is reflected in "Romans 1: 18 For the wrath of God is revealed from heaven against all ungodliness and unrighteousness of men, who hold the truth in unrighteousness; 19 Because that which may be known of God is manifest in them; for God hath shewed it unto them. 20 For the invisible things of him from the creation of the world are clearly seen, being understood by the things that are made, even his eternal power and Godhead; so that they are without excuse: 21 Because that, when they knew God, they glorified him not as God, neither were thankful; but became vain in their imaginations, and their foolish heart was darkened. 22 Professing themselves to be wise, they became fools, 23 And changed the glory of the uncorruptible God into an image made like to corruptible man, and to birds, and four-footed beasts, and creeping things. 24 Wherefore God also gave them up to uncleanness through the lusts of their own hearts, to dishonour their own bodies between themselves: 25 Who changed the truth of God into a lie, and worshipped and served the creature more than the Creator, who is blessed for ever. Amen."

Indeed, God shall not be mocked, but this is happening all around us, all the time. This is the time we are living in. A time of the great falling away. A time of apostasy and rebellion. Paul writes in "Galatians 1: 8 But though we, or an angel from heaven, preach any other gospel unto you than that which we have preached unto you, let him be accursed. 9 As we said before, so say I now again, if any man preach any other gospel unto you than that ye have received, let him be accursed."

Indeed, cursed are those who preach any other doctrine except the one preached by the Apostles, most of whom learned directly from the Lord when He walked the earth. And the apostasy and heresies will only get worse. More than ever, the Lord has revealed that the levels of apostasy and even heresy within churches will continue to intensify and leave many utterly shocked at the levels of depravity and falling away from truth.

These will truly be the days of 1 Kings 18 where one prophet stood in the presence of God, opposing 850 false prophets. These are the days of 1 Kings 22, where the king of Judah and the king of Israel received false word from 400 'prophets', with only one true servant of God speaking the truth of the Lord.

Yes, these are such days, says the Lord. More than ever, we will be witnessing the apostasy as spoken by Paul. It is the level of outright rebellion as seen in Ezekiel 8. So terrible will be apostasy within the church that indeed, we will be left shocked, and the apostasy and the rebellion will be done with greater arrogance and with greater aggression. Yet nothing is new under the sun – this is a call for great discernment.

The occasion of Paul's writing to the Thessalonians was to correct some of the errors concerning the end times that the believers had heard from false teachers. Among the falsehoods was that "the day of the Lord has already come" (verse 2). The Christians in Thessalonica were afraid that Jesus had already come, they had missed the rapture, and they were now in the tribulation. Paul had already explained the rapture to them in his first letter

(1 Thessalonians 4:16–17). Paul writes his second letter to assure them that, contrary to what they had heard, and despite the persecution they were enduring, the "day of Christ" had not yet come.

In 2 Thessalonians 2:3, Paul, therefore, makes it clear that the day of the Lord, a time of worldwide judgment (Isaiah 13:6; Obadiah 1:15), will not transpire until two things happen. First, the falling away, or great apostasy, must occur. Second, the "man of lawlessness" must be revealed, he who is called the "son of perdition," also known as the Antichrist.

Peter of course also spoke about the coming apostasy/falling away in "2 Peter 2: 1 But there were also false prophets among the people, even as there will be false teachers among you, who will secretly bring in destructive heresies, even denying the Lord who bought them, and bring on themselves swift destruction. 2 And many will follow their destructive ways, because of whom the way of truth will be blasphemed. 3 By covetousness they will exploit you with deceptive words; for a long time their judgment has not been idle, and their destruction does not slumber."

The King James Version speaks of damnable heresies, and the NIV speaks of destructive heresies. Whatever the correct translation, it is destructive or damnable. So Peter was saying that we need to be aware of false teachers and false prophets who introduce a 'truth' that will be destructive and even damnable. Remember, the word "heresies" in the above Scripture means "to choose" in Greek. It carries the understanding that when people decide they will believe in a false doctrine, it is by their own free will.

Shocking as it is, apostasy will abound in churches because of free will and because of a choice. On Mount Carmel, Elijah cried out to the prophets to choose whom they would serve, yet he was met with silence. Just so the indifference in churches among believers is deafening, as we remain lukewarm and silent to the butchering of God's Truth, but those who mind not to be cursed.

Something destructive cannot be taken lightly. We cannot read in the Bible that something is destructive, and just mark that off or think it doesn't matter. Peter speaks to the reality of false prophets and false teachers. Their work is destructive; they not only do not edify, but they also destroy and tear down. And this is the work of apostasy and the work of rebellion, which is like the sin of witchcraft.

According to Peter, these false teachers and preachers will bring in something within the church that is destructive. And this is already happening at an alarming rate. False prophets and false teachers will and are introducing something destructive, bringing upon those involved swift destruction. It involves shame, exploitation and condemnation. This is not something you can just overlook. This is not a simple difference in opinion or judgment or some sincere soul who just hasn't learned something yet. This is the bringing in of error, which is called "destructive heresies," and that is deserving of "condemnation."

This is the apostasy as spoken about by Paul. This is the outright rebellion that will befall the church before the coming of the Lord. And this outright rebellion will become ever so clear. It is already here. Jesus warned the disciples concerning the final days in Matthew 24:10–12: "At that time many will turn away from the faith and will betray and hate each other, and many false prophets will appear and deceive many people. Because of the increase of wickedness, the love of most will grow cold."

He also said the following in "Matthew 24:24 For false christs and false prophets will rise and show great signs and wonders to deceive, if possible, even the elect." Take note that even the elect will be deceived. Yes, the devil deceived Adam and Eve, and will surely try to deceive every believer. Judging by the myriad of false teachings and preaching in the church these days, it is clear Matthew 24:24 has become a stark reality. We live in a time where the great apostasy is hastened by false signs of power and lying wonders.

It says in "1 John 4: 1 Beloved, believe not every spirit, but try the spirits whether they are of God: because many false prophets are gone out into the world. 2 Hereby know ye the Spirit of God: Every spirit that confesseth that Jesus Christ is come in the flesh is of God: 3 And every spirit that confesseth not that Jesus Christ is come in the flesh is not of God: and this is that spirit of antichrist, whereof ye have heard that it should come; and even now already is it in the world. 4 Ye are of God, little children, and have overcome them: because greater is he that is in you, than he that is in the world. 5 They are of the world: therefore speak they of the world, and the world heareth them. 6 We are of God: he that knoweth God heareth us; he that is not of God heareth not us. Hereby know we the spirit of truth, and the spirit of error."

Let us pause here for a minute – John writes that those who know God hear them (the disciples teaching the Gospel of the Lord), yet they who are of the world hear them not. Then he concludes by saying "hereby know we the spirit of truth, and the spirit of error".

The Amplified Bible's translation is as follows: 5 They [who teach twisted doctrine] are of the world and belong to it; therefore they speak from the [viewpoint of the] world [with its immoral freedom and baseless theories—demanding compliance with their opinions and ridiculing the values of the upright], and the [gullible one of the] world listens closely and pays attention to them. 6 We [who teach God's word] are from God [energized by the Holy Spirit], and whoever knows God [through personal experience] listens to us [and has a deeper understanding of Him]. Whoever is not of God does not listen to us. By this, we know [without any doubt] the spirit of truth [motivated by God] and the spirit of error [motivated by Satan].

So what was John saying? He said those who truly know the Lord will hear the truth as spoken by those walking in the truth, yet those who do not know the Lord will not listen to the truth, for their ears are turned towards the world. For those who know the Lord, they will want to listen to the truth of the Lord, which is the spirit of truth, and those who choose not to listen to the Lord and His Truth are thus still of the world, which is the spirit of error. Paul warns about it in "Galatians 1: 9 As we said before, so say I now again, if any man preach any other gospel unto you than that ye have received, let him be accursed."

Let us connect what John wrote to "2 Timothy 4: 3 For the time will come when people will not tolerate sound doctrine and accurate instruction [that challenges them with God's truth]; but wanting to have their ears tickled [with something pleasing], they will accumulate for themselves [many] teachers [one after another, chosen] to satisfy their own desires and to support the errors they hold, 4 and will turn their ears away from the truth and will wander off into myths and man-made fictions [and will accept the unacceptable]."

So if you take into consideration what John and Paul wrote, we see clearly the manifestation of the spirit of error within churches. After all, as Paul mentioned, a time will come "when people will not tolerate sound doctrine and accurate instruction." This means their ears are no longer turned to the truth, for they wish not to listen to those who are still standing and preaching the Truth. John makes it clear they, therefore, do not even know God or is of God.

It says in "Romans 8 (KJV): 9: Now if any man have not the Spirit of Christ, he is none of his." Let us take stock of this. In Romans 8, Paul is writing about a life led by the Spirit of the Lord and not the dictates of the flesh. He, therefore, said that those who do not have the Spirit do not belong to the Lord (take into consideration the Lord's teaching in John 3 regarding the importance of being reborn in the Spirit). These are harsh words, but it is about the same as what John said. He said those who do not listen to the Truth are not of God. Remember, the Spirit of the Lord was poured out to lead us in all truth. So if we truly are led by the Lord, we are then led by the Spirit, and then our ears should be turned to the truth, and we should be embracing the truth. If our ears are turned away from the truth, then how can we truly be in the Spirit, and therefore how can we belong to the Lord?

Apostasy in the last days is marked by large-scale deceptions and false teachings. It is the days as described by Paul regarding the itching ears turning to many teachers ... this then also implies the teachers are also false because the itching ears are turning away from the Truth. After all, we read they are turning away their ears to satisfy their own desires and to support the errors they hold and will turn their ears away from the truth and will wander off into myths and man-made fictions [and will accept the unacceptable]. Again, we see the connection between what Paul wrote and what John wrote regarding the error. Of course, what they warned about links up to the false prophets and teachers as described by Peter in 2 Peter 2. Yes, apostasy is rife in churches because so many are turning away their ears to listen to the spirit of error, instead of the spirit of truth.

So Apostasy is very much characterised by the spirit of error because so many are turning away from the Truth as taught by Jesus and the first disciples. Again, if our ears are turned away from the Truth, as we see happening more and more in churches, then you have to wonder who truly belongs to the Lord. After all, if we belong to the Lord, we shall know the voice of the Shepherd (John 10), and we shall be led by the Spirit who leads us in all truth.

Again, a mark of a true believer is one who turns his ears to the Truth, who seeks the truth, and who speaks the truth of the Lord. After all, a true disciple worships in spirit and truth and therefore walks in the spirit of truth and not the spirit of error. One should remember that apostasy deals with a falling away from key and true doctrines of the Bible into heretical teachings that proclaim to be "the real" Christian doctrine, and also to a complete renunciation of the Christian faith, which results in full abandonment of Christ. The latter is the goal of the devil – to get the believer in a position where he becomes so confused and deceived that he even abandons God. Think it cannot happen? We need to wake up then, for it is happening all around us, and many who are preaching on the pulpit are even questioning God or are not even walking in the Spirit of the Lord!

We are living more than ever in such a time of apostasy. A time of false prophets and false christs WITHIN the church. We are living in the time of 2 Timothy 4, where more than ever those within the church system are abandoning sound doctrine to believe fables and myths, and they are lured away and deceived by the lying wonders and false power and signs.

It is interesting to note that the apostasy will be accompanied by great signs and wonders. It says in "Revelation 13:13-14 of the beast that comes out of the earth:

"He performs great signs, so that he even makes fire come down from heaven on the earth in the sight of men. And he deceives those who dwell on the earth by those signs which he was granted to do in the sight of the beast, telling those who dwell on the earth to make an image to the beast who was wounded by the sword and lived."

It also reminds me of the warning of Jesus in John 4: When he heard that Jesus had come out of Judaea into Galilee, he went unto him, and besought him that he would come down, and heal his son: for he was at the point of death. 48 Then said Jesus unto him, Except ye see signs and wonders, ye will not believe.

And also "Matthew 12: 38 Then certain of the scribes and of the Pharisees answered, saying, Master, we would see a sign from thee. 39 But he answered and said unto them, An evil and adulterous generation seeketh after a sign; and there shall no sign be given to it, but the sign of the prophet Jonas."

We cannot deny that the Charismatic Movement is now all about the experience instead of the Word. People flock to churches for signs and wonders as if that validated the authenticity of the pastor. The promise of signs and wonders is used as some kind of marketing tool, for indeed, we sit with a church that seeks signs and wonders above the reality of the Lord or the reality of the Word (Sound Doctrine). Signs and wonders are all about the experience, the feeling and the hype, yet we drift further away from the fundamentals of the Truth of the Lord. And without discernment, we forget even the devil will use signs and wonders to deceive many because, in the end, we trust in the work, outcome and manifestation of the sign and wonder instead of being grounded in the Word. Can we see the problem? If the sign and wonder are fake, or even demonic, we would rather trust in the tangible reality of it and what it means to us instead of being led by the Spirit and the Word.

Mark 16: 17 And these signs shall follow them that believe; In my name shall they cast out devils; they shall speak with new tongues; 18 They shall take up serpents; and if they drink any deadly thing, it shall not hurt them; they shall lay hands on the sick, and they shall recover. Signs and wonders are never really about assuring the believer, but it is about the validation and the authentication that the Kingdom of God is one of power that saves, restores and delivers those in darkness unto the light. For it says in

Acts 2:43: "Then fear came upon every soul and many signs and wonders were done through the apostles."

We are never called to follow after signs and wonders, but according to Mark 16, signs and wonders should follow those who believe. For what reason? So that we can be exalted, glorified or praised? Of course not! It is so that the Kingdom of God is manifested to a broken world, and that people can be delivered from the bondage of the devil. The reality of our spiritual walk should not be grounded in signs and wonders, but in the Lord, who is the Word, and for this reason, Jesus withstood the devil by stating, "It is written". The devil tried to fool and trick the Lord with signs and wonders of power, but the Lord remained steadfast in the Word.

Strangely enough, if you are strong in faith, you don't need signs and wonders to know that the Father cares for you. You don't need to be further convinced of God by exhibiting power. We don't need signs and wonders to prove that He exists or that He hears our prayers. Faith comes by hearing the word about Christ (Romans 10:17). Without seeing any evidence of supernatural manifestations, we can believe because God has granted us grace to believe based upon the testimony of His Word. Faith is to work from his word. The Lord requires faith; however, we are more blessed who believe without seeing (John 20:29). Faith is the foundation upon which rests everything we receive in our spiritual life.

Scripture and history prove that signs and wonders do not instil faith, just the opposite, for lack of faith prompts one's desire to see signs and wonders. John 12:37 But although He had done so many signs before them, they did not believe in Him. John 4:48 Then Jesus said to him, "Unless you people see signs and wonders, you will by no means believe." Jesus was therefore disappointed that it took the miraculous for people to listen to his teachings or follow.

The problem is that some people seek signs and wonders because they want confirmation of the truth of God. There is nothing inherently wrong with this desire. God willingly gave signs to Moses (Exodus 4:1-9) and Gideon (Judges 6:11-22) to confirm His word. Miracles can aid a person's coming to faith, as in John 2:23, "Many people saw the miraculous signs he was doing and believed in his name." Yet, it becomes a problem when our very spiritual reality is solely determined by signs and wonders that we perceive through our physical senses.

Some people also seek after signs and wonders because they are curious thrill-seekers. Like the crowds in John 6:2 and King Herod in Luke 23:8, they want to see something sensational, but they have no real desire to know the truth of Christ. And then you get those who seek after signs and wonders because they hope to get something for themselves. After Jesus fed the multitudes, a large crowd followed Him to the other side of Galilee. Jesus saw their true motivation, however, and rebuked it: "I tell you the truth, you are looking for me, not because you saw miraculous signs but because you ate the loaves and had your fill" (John 6:26). The crowd's desire was not to know Christ or even to see more miracles; it was simply to fill their stomachs again.

Yes, our God is a God of wonders (Psalm 136:3-4). As the Creator and Sustainer of all that is, God has the power to suspend natural laws to fulfil His purposes. Miracles were a part of the ministries of Moses, Elijah and Elisha, and of course Jesus and the apostles, and their miracles primarily served the purpose of confirming their message as being from God (Hebrews 2:3-4). Today, many people still seek to experience the miraculous, and some will go to great lengths to have that experience. But our walk with God is not about the experience or the feeling or what we perceive with our senses, but in our relationship with God, which is solidified by our faith.

And so the devil has used signs and wonders to lead people astray, for they trust in the experience instead of building their spiritual life upon the Word by abiding in Christ. The danger for the church has always been extremes – the extreme of intellectualism and the extreme of emotionalism. We are called to walk a balanced spiritual life as worshippers in Spirit and Truth, for then we shall not be deceived and be led astray by doctrines that promote apostasy.

There is nothing new under the sun, so false teachings and doctrines have always been a mark of the church. Yet Paul warns of the final and great rebellion – a large-scale abandonment of the truth.

The apostasy that we see in the churches these days, in the form of false doctrines and false teachings, highlighted in 2 Peter 2, has been around for a long time. It is only that we are seeing these false doctrines and teachings being accepted on a much larger scale, engulfing and enveloping so many believers. Mass communication, aided by swift advancements in technology, has aided the promotion and promulgation of these false teachings that have fanned the profane flame of apostasy.

As mentioned, a great threat to sound doctrine is the doctrine of Oneness, or the Jesus Only movement, which claims God is not a Trinity. Deceptive teachings on the Trinity of God are not new. Back in the years 250 to 336AD, Arius, a Christian priest from Alexandria, Egypt, who was trained at Antioch in the early fourth century, accused Bishop Alexander of Alexandria of subscribing to Sabellianism, a false teaching which asserted that the Father, Son, and Holy Spirit were merely roles or modes assumed by God at various times. Arius was determined to emphasise the oneness of God; however, he went too far in his teaching of God's nature.

Arius denied the Trinity and introduced what appeared on the surface to be an inconsequential difference between the Father and Son.

Arius argued that Jesus was not homoousios (of the same essence) as the Father, but was rather homoiousios (of similar essence). Only one Greek letter – the iota – separated the two. Arius described his position in this manner: "The Father existed before the Son. There was a time when the Son did not exist. Therefore, the Son was created by the Father. Therefore, although the Son was the highest of all creatures, he was not of the essence of God."

Even though "Arianism" might suggest that Arius was the originator of the teaching that bears his name, the debate over the Son's precise relationship to the Father did not begin with him. This subject had been discussed for decades before his advent; Arius merely intensified the controversy and carried it to a Church-wide audience.

Then there was Peter Abelard (1079–1142), who was the pre-eminent philosopher and theologian of the twelfth century. He is regarded, arguably, as the greatest logician of the Middle Ages and is equally famous as the first great nominalist philosopher. He championed the use of reason in matters of faith (he was the first to use 'theology' in its modern sense). He came under fire for this reasoning regarding the Trinity, with his views bordering on Tritheism, which is the belief that cosmic divinity is composed of three powerful entities. In other words, he suggested three different gods.

Arius and Abelard (who was opposed by the sound doctrine as preached by St Bernard) represented a form of apostasy which encapsulated a denial of key Christian truths (such as the divinity of Christ) that begins a downhill slide into a full departure from the faith, which is the second form of apostasy. It is important to understand that the second form almost always begins with the first. A heretical belief becomes a heretical teaching that splinters and grows until it pollutes all aspects of a person's faith, and then the end goal of Satan is accomplished, which is a complete falling away from Christianity.

In A.D. 325, the Council of Nicaea convened primarily to take up the issue of Arius and his teaching. Much to Arius's dismay, the result was his ex-communication and a statement in the Nicene Creed that affirmed Christ's divinity: "We believe in one God, the Father Almighty, maker of all things visible and invisible; and in one Lord Jesus Christ, the Son of God, the only-begotten of his Father, of the substance of the Father, God of God, Light of Light, very God of very God, begotten not made, being of one substance with the Father."

The reality is that apostasy abounds in our churches, and there are even those who are still in ministry yet who have abandoned their faith! A 2010 study was done by prominent atheists Daniel Dennett and Linda LaScola called "Preachers Who Are Not Believers." Dennett and LaScola's work chronicles five different preachers who, over time, were presented with and accepted heretical teachings about Christianity and now have completely fallen away from the faith and are either pantheists or clandestine atheists. One of the most disturbing truths highlighted in the study is that these preachers maintain their position as pastors of Christian churches, with their congregations being unaware of their leaders' true spiritual state.

The dangers of apostasy were also warned about in the book of Jude, which serves as a handbook for understanding the characteristics of apostates like those chronicled in Dennett and LaScola's study. Jude's words are every bit as relevant for us today as they were when he penned them in the first century.

He writes: "3 Beloved, when I gave all diligence to write unto you of the common salvation, it was needful for me to write unto you, and exhort you that ye should earnestly contend for the faith which was once delivered unto the saints. 4 For there are certain men crept in unawares, who were before of old ordained to this condemnation, ungodly men, turning the grace of our God into lasciviousness, and denying the only Lord God, and our Lord Jesus Christ."

Jude was the half-brother of Jesus and a leader in the early church. In his New Testament letter, he outlines how to recognise apostasy and strongly urges those in the body of Christ to contend earnestly for the faith (vs. 3). The Greek word translated "contend earnestly" is a compound verb from which we get the word "agonise." It is in the present infinitive form, which means that the struggle will be continuous. In other words, Jude is telling us that there will be a constant fight against false teaching and that Christians should take it so seriously that we "agonise" over the fight in which we are engaged. Moreover, Jude makes it clear that every Christian is called to this fight, not just church leaders, so all believers must sharpen their discernment skills so that they can recognise and prevent apostasy in their midst.

After urging his readers to contend earnestly for the faith, Jude highlights the reason: "For certain persons have crept in unnoticed, those who were long beforehand marked out for this condemnation, ungodly persons who turn the grace of our God into licentiousness and deny our only Master and Lord, Jesus Christ" (vs. 4). In this one verse, Jude provides Christians with three traits of apostasy and apostate teachers.

First, Jude says that apostasy can be subtle. Jude uses the word "crept" to describe the apostate's entry into the church. The word means "slip in sideways; come in stealthily; sneak in; hard to detect." In other words, Jude says it is rare that apostasy begins in an overt and easily detectable manner. Instead, it looks a lot like Arius' preaching in which, nonchalantly, only a single letter differentiates his doctrine from the real teaching of the Christian faith.

Second, Jude describes the apostates as "ungodly" and as those who use God's grace as a license to commit unrighteous acts. Beginning with "ungodly," Jude describes eighteen unflattering traits of apostates so his readers can more easily identify them. Jude says the apostates are ungodly (vs. 4), morally perverted (vs. 4), denying Christ (vs. 4), ones who defile the flesh (vs. 8), rebellious (vs. 8), people who revile angels (vs. 8), who are ignorant about God (vs. 8), those who proclaim false visions (vs. 10), self-destructive (vs. 10), grumblers (vs. 16), fault finders (vs. 16), self-satisfying (vs. 16), people who use arrogant words and false flattery (vs. 16), mockers of God (vs. 18), those who cause divisions (vs. 19), worldly-minded (vs. 19), and finally (and not surprisingly), devoid of the Spirit/unsaved (vs. 19).

Third, Jude says apostates "deny our only Master and Lord, Jesus Christ." How do apostates do this? Paul tells us in his letter to Titus, "To the pure, all things are pure; but to those who are defiled and unbelieving, nothing is pure, but both their mind and their conscience are defiled. They profess to know God, but by their deeds they deny Him, being detestable and disobedient and worthless for any good deed" (Titus 1:15-16, emphasis added). Through their unrighteous behaviour, the apostates show their true selves. Unlike an apostate, a true believer is someone who has been delivered from sin to righteousness in Christ.

Ultimately, the sign of an apostate is that he eventually falls away and departs from the truth of God's Word and His righteousness. The apostle John signifies this is a mark of a false believer: "They went out from us, but they were not really of us; for if they had been of us, they would have remained with us; but they went out, so that it would be shown that they all are not of us" (1 John 2:19).

That God takes apostasy and false teaching seriously is evidenced by the fact that every New Testament book except Philemon contains warnings about false teaching. Why is this? It should be remembered that Satan did not come to the first couple in the Garden with an external armament or supernatural weapon; instead, he came to them with an idea. And it was that idea that condemned them and the rest of humankind, with the only remedy being the sacrificial death of God's Son.

Sadly, until Christ returns and every last spiritual enemy has been removed, we will deal with apostasy in the church, which has become worldwide. This reminds us of Matthew 13: 24 Another parable put he forth unto them, saying, The kingdom of heaven is likened unto a man which sowed good seed in his field: 25 But while men slept, his enemy came and sowed tares among the wheat, and went his way.26 But when the blade sprang up, and brought forth fruit, then appeared the tares also. 27 So the servants of the householder came and said unto him, Sir, didst not thou sow good seed in thy field? From whence then hath it tares? 28 He said unto them, An enemy hath done this. The servants said unto him, Wilt thou then that we go and gather them up? 29 But he said, Nay; lest while ye gather up the tares, ye root up also the wheat with them. 30 Let both grow together until the harvest: and in the time of harvest I will say to the reapers, Gather ye together first the tares, and bind them in bundles to burn them: but gather the wheat into my barn.

It is therefore critical, now more than ever, that every believer pray for discernment, combat apostasy, and contend earnestly for the faith that has once and for all been delivered to the saints.

In conclusion, let us ponder on what Paul wrote in 2 Thessalonians 2, which we should take to heart and consider deeply in our times of apostasy: 15 Therefore, brethren, stand fast, and hold the traditions which ye have been taught, whether by word, or our epistle. 16 Now our Lord Jesus Christ himself, and God, even our Father, which hath loved us, and hath given us everlasting consolation and good hope through grace, 17 Comfort your hearts, and establish you in every good word and work.

Yes, let us stand fast, as Paul also wrote in Ephesians 6 and let us endure by preaching sound doctrine. Indeed, let us stand and not compromise. God wants a committed love relationship with us, and He is not prepared to share our affections with any other. He will not tolerate what might be called an "open relationship" in today's terms – He is strictly monogamous.

Rise of the true worshippers

God is calling for His end-time Bride to return to the heart of worship, which is more than just singing songs. It is about fellowship, communion, intimacy and abiding in the Lord. We are called to be worshippers in Spirit and truth, meaning true worshippers have a heart for God, seek His presence above all and seek to glorify Him with their entire being!

True worshippers speak of servants willing to serve God in complete obedience. They seek intimacy with God, and they shall not bow to other idols. Yet, they are sold out to God, for God is their only King and their first love! True worshippers are arising out of the ashes. While service to act is indeed an act of worship, many true worshippers will glorify and exalt God through song, dance, and their creative artistry! Indeed, such worshippers will stir the spiritual realm, ushering in God's presence, for they shall glorify God with a true and humble heart of worship!

The Heart of Worship, a song by Matt Redman, sums it up beautifully: When the music fades, all is stripped away and I simply come, longin' just to bring something that's of worth, that will bless Your heart, I'll bring You more than a song for a song in itself is not what You have required, you search much deeper within, through the ways things appear, you're looking into my heart, I'm comin' back to the heart of worship, and it's all about You, it's all about You, Jesus, I'm sorry, Lord, for the thing I've made it when it's all about You, it's all about You, Jesus.

For the true worshippers, it is all about Jesus, and nothing else! True worshippers are those who enjoy a loving and real relationship with the Lord. They are submitted, yielded, and surrendered unto His glory, beauty and majesty. They have truly died to the self to see Adonai glorified! True worshippers, be they singers, dancers, prophetic flag bearers, or just disciples serving God, are those who seek to be a living sacrifice unto God, so that His fires may burn within us through the indwelling presence of the Holy Spirit. True worshippers are those who seek to become a pleasing offering unto Him, and, therefore, a sweet aroma. Yes, they burn with God, and they seek only His Spirit. Yes, they long and yearn to be in His Presence and to lift Him higher!

The heart of worship is relationship. God has not called us to follow a religion, which is a man-made system of rules, regulations and traditions. He calls us to follow Him and to be WORSHIPPERS OF SPIRIT AND TRUTH. Worship is far more than raising your hands and lifting your voice to the Lord; it is about a heart seeking the Lord, a heart loving the Lord, and a heart yearning for the Lord. King David had such a heart for the Lord. The Hebrew word for worship is Shachah - "to depress, meaning prostrate (in homage to royalty or God): bow (self) down, crouch, fall down (flat), humbly beseech, do reverence, make to stoop, worship."

There are three Greek words for worship. They are a) Proskuneo (to fawn or crouch, pay homage, it originally carried with it the idea of subjects falling to kiss the ground before a king or kiss their feet), b) Sebomai (to reverence, hold in awe), c) Latreuo (to render service of homage).

True worship, therefore, begins with deep respect or reverence for God, a frame of heart and an attitude. It speaks of reverent submission and bowing before the true King of kings. Worship is about a lifestyle. It is about intimate relationships. It is about consecration and being set apart for His Glory and to His Glory. We can only walk in such reverence, in such a manner and in such a relationship once we die to the Self, once we lay down our crowns and in love and Spirit to seek Him and follow Him above all else.

In the end times, true relationship with the Lord, true worship, true intimacy, and the value of the Covenant of Blood have become lost and blurred amid all the noise, smoke and mirrors of religion, traditions and worldly attractions. It is time to restore the heart of worship. It is time to restore God to the throne of our hearts, for then, as a worthy sacrifice unto the Lord, the fire shall fall and cleanse, purify and refine us. For then, as we become a "pleasing offering" by the fire of heaven and the cleaning of the Blood, we worship Him in Spirit and truth.

The Scriptures speak about loving God with all your heart (Mark 12:30) and trusting God with all your heart (Proverbs 3:5). Yes, there are hundreds of Scriptures dealing with the heart – such as writing His laws upon one's heart and about guarding one's heart. The heart is very important, for it is not just the source of our life, but it speaks of a God of all creation who calls all creation to love Him and to worship Him. Our hearts need to be renewed as we reconnect with God, the one who has made us wonderfully in the secret place (Psalm 139).

Do you know the heart has four chambers? Yes, and each chamber has a specific function, yet the heart acts as one, just as the brain is made up of three areas of functionality, yet operates as one. In the Bible, four always speaks of creation, since in creation there are four seasons, four wind directions and four elements (wind, fire, earth, water). The four living creatures in the Bible standing around the Throne represent Creation, as they come in the appearance of man, a lion, an ox, and the flying eagle (Revelation 4:7). God made the heart with four chambers, for it reminds us that at the heart of God's creation is man. We have been made, thus created, in His image. We are His masterpiece. God has placed our heart with four chambers within us, for it speaks of man being the focal point of creation, for we are God's creation. Just so the heart, created by the Creator for His creation, keeps us as His creation alive and functioning. All of creation speaks of the God of Life. The Scriptures also say life is in the Blood, so for this reason, the focal point of creation – man – is kept alive by every beat of the heart that pumps blood, for blood is life.

Thus, the heart of the Creator beats for mankind – His creation – so that they worship and love Him. And we do so when we love Him as His creation with all our heart, for this is the mark of our creation by the Creator. He has called us to adore Him, just as the elders worship Him around the throne. We are called as His creation now and for all eternity to praise Him, singing Hallelujah and Glory unto our Creator. And so within us beats a heart – a heart of four chambers – to remind us of the God of all creation, of the God of life, and the One who has made us all.

Jesus shed His Blood so that we as God's creation may live, so that our hearts may beat as one with God, and so that we may be redeemed, restored and saved. To say we must love God with all our heart and to trust Him with all our heart speaks of loving God fully as His creation, for our heart represents God's Life and God's Sovereignty as the Creator of all. And we honour Him for His Blood gives us new life, just as our heart constantly pumps blood throughout our body to keep us alive. This is when we engage in true worship.

We are called to worship Him in Spirit and truth, with our heart that speaks of creation beating in unison with the heart of the Creator. This is the epitome of abiding in God, and so we then grasp how God longs to tabernacle with us. The Lord is calling His Bride to worship and prayer. We need to know worship – it is the act of prostrating oneself in utter abandonment, humility, consecration and obedience unto the Lord. It implies leaning towards the Lord, drawing closer to Him with all our strength and might. We need to again fall prostrate before Him in our daily lives, submitting to Him, yielding, yielding, and yielding - we need to bow, and we need to search for Him.

From true worship flows all - from worship flows the hunger for the Lord, and from worship flows obedience, submission, love, compassion and a heart aching for the lost and dying. The saints are called to worship, worship and worship - fall before Him, seek him, call Him, for He draws near to those who draw near to Him. In worship, the Lord speaks, in worship the Lord moves in our Spirit and in worship the Lord reveals Himself. In worship, we lean towards Him and we are taught His principles, His laws, His ordinances, His statutes, His constitution and His precepts. Worship has been distorted into a concept of noise, performance, showmanship and emotionalism. Big noise, big lights and big events do not catch the attention of YHVH.

A still humble heart, captivated by the beauty of the Father, is what stirs the heart of the Master. A heart moved by the lost and the broken and the hurting stirs the Father's heart. A heart seeking to know the beauty of salvation and the delivering power of truth stirs the Father's heart.

Only when the children return to the Father will they be taught how to worship in Spirit and Truth? True worship takes place before the Mercy Seat in the Holy of Holies. For there, in that place of worship, the true bond of Father and child grows strong. True worship is the inward journey to where the Father dwells in our Spirit. True worship is when we abandon all, not only in the Holy of Holies but also in life, to worship Him. In that silence, one's spirit is embraced by His Spirit and quickened. Indeed, the flesh profits none.

Our spirit is moved then not by words or manifestation, but by His mere presence. It is not moved by needs, wants or desires, but by simple adoration. Let us draw closer and look upon His face. God seeks humble, pure-in-spirit Crusaders (disciples loving God), called to free the lost from the clutches of darkness through the Blood of Jesus. He seeks crusaders walking in love, truth and honesty, seeking no glory but only His will. Let the Crusaders not walk in hate, intolerance and anger. Let the glory come down. His presence brings you to your knees. It strips away all vanity and pride. It crushes all worth and arrogance. Oh God, arise in our midst!

God calls for true worshippers who love His holiness, for in the Holy of Holies, there is perfect union with Father and child. Truth dwells in the Holy of Holies. As we are in union with the Lord, we are in union with the Word, who is Jesus, who is the Bread of Life (manna) and the Truth (Commandments) and who came to give us life through grace. Union with the Lord leads to obedience and willingness unto His commandments and precepts. Such obedience comes not from duty or obligations, but because those who dwell in the Holy of Holies walk in the sweet surrendered union with the Father, His Spirit and Son. Out of such union flows intimacy, and in intimacy is true power.

In the Holy of Holies, our spirit calls unto deep and we flow in His Spirit. Oh, why do we seek noise when the Holy of Holies is silent? Why do we need performance when the Lord seeks truth and honesty? The Lord is present in the silence. He is in the stillness of the spirit. He dwells in the realms where a contrite spirit stirs Him. We behold Him as we draw towards Him in the Holy of Holies. There, in His loving embrace, He captivates our spirit as He draws us closer to knowing the truth in Spirit. It is in the Holy of Holies where we taste that commanded moment of surrender and perfect union, producing a clarity that rises like the dawn and where revelation is birthed like creation. If we live a life of true union with the Father, thus walking in the sweet ways of the Holy of Holies, then our strength will soar like an eagle, and we will run and not grow faint, and we will walk and not grow weary.

The great heresy of the church today is that we think we're in the entertainment business. A.W. Tozer believed this to be true back in the 1950s and '60s. Church members "want to be entertained while they are edified," he said in 1962. Tozer grieved, even then, that it was "scarcely possible in most places to get anyone to attend a meeting where the only attraction was God." Yes, we have replaced the true heart of worship with cheap tricks, emotionalism, gimmicks and shallow entertainment.

Like Tozer, we should be concerned that so many people in our churches want to be entertained while they worship. We should be concerned when we no longer recognise the difference between the two. Hallowedness has given way to shallowness. True worship is not about worship styles. What God is restoring is the heart, focus and intent of worship. Are we truly loving God? Are we truly adoring Him? We are not called to have a good time, but to love Him, adore Him, praise Him and revere Him! Yes, He must be our all and our everything, and He must consume us for He is an all-consuming fire! Let the true worshippers arise with a glorious song, with a heavenly melody, and may the dancers praise His holy Name! Yes, may we all as disciples be true worshippers who love Him!

In conclusion, true worship reminds me of that beautiful song called Dance With Me.

It says: *Behold You have come over the hills, upon the mountain to me, You will run; My Beloved, You've captured my heart; behold You have come over the hills, upon the mountain to me, You will run; My Beloved, You've captured my heart, won't You dance with me Oh, Lover of my soul to the song of all songs? For the Church, God should be our first love, our Fair One, for only He deserves all our praise. Yes, praise Him, for indeed "'Holy, holy, holy is the Lord God Almighty,' who was, and is, and is to come."*

Rise of God's end-times messengers

It has been placed in my spirit of late that God is not only establishing His end-time Bride to endure and overcome perilous times, but also to raise messengers/witnesses for such a critical time. After all, we know the end times will be spiritually very intense, as the spiritual war wages and deception along with rebellion deepen to incredible levels of apostasy (especially within the Babylonian church system).

The true Bride, therefore, the remnant who has not bowed the knee to Babylon like the 7000 mentioned by God when encouraging Elijah, needs to be fully prepared, trained, equipped and empowered to stand (in accordance with Ephesians 6) for such times. Paul warned in 2 Thessalonians 2 that BEFORE the coming of Christ, we will see the great falling away (which applies to the church, also see 2 Timothy 3, 2 Timothy 4, of rejecting truth) and then the man of sin/lawlessness will be revealed. The rebellion in the church has been in motion for a long time, yet the intensity of the apostasy is quickening and bounds unchecked; it seems to be heading into greater calamity and spiritual conflict (also read 2 Peter 2, Book of Jude).

In such times, the remnant will be called to not only remain standing and resisting the agendas, schemes and brainwashing of the devil but also to overcome and fulfil the Great Commission in the power of God. After all, the urgency of OVERCOMING is highlighted in the letters to the churches in Revelation. The remnant will need to know how to OVERCOME, how to thrive in the storms, and how to remain standing in the truth and not bow to the spirit of error, deception, wickedness and lawlessness.

Matthew 24 says, "4 And Jesus answered and said to them: 'Take heed that no one deceives you." Wherever you look, there is a great deception at work. Because we live in the last of the last days and are rapidly heading towards the end of the age, we must be alert to the fact that the devil is attempting to groom and modify both the church and the world to receive the man of lawlessness, who is, of course, the Antichrist. A massive undertaking is being executed to lead mankind into a state of epic lawlessness (rebellion), which will open the doors to greater demonic onslaughts.

We can see how people's minds are being inundated with false information and a celebration of various forms of lies and deception, including a deluge of false propaganda about human sexuality, Christianity, religion, the true and the false, and the good and the bad. This is a last-day attack of seducing spirits bent on modifying the collective mind of society and those whom satan will take captive, within the church, to do his will - yes, in the church. Thus creating a way of thinking that is free of moral restraint.

In the midst of all of this, God is raising end-time messengers/witnesses to equip and prepare the remnant. This will also include messages of correction and rebuke, for we have strayed dangerously away from God's ordained ancient paths. We need to understand that such messengers are specifically called for a specific task, and this is different to the mandate given to all disciples to be messengers of the Gospel in accordance with the Great Commission.

For this, we have been empowered (Acts 1:8), which is to show Christ to the world. Yet the message of the Gospel is for the lost and unsaved. The end-time messages are for the church specifically, similar to the letters to the seven churches in the Book of Revelation.

Paul wrote in "2 Timothy 4:17 But the Lord stood with me and strengthened me, so that the message might be preached fully through me, and that all the Gentiles might hear." Paul was called to be a messenger to the Gentiles of the Gospel, so that the Gentiles may also be saved by the Blood of the Lamb. He fulfilled this task diligently (see Acts 20:7). Yet the end-time messengers/witnesses will deal specifically with the remnant and be carriers of various but very specific messages. They are born for a time like now.

It needs to be made clear that such messengers are not necessarily prophets. And not all prophets are end-time messengers. Such messengers carry different callings and mandates. They are each uniquely gifted and empowered with natural and spiritual gifts. God is restoring intercession (prayer) and worship in the remnant (who is the true Bride/Ecclesia). He is restoring the truth of His Kingdom in the hearts of the true worshippers of Spirit and truth. The remnant shall be prepared and equipped for spiritual warfare. There will be many messages vital for preparation and equipping, which means messengers of all gifting and calling will be raised for such end times.

Such messengers and messages do not negate the great need to continue training and equipping the Bride to be true disciples in service of the Kingdom. Ephesians 4 makes it clear God has empowered some individuals (what we know as the apostles, prophets, evangelists, shepherds and teachers) to train disciples for the work of ministry. It should be noted that there is no such thing as the clergy vs laity (this is a man-made concept). All disciples of God are called to be activated and mobilised to fulfil the Great Commission, which includes being witnesses of the Gospel and making disciples.

John, who wrote the Book of Revelation, was an end-time messenger, for the end time already started with the ascension of Jesus and the outpouring of the Spirit. God used the apostle John to write messages addressed to seven notable church leaders, and these leaders would then share the messages with the rest of the church. His message is very specific and is still used to prepare and train the Bride in wisdom and knowledge of how to overcome and be prepared.

John the Baptist was also a messenger, for he came to prepare the way for the Lord and to declare the powerful message of repentance and baptism. Such messengers God is now raising will be like both John, for they shall prepare for the coming of Christ. Others will be like John, who wrote Revelation, for their visions, dreams, and revelations will serve to strengthen the remnant with knowledge and truth. Indeed, such messengers will be writers, some will be speakers, some will dream, some will see visions, some will be prayer warriors, some will be worshippers, and some will prophesy, some will teach, and some will just walk in God's manifested power! As John was sold out, these end-time messengers would be called to be sold out for God. As God separated John from the world, just so do not be surprised that God will separate such messengers in the end-times from the world. After all, God's Kingdom is not of this world! Yes, they must burn in the Spirit for God, seeking holiness, truth, and God's will, way and Kingdom above all.

The validity and importance of such messengers shouldn't come as a surprise, since angels function as messengers. Revelation 14:6-12 deals with the proclamations of three angels. One says, "Fear God and give glory to Him, for the hour of His judgment has come; and worship Him who made heaven and earth, the sea and springs of water," the other proclaimed "Babylon is fallen, is fallen, that great city, because she has made all nations drink of the wine of the wrath of her fornication," and the third angel said, "If anyone worships the beast and his image, and receives his mark on his forehead or on his hand, he himself shall also drink of the wine of the wrath of God, which is poured out full strength into the cup of His indignation." So we find the angels sharing specific messages designed for a specific and yet powerful purpose and function.

Revelation 1:20 says, "The mystery of the seven stars which you saw in My right hand, and the seven golden lampstands: The seven stars are the angels of the seven churches, and the seven lampstands which you saw are the seven churches." The Greek word angelos simply meant "messenger"; usually the word was used for supernatural "messengers" from God. However, sometimes the word was applied to human messengers of God's Word: John the Baptist is called an "angelos" in Matthew 11:10 (Kings James).

In the last of the last days, such divine activity to prepare the Bride and declare God's truth shall be accomplished through heavenly and natural messengers. They shall walk and function with God's servants for together the remnant in unity and love shall accomplish God's end-time purposes.

They shall not function as lone guns but will be supported and ministering with the watchmen, the intercessors, the worshippers, and those called to train the Bride in the Word of God (known by some as the five-fold ministry). The messengers shall not endure isolation, for the devil roams and seeks to devour. They shall become an integral part of God's remnant, seeking to strengthen other witnesses/messengers, and helping the remnant to overcome, thrive and be victorious in her mandate.

In Revelation 11:3–12, we find a description of two individuals who will help accomplish God's work during the tribulation: "I will appoint my two witnesses, and they will prophesy for 1,260 days, clothed in sackcloth" (verse 3). Nowhere does the Bible identify these two witnesses by name, although people through the years have speculated. Some say Moses and Elijah because of the nature of the miraculous powers to accompany their message (Revelation 11:6).

What is important is that no one will be able to stop them in their work (verse 5) until God's purpose for them has been fulfilled. They may be killed, but we read how they will be resurrected and, in full view of their enemies, ascend to heaven (verses 11–12). God has placed it on my heart that we will not only witness TWO such messengers in the last of the last days, but there will be many more. They have a specific task, carrying specific messages, and God will empower them mightily to fulfil His mandate.

What is important is that many messengers/witnesses will be known for signs, wonders and miracles, for God's power will flow through them to fulfil the purpose of the message. This calls for such messengers to be sold out for God, to seek Him, to become more sensitive to His Spirit, and to yearn for His Presence. They must remain humble, pure of heart, and completely yielded to God, for they are not special, but simply chosen for a time like this. God, in His Sovereignty, like He chose Cyrus, is preparing his end-time Bride, and He is choosing individuals to fight the good fight like never before.

We may live in perilous and intense times of danger and threats, but intense also will be the power of God working through the messengers! After all, Revelation 1:20 reminds us that the "stars" are held in Jesus' "right hand", which reminds us that the Lord Himself protects, upholds, and guides those who serve Him with His strength and wisdom.

Rise of prayer warriors, intercessors

The need for prayer warriors and true intercessors is of critical importance in the end times. The end-time remnant, therefore, the true Bride of Christ, is going to need a lot of prayers to remain standing, to endure, to overcome and also to fulfil its task of fulfilling the Great Commission. A lot of fervent prayers are also needed to pray for the lost, the forgotten, the broken, and the downtrodden.

It says in "James 5:16: The effective, fervent prayer of a righteous man avails much." We are involved in a spiritual war (whether we like it or not), and we live in terrible and perilous days of darkness, but those who seek His righteousness and follow God can stand upon the Word that one's prayer avails much! Prayer of the righteous will thus be useful and beneficial, all to the glory of God.

One man who knows about the power of prayer in difficult times is John Knox, who was born in Scotland in about 1514. Converted to Protestantism from Roman Catholicism in 1543, Knox lived during a time when it was often very dangerous to be a follower of Christ.

When the Roman Catholic Mary Tudor (also known as "Bloody Mary" because of her ruthless persecution of the Protestants) became queen in 1553, Knox, who was in England at this time, was forced to hide. He eventually landed in Geneva, where he met John Calvin, who became his mentor. Knox returned to Scotland in 1559, the year after Queen "Bloody Mary" died and was succeeded by the Protestant Queen Elizabeth. He remained in Scotland, bringing reformation to the church until his death in 1572.

Today, people remember Knox as the leader of the Protestant Reformation in Scotland and the founder of Scottish Presbyterianism. But what others don't realise is that by the end of his ministry, he became better known for his prayer than for his other ministries. The devout Catholic Mary, Queen of Scots, is reputed to have said, "I fear the prayers of John Knox more than all the assembled armies of Europe."

She saw the impact of Knox's prayer. From a human point of view, it was the prayer of Knox that sparked the Reformation in Scotland. His prayer became the fuel of the ongoing reformation during his time. His prayer shook the land of Scotland, causing a revival among God's people.

Perhaps of all the prayers of Knox, "Give me Scotland, or I die" is the most quoted one. It was not an arrogant prayer but a passionate plea, showing his intense desire for the conversion of the people of Scotland. His prayer was an expression of his great confidence in God. His prayer also echoes the Apostle Paul's prayer in Romans 10:1, "my heart's desire and prayer to God for Israel is, that they might be saved."

Knox remained prayerful even to death. It is said that during his dying hours, he was much engaged in meditation and prayer. Knox was not perfect, but we can definitely learn from his prayer life.

Prayer is not an option for the believer. It is a necessity to fulfil God's purposes in the world and in our individual lives. Time spent in prayer is not time wasted but time invested. As we embrace the will of God, as we live before Him in the righteousness of Christ, as we seek to fulfil His purposes, nothing will be able to hinder our prayers, and we will begin to understand Jesus' saying, "With God all things are possible" (Matthew 19:26).

Indeed, we need prayer warriors like John Knox! We need true intercessors who have spent time at God's feet, lifting up the Bride, and praying for the lost to find their home in Christ!

It says in "Ephesians 6: 17 And take the helmet of salvation, and the sword of the Spirit, which is the word of God; 18 praying always with all prayer and supplication in the Spirit, being watchful to this end with all perseverance and supplication for all the saints— 19 and for me, that utterance may be given to me, that I may open my mouth boldly to make known the mystery of the gospel, 20 for which I am an ambassador in chains; that in it I may speak boldly, as I ought to speak."

We often read about the armour of God, but so often we neglect a very important piece of the armour – prayer! And remember, the armour of God is critical to understand and grasp because in this spiritual war, we always need to wear it and keep the armour polished and functional. We are urged to pray always with all prayer and supplication in the Spirit.

A dedicated and functional prayer life is vital in our dangerous times, as we continuously seek the Lord's will, His ways and His truth. And when we speak by the Spirit, this can imply always praying as led by the Spirit, or speaking in the heavenly languages as given by the Spirit. Either way, Romans 8:26 holds true: "In the same way, the Spirit helps us in our weakness. We do not know what we ought to pray for, but the Spirit himself intercedes for us through wordless groans." The most powerful prayer is one prayed in the Spirit, even if it is in your earthly language, because it is driven by God Himself. There is great power in prayer!

Prayer is of critical importance! After all, there are dozens of real-life accounts in the Bible where Jesus and other disciples battled in prayer. God shut the heavens and prevented rain from falling for three years at Elijah's request. He parted the Red Sea for Moses to lead His people through. He cast out demons; Jesus healed the sick and gave sight to the blind, and on more than one occasion, raised people from the dead, like Lazarus.

The power of prayer isn't in the words you utter. It's not about what you pray or even how you pray. Prayer can be defined as talking to God, but it is much more than that. Prayer is an act of worship that glorifies God and reinforces our need for Him. Through living a life of prayer, we communicate with the very source of and purpose for our existence. Prayer flows from intimacy, from fellowship with God and a deep love for Him.

David was one of the greatest men who ever lived. He was a man after God's heart. He was a descendant of Abraham, Israel and Judah. He was a great warrior, builder and king. He was the first of his dynasty, which was chosen by God to bring forth the Messiah, the ultimate King of Israel and the nations. David was a prophet. And he was a poet and musician. And he prayed a lot – about everything. He wrote down many of his prayers and put them to music, creating the Book of Psalms.

He wrote most of the book of Psalms, which has been the prayer book of Israel and the Church for 3,000 years. David knew how to pray.

Following Pentecost and at the time of the birth of the Church, in Acts 2, we read of how the disciples would regularly meet to fellowship. The church experienced a vital growth, not only because it adhered to the truth, but because it continued steadfastly in prayer. When facing great danger, the early disciples sought the Lord and prayed. Yes, prayer is powerful! It is also vital, and as believers in Christ, we need to pray more. As believers, we are constantly facing threats, so as the corporate Bride, we need to seek the Lord in prayer. This calls for unity, just as the disciples, in the beginning, were united with Christ and each other.

Years ago, the Lord placed in my heart the absolute necessity for 24-hour prayer houses. God calls for a praying Bride, who seeks His will day and night. The devil knows that the fervent prayer of a righteous man avails much. He wants believers to stop praying or to pray less. He keeps us busy, for if we start praying collectively as the Bride, then surely the gates of hell shall be shaken!

Our English word "intercession" is derived from the Latin for "to come between," which means both "obstruct" and "to interpose on behalf of" someone. Christ stands between us and the Father. That's why we pray "in Jesus' name" because it's by His sacrifice that we are made righteous and can approach the throne of God. Believers are, therefore, able to bring the needs of other people before God through Christ.

While we may not all be gifted as intercessors to be steadfast in prayer (Colossians 4:2), we are all called to pray. Paul exhorted the church to pray that he would boldly declare the gospel (Ephesians 6:19). He told the church to pray for one another with "supplications [...] and thanksgivings," (1 Timothy 2:1), and he prayed for them too. "We give thanks to God always for all of you, constantly mentioning you in our prayers, remembering before our God and Father your work of faith and labor of love and steadfast hope in our Lord Jesus Christ" (1 Thessalonians 1:2). We all need intercession, even believers. Paul was moved and encouraged by prayer on his behalf.

You can say intercession is a prayer that pleads with God for your needs and the needs of others. But it is also much more than that. Intercession involves taking hold of God's will and refusing to let go until His will comes to pass. Intercession is warfare—the key to God's battle plan for our lives. But the battleground is not of this earth. Intercessory prayer takes place in this spiritual world where the battles for our own lives, our families, our friends and our nation are won or lost.

Intercessory prayer is simply a pointed, persistent pleading on behalf of someone else for a deep need. Specifically, in the New Testament, we read that Jesus and the Holy Spirit interceded on behalf of God's people for various reasons.

The reality is that we need a lot more intercessory prayer in the Body of Christ, and especially intercessors to heed the call for 24-hour prayer houses. We live in times of so much deception that all believers need prayer right now, and we need to pray day and night for the lost and the broken.

Remember, the Lord or the devil doesn't sleep. While we are human, we are also many in the Body of Christ. More than ever, there should be greater unity in the Body of Christ, where together believers take hands to pray and to stand in the gap. Through prayer, particularly intercession, the Body of Christ truly takes up its place on the watchtower while the spiritual war wages and the ancient dragon seeks to devour. In prayer, we must declare God's will, His glory and truth.

Intercession is vital these days as it has always been important throughout the Bible. Abraham interceded on Lot's behalf to save him from the destruction of his home town (Genesis 18-19), Jonah (though begrudgingly) interceded for the town of Nineveh (Jonah 3), and in the greatest act of intercession, Jesus came down to earth to live as one of us and interceded for our salvation (John 17:20-26; Luke 23:34).

As believers, we are not praying enough. 24-hour prayer houses are of critical importance, for the devil is on a rampage to destroy, kill and steal. Now is the time to pray for the youth, marriages, the Bride of Christ and for those still lost in the wilderness. It is time that all believers continue steadfastly in prayer, with the intercessors at the forefront of this mighty battle.

There is great power in prayer. We cannot only be occupied with preaching and teaching God's word, but we need to pray the word, and we need to seek the face of the Almighty day and night! 24-hour prayer houses. It is time. In every city and every town. Constant prayer across the globe, interceding and seeking the Lord's will and that His hand shall move in power.

Standing in the gap in these perilous hours

Ezekiel 22 says the following: "30 I searched for a man among them who would build up the wall and stand in the gap before Me for [the sake of] the land, that I would not destroy it, but I found no one [not even one]."

Ezekiel 22 summarises the sins and abuses of the nation. As punishment for Israel's sins, God says He will disperse them among the nations. In the ancient world of the Bible, cities had walls surrounding them to protect them from enemies. When the wall was breached, the city was vulnerable to destruction; the only way to secure it was for people, at times, to risk their lives by literally standing in the gap in the wall and fighting the enemy. Another option was for the gap to be repaired as soon as possible. If a breach were left unattended or unrepaired, the city would fall.

So in Ezekiel 22, the "gap" here represents the danger facing Jerusalem: God's wrath is about to break through in judgment on the sinful city. So the Lord asked if there was anyone who would, in righteousness, intercede on behalf of the city and seek God's mercy. If the gap is not repaired, then destruction is imminent. God searched for such a defender, but He could find none. It seems that, if someone had been willing to "stand in the gap," the destruction of Jerusalem could have been avoided. Since no one was available or willing to defend the breach and rebuild the wall, judgment fell.

This is similar to the Genesis account of the destruction of Sodom and Gomorrah. God reveals to Abraham that Sodom and Gomorrah are to be destroyed for their grave sins (18:20). Abraham pleads for the lives of any righteous people living there, especially the lives of his nephew, Lot, and his family.

Still today the question echoes of who will in this last hour of perilous times (2 Timothy 3:1), like Abraham, be willing to stand in the gap of the Church? Make no mistake, there are plenty of "gaps" in the church walls, and the church is facing the danger of being overrun by the enemy and even judgement at the hands of God for her idolatry, treachery and devious ways.

There is just no more room for us to argue that it is OK with the church. The enemy is no longer at the door but has been allowed to breach the walls. Sin, iniquity, witchcraft and all other forms of rebellion and carnal behaviour are evident in this Church, once described by Augustine as the City of God.

It is time to again take a stand on the walls and declare God's Word and God's Truth. It is time again to stand at the city gates and declare what is proper, holy and pure. It is time again to stand in the gap, and to defend God's holy ways and truth no matter the cost. Who is prepared in this hour to be true watchmen, to be a rebuilder of what is broken and a restorer of what the enemy (John 10:10) has stolen and trampled upon?

In the days of Ezekiel, Jerusalem was accused of several repulsive acts. This includes idolatry, shedding blood in the city and sexual immorality. It also says the following in "Ezekiel 25: 25 There is a conspiracy of her [false] prophets in her midst, like a roaring lion tearing the prey. They have devoured [human] life; they have taken [in their greed] treasure and precious things; they have made many widows among her. 26 Her priests have done violence to My law and have profaned My holy things. They have made no distinction between the holy (sacred) and the profane (secular), they have not taught [people] the difference between the unclean and the clean. 27 Her princes within her are like wolves tearing and devouring the prey, shedding blood and destroying lives in order to get dishonest gain. 28 Her prophets have smeared whitewash for them, seeing false visions and divining lies for them, saying, 'Thus says the Lord God'—when the Lord has not spoken. 29 The people of the land have practiced oppression and extortion and have committed robbery; they have wronged the poor and needy and they have oppressed the stranger without justice."

If we look at the state of the Church these days, then the similarities with Jerusalem are shocking. The Church also sits with a priesthood (all believers) who are struggling to distinguish between the holy (sacred) and the profane (secular).

We simply do not even know the truth anymore. We also sit with the counterfeit prophetic movement that has caused immense harm with so many false and misguided instructions and promises. Who can deny so many ministries and churches run like a business, where extortion, spiritual abuse and manipulation are rife in the quest for self-enrichment and self-glorification? Who can deny that so many believers have been oppressed from truly following their calling and mandate because of religious control (for even manipulation is a form of witchcraft). And while we may not have shed physical blood (even though the Church has done so hundreds of years ago during the wars between the Catholics and the Protestants), we have indeed done incredible spiritual harm through our dubious church practises, traditions and erroneous teachings. Jesus levelled such an accusation against the Pharisees and Sadducees in Matthew 23. Also read 2 Timothy 3, 2 Timothy 4, 2 Peter 2 and the Book of Jude.

Of Jerusalem, the Lord said: "4 I have made you an object of scorn to the [pagan] nations and a thing to be mocked by all countries. 5 Those who are near and those who are far from you will mock you, you [infamous one] of ill repute, full of turmoil." Can we not see or realise the Church has lost its credibility in the world? We are also in turmoil? The church's reputation is also if ill-repute.

Can we not see we have also become a laughingstock because the Church looks so much like the world and our action is these days more worldly than godly? Yes, this world mocks the Church for our shameful actions, falseness and hypocrisy. How can we indeed be victorious if we look so much like the enemy and the world? So who is willing to stand in the gap for the Church in these last days? Who is willing to stand for the truth? Who is willing to preach and teach the Word of God without compromise? Who is willing to seek the ancient of paths (Jeremiah 6:16)?

The one person who should be willing to stand in the gap is the prophet. After all, the prophet should be able to know what the danger is and where the 'wall' has been breached, what are the threats, what is God saying about it all and what God is instructing. This applies to the Church more than ever in this time and hour.

The prophet has the task of speaking God's will, His instruction, His correction, His truth and His message to repair the gap where needed, to mend the wall, to repel the attacks and to guard the gates. Such a task rests most assuredly with the prophetic, for the prophet should indeed be able to see, to know, to discern, and to understand the reality of the situation. And the prophet should be able to act according to God's will and God's plan and mandate.

A false prophet will not be able to discern, for by implication such a prophet walks not in alignment with God's thoughts, His will or even His reality. Such a prophet will act erroneously and even out of the will of God, causing greater harm and damage to the Body of Christ. Only a true prophet hears from God – be it directly or through dreams or visions. Such a prophet will not be misled by the flesh or the imagination or demonic forces, but the true Word and Will of the Lord Almighty.

Standing in the gap is thus an important function and role of the prophet. And thus the prophet is able to fulfil this role simply because of his or her mandate and calling. The prophet sees, hears and discerns as God leads and guides, and thus can operate sufficiently and effectively to accordingly fulfil God's commands. No action can be taken without clear understanding and discernment, which should flow from the true prophet.

Similar wording of standing in the gap is found in Psalm 106:23. This psalm summarizes the sins of Israel in the wilderness, primarily concerning the golden calf. Verse 23 explains, "So [God] said he would destroy them—had not Moses, his chosen one, stood in the breach before him to keep his wrath from destroying them." Moses "stood in the gap" and saved the people of Israel with his petition on their behalf. In standing in the gap, he "stepped between the LORD and the people" (Psalm 106:23, NLT). Moses had been chosen for that very purpose. The original story of Moses standing in the gap is found in Exodus 32:9–14: To stand in the gap is, therefore, to intercede and plead for God's mercy.

In Ezekiel's day, there was no Moses. No one interceded for Israel. No one understood the danger God's people were in. With no intercessor to stand in the gap, the destruction of Israel would be carried out. Not even the prophets were willing to stand in the gap. In Ezekiel 13 we read of the prophets: "4 O Israel, your prophets have been like foxes among the ruins. 5 You have not gone up into the gaps or breaches, nor built the wall around the house of Israel that it might stand in the battle on the day of the Lord." Sadly, instead of standing in the gap, the prophets simply denied that judgment was going to come. They were prophesying all is fine and declaring 'peace, peace' when there was no peace. They were speaking out of the imagination or even worse, by a different spirit. They were creating a false reality. Glory to God, these days there are still true prophets who are standing on the watchtower and many of them are willing to stand in the gap, praying and interceding. For the true prophets know the church is in danger. For the true prophets know there is no 'peace, peace' for idolatry and immorality is rife. Such prophets are declaring God's will, His Word and truth in the Spirit in such perilous days. But many have also turned a blind eye or have been seduced by a different reality or truth. Woe indeed to us.

Like Moses and Abraham, over the years, there have been those in the Church's history who have had the courage and insight to "stand in the gap" and intercede for others. Just think of the Reformation and of men like Martin Luther and Jan Hus.

We need once again more people like Stephen who prayed for those stoning him (Acts 7:60). Paul prayed for Israel's salvation (Romans 10:1), and so we need to stand up for God, for His Kingdom and intercede in prayer without ceasing in such perilous times. And so the Lord is looking for those who are willing to stand in the gap. The Lord Jesus is the master of standing in the gap, praying from the cross, "Father, forgive them, for they do not know what they are doing" (Luke 23:34) and continuing to intercede for us (Hebrews 7:25).

We follow Jesus, and thus we must also be standing in the gap right now, willing to give it all, no matter what, lest darkness fall upon us. James 5:16 KJV says the "effectual fervent prayer of a righteous man availeth much." How God is looking for people to stand for righteousness, to stand in faith and in truth. God doesn't need an army to stand in the gap, but only those who are willing to be obedient, faithful and willing to be a living sacrifice to the glory of God. This was proven by David, who slew Goliath, Gideon, who routed an entire army with a few men, and with Samson, who sowed fear in the hearts of the Philistines. Jesus picked only 12 disciples. We are only men and women filled by the Spirit again who will not back, or who will go quietly into the night!

John Knox is known as the leader of the Protestant Reformation in Scotland and the founder of Scottish Presbyterianism. By the end of his ministry, he became better known for his prayer than for his other ministries. The devout Catholic Mary, Queen of Scots, is reputed to have said, "I fear the prayers of John Knox more than all the assembled armies of Europe." She saw the impact of Knox's prayer. From a human point of view, it was the prayer of Knox that sparked the Reformation in Scotland. His prayer became the fuel of the ongoing reformation during his time. His prayer shook the land of Scotland, causing a revival among God's people. Perhaps of all the prayers of Knox, "Give me Scotland, or I die" is the most quoted one. It was not an arrogant prayer but a passionate plea, showing his intense desire for the conversion of the people of Scotland.

How God is looking for such men and women today, like Knox, who is willing to stand in the gap. A healthy Church leads to a healthy society and a healthy nation! Who is willing to fight for the soul of the church? Who is willing to intercede, to plead and speak God's word of truth? For correction is not done for judging, but to bless, for in correction comes the blessing. In God's wisdom and sovereignty, He has chosen to use the prayers of people to accomplish His will. He still seeks those who will stand in the gap for friends and family, for people groups and nations. And especially those who are willing to stand in the gap for the Church.

Like Abraham and Moses, we should be willing to stand in the gap, asking God to spare and save us. We must seek God's will, turn our ears more than ever towards God and be willing to follow where He leads. And this applies, as mentioned, most definitely, to the prophet. May the true prophets arise to stand in the gap, to act as the Lord leads and to even close the gap where necessary and in the will of God.

End-time watchmen to watch and pray

Today, in a spiritual sense, the Lord is also calling for watchmen, and in truth, every believer is a watchman. We have all, in varying ways, been tasked to keep guard, to watch, to be alert and to be aware of any dangers or threats against the Bride of God, against our families, our nation, our marriage and our very own lives. We need to stand guard against what is false, what is deception, counterfeit, unholy, profane, carnal and rebellious in nature.

We find watchmen of all kinds of nature, and of calling and of importance and of ability. Just as in the days of Israel, we too find in the church-appointed watchmen who keep watch over the local congregation from an external point of view similar to one standing on a rooftop gazing over the fields, and we also find those watchmen who are more internally involved in the flow of spiritual matters, making sure that no idolatry, rebellion or lawlessness takes hold internally.

We also find watchmen who keep watch and guard corporately over the Bride, and we also find watchmen who are stationed in the "countryside", meaning the marketplaces of this world, where a lot of the saints are in operation. The end-time remnant will be characterised as a people who watch and pray. Jesus used the phrase "watch and pray" on a couple of different occasions. Once was the night before the crucifixion. Jesus took Peter, James, and John with Him to the Garden of Gethsemane, where He prayed that "this cup be taken from me" (Matthew 26:39). After the prayer, He found

His disciples sleeping. He was grieved that they could not even pray with Him for an hour and warned them to "watch and pray so that you will not fall into temptation. The spirit is willing, but the flesh is weak" (Matthew 26:41).

Another occurrence of the phrase "watch and pray" is found earlier in Jesus' ministry when He prophesied about the end times. Luke chapter 21 details many of those events, and Jesus warns that they would happen suddenly: "Be careful, or your hearts will be weighed down with carousing, drunkenness and the anxieties of life, and that day will close on you suddenly like a trap" (Luke 21:34). He then says, "Be always on the watch, and pray that you may be able to escape all that is about to happen, and that you may be able to stand before the Son of Man" (verse 36).

The word translated "watch" means "to have the alertness of a guard at night." A night watchman must be even more vigilant than a daytime guard. In the daytime, danger can often be spotted from a distance. But at night everything is different. A night watchman must use senses other than sight to detect danger. He is often alone in the darkness and without the defences, he would otherwise employ. There may be no indications of an enemy attack until it happens, so he must be hyper-vigilant, suspecting it at any moment. That is the type of watching Jesus spoke about.

Jesus warned us that we are too easily distracted by the physical and will be caught unaware if we do not continually discipline ourselves. In the Garden of Gethsemane, sleepiness overcame the disciples. Their physical need overpowered their desire to obey Him. He was grieved when He saw this, knowing what was ahead for them. If they did not remain spiritually vigilant, in tune with Him (John 15:5) and ready to deny the flesh, they would be overcome by the evil one (1 Peter 5:8).

Jesus' disciples today must also watch and pray. We are easily distracted by this world, our fleshly needs and desires, and the schemes of the enemy (2 Corinthians 2:11). When we take our eyes from Jesus and His soon return, our values begin to shift, our attention wanders, and soon we are living like the world and bearing little fruit for God's kingdom (1 Timothy 6:18–19). He warned us that we must be ready at any moment to stand before Him and give an account of our lives (Romans 14:12; 1 Peter 4:5; Matthew 12:36).

We can only remain faithful when we are devoted to prayer. In prayer, we continually allow God to forgive us, cleanse us, teach us, and strengthen us to obey Him (John 14:14). To keep watch, we must pray for endurance and freedom from distractions (Hebrews 12:2; Luke 18:1; Ephesians 6:18). We must pray without ceasing (1 Thessalonians 5:17). When we live with the eager expectation of the Lord's return and expect persecution until then (2 Timothy 3:12; Matthew 24:9; 1 Peter 4:12), we are more likely to keep our lives pure and our hearts ready to meet Him.

We after all need the discernment of times and seasons and so we need to know what is also happening in the world and how it affects the church – especially when it comes to the economy, philosophy, religions and politics. Such watchmen were of critical importance during the hundreds of years of religious conflict and in the turbulent ages when the world saw many social, political and economic upheavals that threatened to destabilize the church.

And why must we watch and pray? Because there is a clear and intentional onslaught against the spiritual 'gates'. This has been revealed by the Lord. This is not an attack for the 'now' but an attack that has always existed. This is an attack that is escalating, intensifying and becoming more vicious than ever before. It is an attack to lead people away from God, thus an attack on the destruction of the person.

And we are talking here about the 'gate' – entry point – of nations, of cities, of homes, of families, and our very lives. A gate is a strategic point. It is a point of legally 'controlling' what goes in and goes out of the 'city'. The enemy is laying siege to gain entry, for once he has entered through the 'gate', he comes to steal, to destroy and to kill. For the Lord has shown the enemy has come like an assassin, like a thief and as a destroyer.

Let us first understand the importance of a gate in the Scriptures. Besides being part of a city's protection against invaders, city gates were places of central activity in biblical times. It was at the city gates that important business transactions were made, the court was convened, and public announcements were heralded. Accordingly, it is natural that the Bible frequently speaks of "sitting in the gate" or of the activities that took place at the gate. In Proverbs 1, wisdom is personified: "At the head of the noisy streets she cries out, in the gateways of the city she makes her speech" (verse 21). To spread her words to the maximum number of people, Wisdom took to the gates.

The first mention of a city gate is found in Genesis 19:1. It was at the gate of Sodom that Abraham's nephew, Lot, greeted the angelic visitors to his city. Lot was there with other leading men of the city, either discussing the day's issues or engaging in important civic business. In the Law of Moses, the parents of a rebellious son were told to bring him to the city gate, where the elders would examine the evidence and pass judgment (Deuteronomy 21:18-21). This affirms that the city gate was central to community action. Another important example is found in the book of Ruth. In Ruth 4:1-11, Boaz officially claimed the position of kinsman-redeemer by meeting with the city elders at the gate of Bethlehem. There, the legal matters related to his marriage to Ruth were settled.

As Israel combatted the Philistines, the priest Eli waited at the city gate for news regarding the ark and to hear how his sons fared in the battle (1 Samuel 4:18). When King David ruled Israel, he stood before his troops to give instructions from the city gate (2 Samuel 18:1-5). After his son Absalom died, David mourned but eventually returned to the city gate along with his people (2 Samuel 19:1-8).

Therefore, in essence, to CONTROL THE GATES OF ONE'S ENEMIES WAS TO CONQUER THEIR CITY. Why? Because it was the place of trade, commerce, and where the judgment was passed. Part of Abraham's blessing from the Lord was the promise that "your offspring shall possess the gate of his enemies" (Genesis 22:17).

When Jesus promised to build His Church, He said, "The gates of Hades will not overcome it" (Matthew 16:18). An understanding of the biblical implications of "gates" helps us interpret Jesus' words. Since a gate was a place where rulers met and counsel was given, Jesus was saying that all the evil plans and schemes of Satan himself would never defeat the Church. Thus, for those who are the Blood, the devil cannot rule, and he cannot control or take up a place of dominion (manifested in the old days as taking control of trade and commerce).

So let us understand, a gate is of great significance. Again, to control the gate means you control the "space" behind the gate. To control the gate(s) of a nation means you can control the nation, for it means you can control governance, business, and even launch an attack against the spiritual strongholds within the nation.

Let us remember the truth that the devil roams like a lion, seeking to devour and to destroy (1 Peter 5:8). This Scripture also speaks about being alert, because the devil is always looking for ways to attack our gates, to attack our homes, our lives and our families. He is constantly roaming like a roaring lion, trying to impart fear, trying to confuse and to deceive. The very tactic of the devil is to lure us away from the Lord, from His Truth and from His Kingdom so that our 'gates' of our nations, the churches, our homes and our lives are exposed to the infiltration, infestation and corruption of the devil. He wants us to move away from the Light of the Lord, from the Blood and the Covering of the Lord by moving into the carnality and depravity of the world. For then the devil can attack and devour and destroy.

Now, let us understand the enemy can either lay siege to a gate or take it by force or the gate can be so seductive that he is ALLOWED LEGALLY through the gate. The enemy is a sly fox, and the reason why there are so many false doctrines and teachings in churches today is that the devil has been allowed through the gate. And once the enemy gains LEGAL entry, he can operate legally to destroy, kill and steal.

This is what happens in countries throughout the world, where the church has not been a watchman and so has allowed the enemy into the nation, into the government and into commerce. The result is a corrupt nation, that suffers violence, lawlessness and anarchy. Why? Because the enemy has been allowed to enter through the gate. Let us understand, the enemy wants to enter through the gate. He wants to control us. He wants to come into our homes and into our families. As Christians, we must be careful and not allow him in, but so great are the onslaught and so intense the attack this is what is happening. If we give way, if we compromise, then we give the devil a foothold.

Just so, our hearts, our minds, and our senses are all gateways into our soul and spirit. All believers in one sense or another are watchmen, firstly as a watchman over our own lives, for it says in Proverbs 4:23: Above all else, guard your heart, for everything you do flows from it. We are called to firstly keep guard over our own hearts, but also to stand guard for our brothers and sisters regarding dangers, threats and any other disabling forces and lastly to keep a watch over the lost who are still held captive by the darkness.

We need to be so aware of our spiritual walk and we need to keep guard over our own "gates". We need to aware and be alert to every danger and threat that attempts to steal God's presence. We need to be wary and alert to such pitfalls, temptations and tests that rise against our brothers and sisters in Christ and we need to be discerning regarding those who are still lost and who are looking to find their way.

It says in "2 Timothy 1: 11 And of this gospel I was appointed a herald and an apostle and a teacher. 12 That is why I am suffering as I am. Yet this is no cause for shame, because I know whom I have believed, and am convinced that he is able to guard what I have entrusted to him until that day. 13 What you heard from me, keep as the pattern of sound teaching, with faith and love in Christ Jesus. 14 Guard the good deposit that was entrusted to you—guard it with the help of the Holy Spirit who lives in us."

In the days of Jerusalem, we find the Lord called for watchmen to stand guard on the walls, at the city gates, on the ramparts and in the countryside – these watchmen were tasked to discern danger, to discern any form of external or internal threat and they were tasked to provide an additional sense of security and peace. The Old City walls contained 43 surveillance towers to guard the 11 gates, illustrating the importance of standing guard over the gates. The concept of watchmen is, however, not only pertinent to Israel's history – during all the wars and conflicts, armies have used sentries and watchmen to keep guard and to stand at the post regarding any dangers.

We read of such watchmen in "Song of Solomon 3: 3 The watchmen found me as they made their rounds in the city", and also in "2 Samuel 18: 24 While David was sitting between the inner and outer gates, the watchman went up to the roof of the gateway by the wall. As he looked out, he saw a man running alone. 25 The watchman called out to the king and reported it."

A prophetic action of a watchman is found in "Isaiah 21: 11 A prophecy against Dumah: Someone calls to me from Seir, "Watchman, what is left of the night? Watchman, what is left of the night?" 12 The watchman replies, "Morning is coming, but also the night. If you would ask, then ask; and come back yet again." And also in Hosea 9:7-9: 7 The days of punishment are coming, the days of reckoning are at hand. Let Israel know this. Because your sins are so many and your hostility so great, the prophet is considered a fool, the inspired person a maniac. 8 The prophet, along with my God, is the watchman over Ephraim, yet snares await him on all his paths, and hostility in the house of his God. 9 They have sunk deep into corruption, as in the days of Gibeah. God will remember their wickedness and punish them for their sins."

We find in the Bible that Ezekiel was charged as a prophetic watchman, meaning one who watches for any internal or external threats spiritually, and he was tasked to keep watch over God's pending judgment as Israel slipped deeper into idolatry and spiritual rebellion.

It says in "Ezekiel 33: 1 The word of the LORD came to me: 2 "Son of man, speak to your people and say to them: 'When I bring the sword against a land, and the people of the land choose one of their men and make him their watchman, 3 and he sees the sword coming against the land and blows the trumpet to warn the people, 4 then if anyone hears the trumpet but does not heed the warning and the sword comes and takes their life, their blood will be on their own head. 5 Since they heard the sound of the trumpet but did not heed the warning, their blood will be on their own head. If they had heeded the warning, they would have saved themselves. 6 But if the watchman sees the sword coming and does not blow the trumpet to warn the people and the sword comes and takes someone's life, that person's life will be taken because of their sin, but I will hold the watchman accountable for their blood.' 7 "Son of man, I have made you a watchman for the people of Israel; so hear the word I speak and give them warning from me. 8 When I say to the wicked, 'You wicked person, you will surely die,' and you do not speak out to dissuade them from their ways, that wicked person will die for their sin, and I will hold you accountable for their blood. 9 But if you do warn the wicked person to turn from their ways and they do not do so, they will die for their sin, though you yourself will be saved."

We perceive therefore that Ezekiel was tasked to warn the people against the "sword", against wickedness and against idolatry. Ezekiel, therefore, understood that he was called to keep guard against wickedness in the sense that the wicked ways of the people invited judgment in the form of the sword. And the words of the Lord are quite harsh, for He warns Ezekiel that if he fails to react to what he sees and he fails to sound a warning then the blood of those who perished are on his hands.

So yes, the onslaught is real. We live in a world of great depravity, where the truth of God has been abandoned for New Age teachings, secularism, and the exaltation of the Self. We live in a world of 2 Timothy 3: But know this, that in the last days perilous times will come: 2 For men will be lovers of themselves, lovers of money, boasters, proud, blasphemers, disobedient to parents, unthankful, unholy, 3 unloving, unforgiving, slanderers, without self-control, brutal, despisers of good, 4 traitors, headstrong, haughty, lovers of pleasure rather than lovers of God, 5 having a form of godliness but denying its power. And from such people turn away! 6 For of this sort are those who creep into households and make captives of gullible women loaded down with sins, led away by various lusts, 7 always learning and never able to come to the knowledge of the truth. 8 Now as Jannes and Jambres resisted Moses, so do these also resist the truth: men of corrupt minds, disapproved concerning the faith; 9 but they will progress no further, for their folly will be manifest to all, as theirs also was.

We need to be alert, we need to be sober, and take guard against the ways of the enemy who seeks to infiltrate, manipulate and cause destruction, and death. It says in "Revelation 22 of the Perfect Life, thus the end of all (the New Jerusalem) and God's final establishment of rule: 3 There will no longer exist anything that is cursed [because sin and illness and death are gone]; and the throne of God and of the Lamb will be in it, and His bond-servants will serve and worship Him [with great awe and joy and loving devotion]; 4 they will [be privileged to] see His face, and His name will be on their foreheads. 5 And there will no longer be night; they have no need for lamplight or sunlight, because the Lord God will illumine them; and they will reign [as kings] forever and ever." Only then will there be no more need to stand guard over the gates, but until then, when darkness is no more, we must remain vigilant and on guard.

Yes, we need the watchmen to arise! For the Lord has shown this is a relentless attack – an attack upon attack. And we need to take note of what the enemy is doing lest we be swept away by the demonic onslaught. This onslaught comes in the form of anything unnatural, unholy, immoral, false, counterfeit, and deceptive. It is an onslaught of great darkness and spiritual destruction. We need to realise modern-day warfare is very similar to spiritual warfare. Where else did man learn about warfare other than from the spiritual realm?

Over the last five decades, while a clear agenda has been pushed to lead the world and the youth down a dark path, the Church at the same time steadily forgot about the devil, about hell, about demons, and instead of acting like a true watchman on the walls declaring God's Truth and sounding the trumpet of warning, the Church has rather chosen a different path. Instead of the Church standing in unity as the entertainment and the social revolution raged on, the Church became more divided, and instead of waging spiritual war against the onslaught, the Church decided to rather preach a "seeker-friendly" message of self-enlightenment and exaltation, tolerance, prosperity and self-enrichment.

Yes, while the world burns with more and more people becoming demonically enslaved and seduced daily, inside the church walls things aren't going so well either. Over the last 50 years there was revival here and there, but in 2015 the Church has become largely ineffective when it comes to waging war in the spiritual realm, because instead of being alert and sober, preaching against the defilement on the world, the church has been preaching humanism, and yes, even New Age teachings regarding the improvement of the Self (law of attractions and so on). Instead of the Church making her voice known while the voices of deception cruelly whisper their incantations of spiritual corruption, the church has allowed herself to be swept up by the tidal wave of the social revolution.

How else to explain churches agreeing on same-sex marriages, condoning pagan holiday festivals, and condoning abortions, all the while deliberately and intentionally twisting the Word of God for their own gain and benefit? Sadly, while the call for sexual immorality has been promoted from all platforms, we see even within the church that the dark tide has hit home. The spirit of lust has been rampant among believers, and yes, so often among church leaders. Adultery and sexual promiscuity are not just the way of the world.

And of course, decade after decade, the Church has lost the fear of God, has systematically shunned the work of the Holy Spirit, and her light has begun to dim dramatically. No wonder the world is ablaze. Is it not because the church itself is ablaze with carnal desires, all the while seeking after the delights of a world that is embraced by the devil himself?

Is the church today acting as a watchman? Not at all. She is too preoccupied with her own kingdoms and self-indulgent vanity, pride and greed. The satanic agenda is still pushed, more ferociously than ever before, and yes, the youth is under attack, so is the family structure, and so is the institution of marriage. Yet, the church remains silent in this spiritual war, where more than ever the devil and his kingdom are denied as being real.

The Lord wants a mighty army, full of God's fire and holiness, full of His Glory and Power. But we need to walk in spirit and truth, and we need to seek Him above all. We can overcome and we can be mighty in battle, but only when we bow the knee to our Supreme Commander and give Him the Glory. How the Lord is looking for an army to march through the lands, fighting in Spirit and Truth, with the high praises in their mouths, and by that praise cause confusion in the camp of the enemy and restore the Lord's ways in the broken lands and homes.

Let us arise, until sheep become lions, until children become men, and until warriors take their place on the Lord's battlefield. Let us arise with the song of Psalm 24 in our hearts. God is indeed calling an army who is willing to watch and pray, to discern, to "see", and to keep guard.

End-time light bearers

In Matthew 5 we read: 13 "You are the salt of the earth; but if the salt loses its flavor, how shall it be seasoned? It is then good for nothing but to be thrown out and trampled underfoot by men. 14 "You are the light of the world. A city that is set on a hill cannot be hidden. 15 Nor do they light a lamp and put it under a basket, but on a lampstand, and it gives light to all who are in the house. 16 Let your light so shine before men, that they may see your good works and glorify your Father in heaven."

As disciples of God, we are called to shine the light of Christ. Of this importance, we must never forget. The Greek word for light, as used in this context of Matthew 5, is Phos, which means to shine or make manifest, especially by rays. The word is especially used to speak of a light that is emitted by a lamp; a heavenly light, such as surrounds angels when they appear on earth; fire, because it is light and sheds light; and a lamp or torch.

Light in the Bible speaks of God being the light (1 John 1:5-8), for light is extremely delicate, subtle, pure and has a brilliant quality. God is the light for God is also the truth and the knowledge, coupled with the spiritual purity, that exposes to the view of all openly and publicly all that is false, wrong and impure. God is the light, for He is the ancient moral and spiritual truth. And so when Jesus said in Matthew 5 that we must be the light, He was speaking of upholding the greater and moral truths of God. Jesus was also speaking about us walking in the light, therefore, in the purity of understanding, purity of hope and truth. He was talking about standing in righteousness, meaning walking according to the Lord's commandments, and in doing so remaining in His will and purpose. After all, in Matthew 6:33, we are urged to first seek God's Kingdom and His righteousness.

We are called to be God's ambassadors on earth, reflecting the image of God. Reflection speaks of light, and so as our light shines in the world we will truly become the reflection of God's glory, truth and honour on earth. The concept behind the word image in the Greek translation is translated as 'stamp bearer'. When we think of a stamp bearer we think of an engraved character or the impress made by a die or a seal, for example, on a coin. The Greek word translated 'nature' denotes the very essence of God.

We are, therefore, called and intended to be reflecting the identity or the essence of Jesus, by walking in His ways, according to His Word and according to the Spirit. For then we will certainly be of value and of worth to the Kingdom. The power of light can also be illustrated by the following example: if you sit in a dark room and if then light a candle, immediately the darkness will recede. Once we light another candle, then the power of two lights will shine even more brightly and bring greater light into the dark room. By the time we have lit three candles, shadows will recede and the reality of what is in the room will be revealed.

Just so, we also live in a world of darkness, strife and chaos. But if we let our light shine, we will be like a candle that shines in that darkened room. And where the light shines, there the darkness will and has to recede. And just so, if we let our light shine, we might cause someone else's light to shine, and so the power of two lights, like two candles, will bring even greater light to a world of falseness and lies. This is why the Lord encouraged us to shine our light. For where there is light, then darkness has and will recede. For where there is light, God's love, truth and purity will shine brightly like a new dawn after a stormy night. And so, as we let our light shine, we will reflect His character and image and, in doing so, bring others closer to God so that the light might shine in them.

More than ever, we need to shine the light of the Lord. More than ever, we need to make disciples so that the light may shine. There has been too much darkness in this world. If there is too much darkness, it simply means there has been a lack of Kingdom labourers shining the light in the darkness. Yet, the Church is absent in a world of chaos and darkness, because so many are not active in declaring the Lord and His Kingdom to a world so broken, so confused and lost. We need active ministers of the Gospel to shine the light and to be salt! This will enable the Church to become alive, to become awake, and thus revived. Therefore, to be bearers of light!

The following Scriptures speak of shining and reflecting God's light:

Romans 13 (New International Version): 11And do this, understanding the present time. The hour has come for you to wake up from your slumber, because our salvation is nearer now than when we first believed. 12The night is nearly over; the day is almost here. So let us put aside the deeds of darkness and put on the armor of light.

1 Peter 2:9 But you are a chosen people, a royal priesthood, a holy nation, a people belonging to God, that you may declare the praises of him who called you out of darkness into his wonderful light.

Yes, we must put on the armour of light, just as we are called to put on the spiritual armour of faith, truth, righteousness and salvation of Ephesians 6. We need to actively and with purpose choose to walk in the light, therefore, in goodness, hope and faith. Our Lord is the light of the world. For it is written in "John 8:12: When Jesus spoke again to the people, he said, 'I am the light of the world. Whoever follows me will never walk in darkness, but will have the light of life.'" The words of our Lord is rooted in Jesus' relationship with His Father. Apart from Jesus, we live in darkness. We have limited capacity to understand who we are or what we see in the world. Life can be wonderful on earth, but not fully complete without Jesus. We are all created to crave the Creator, our Father, and only through a relationship with our Saviour Jesus can the dark parts of our hearts brighten.

The Light of the world paid for our freedom on the cross. He paid for our salvation. And in Him we see the beauty of salvation, of redemption and hope. And so we need to let our light shine so that the entire world may see and know the greatness of God, the power of the Blood and that there is always love, hope and joy. For His Name is Jesus. Indeed, we are called to walk properly according to Romans 13, which means walking in the ways of the Kingdom, and not in religion which breeds the works of the flesh and thus fulfils the lusts of the flesh.

As Christians, we are called to walk in light, not darkness! We must keep ourselves separated from the darkness, for this is God's order. To walk in the light means walking in holiness and purity, for God is holy and pure. In the eyes of God, there is separatism between the holy and the unholy, the common and the uncommon and the immoral from the moral. This is Paul's argument in "2 Corinthians 6: 14 Do not be unequally bound together with unbelievers [do not make mismatched alliances with them, inconsistent with your faith]. For what partnership can righteousness have with lawlessness? Or what fellowship can light have with darkness? 15 What harmony can there be between Christ and Belial (Satan)? Or what does a believer have in common with an unbeliever? 16 What agreement is there between the temple of God and idols? For we are the temple of the living God; just as God said: "I will dwell among them and walk among them; and I will be their God, and they shall be My people. 17 "So come out from among unbelievers and be separate," says the Lord, "And do not touch what is unclean; And I will graciously receive you and welcome you [with favor]."

So there must be a separation between the believer and the world. We must remain united in Christ, thus united in the light to be the light. Right in the beginning at the creation of all things, God separated for example night from day, the land and water, and land and the sky. There was a reason for this, just as there is a reason for God separating and God uniting. Yet the devil will always try to attack God's order and bring about a different and false order. We need to show the world there is a separation between what is right and wrong, and between what is light (good) and what is dark (evil).

Plato, the Greek philosopher, once said: "We can easily forgive a child who is afraid of the dark; the real tragedy of life is when men are afraid of the light." So true. And it seems more and more people are turning away from the true light – Jesus – and are turning to the false light of the devil. People are not just turning away, but they seem not to want the true light. Martin Luther King Jr also once said, "Darkness cannot drive out darkness: only light can do that. Hate cannot drive out hate: only love can do that." So if more people are turning away from the light or are afraid of the true light, then we will see greater darkness descend on the earth.

The disciple John said in "1 John 1: 6 If we say that we have fellowship with Him, and walk in darkness, we lie and do not practice the truth." Thus, we need to walk as ministers of worth, meaning we can back up our talk in the reflection of how we live and act and speak. In times of great darkness, God ensures that Light will always shine, as in the late 1500s when the spiritual light shone when men like Wycliffe, Martin Luther, John Huss and John Calvin challenged the apostate way of politics and the church. It ultimately led to greater movements of reformation, restoring salvation through faith while men like George Fox opened the doors for the Holy Spirit to work. And so in our times of rebellion and apostasy, it is time for the true believers to stand up, and to walk in the true light! For only then will the darkness be driven back! It is time for the world that is so afraid of the true light to know that Jesus is the Light of the world and in Him, there is no darkness. In Him, there is also forgiveness, hope, redemption and love.

So let us stop being afraid of what the world says or thinks, and let our light shine. And let us be true unto the Word, unto the Kingdom and unto our Lord, for darkness and light has no fellowship. For indeed, as the light shines, then darkness shall flee. Let us show people the way to the true light, and that there is nothing to fear.

By being bearers of the light, we shall surely "pierce the darkness". This phrase was made popular by Frank E Peretti's novel of the same name, which was a sequel to This Present Darkness. Peretti's books explore the spiritual realm and the war that wages in the heavenly. The phrase "pierce the darkness" applies very much to spiritual warfare.

Wherever you look these days, you see darkness. Not physical darkness, but a darkness of a spiritual nature. The world has become very cruel, violent, selfish, and cold in terms of showing real love. It is a world of spiritual malnourishment as so many people have turned their backs on God and have decided to follow their will, way and brand of truth. People are walking in darkness, meaning they are confused and disoriented regarding the truth is. Such darkness has resulted from spiritual blindness, and it translates into one's conduct. 2 Timothy 3 is a prophetic declaration of how 'dark' the end of days will be as morality and truth are trampled upon.

Romans 1 speaks of such darkness when people seek not to follow God but rather choose to follow their own path. "21 For although they knew God, they neither glorified him as God nor gave thanks to him, but their thinking became futile and their foolish hearts were darkened. 22 Although they claimed to be wise, they became fools 23 and exchanged the glory of the immortal God for images made to look like a mortal human being and birds and animals and reptiles. 24 Therefore God gave them over in the sinful desires of their hearts to sexual impurity for the degrading of their bodies with one another. 25 They exchanged the truth about God for a lie, and worshipped and served created things rather than the Creator—who is forever praised. Amen."

In such perilous times that we are living in now, as Christians, we are called to shine our light as taught by the Lord in Matthew 5. We are called to fulfil the Great Commission, and we do so by leading people to Jesus. If we are obedient to the Great Commission of telling the world about Jesus and making disciples, then we shall lead them out of darkness and into the light. We then see the reality of piercing the darkness in this spiritual war.

Most children are afraid of the dark. By the time we become adults, we know, on a rational level, that there's no reason to be scared when the lights are off. Yet, some adults are still scared of the dark. This is because if we are a child or an adult, darkness makes us uncomfortable. It impairs our vision, so we are more afraid of what we cannot see in the darkness. The reality is that we are more comfortable in the light, for light brings warmth. In the light, we can see, and what we see provides a sense of calmness and security. Some people are so used to their spiritual darkness that it becomes the norm, yet they are blinded to the beauty of the light and that the light is always better than the dark. For this reason, as believers, we must keep on speaking about Jesus, for He is the Light. John 3:3 speaks about seeing the Kingdom of God for those who are reborn because such disciples walk and live in the light and are not blinded by the darkness.

How then do we piece the darkness, meaning piercing the veil of confusion, fear, anxiety, disorder, chaos, and spiritual bankruptcy that spiritually blinds so many people? Simple, we shine the light of Christ, and we shine the light by declaring the true goodness and Gospel of our Lord and Saviour. The greatest weapon we can wield in this war is to speak of Jesus, showing His love and shining His light so that people may come out of the darkness into the light of God's glory and majesty. Isaiah 60:19 says, "The sun will no more be your light by day, nor will the brightness of the moon shine on you, for the Lord will be your everlasting light, and your God will be your glory." Of Jesus, it says in "Colossians 1:13 For he has rescued us from the dominion of darkness and brought us into the kingdom of the Son he loves."

John 9:5 says of Jesus: "While I am in the world, I am the light of the world." The Lord also said in John 8:12 that He is the Light of the world. In declaring Himself to be the Light of the world, Jesus was claiming that He is the exclusive source of spiritual light. No other source of spiritual truth is available to mankind. We need to remember that light is always greater than darkness, for darkness only exists where light is absent. Where Jesus is present, there is no darkness. John 1:5 says, "The light shines in the darkness, and the darkness has not overcome it."

When we are born into this world, we perceive physical light, and by it we learn of our Creator's handiwork in the things we see. However, although that light is good, there is another Light, a Light so important that the Son of God had to come to both declare and impart it to men. John 8:12 records, "When Jesus spoke again to the people, He said, 'I am the Light of the world. Whoever follows me will never walk in darkness but have the light of life.'" The allegory used by the Lord in this verse speaks of the light of His Truth, the light of His Word, the light of eternal

Life. Those who perceive the true Light will never walk in spiritual darkness.

We take a candle into a room to dispel the darkness. Likewise, the light of Jesus Christ has to be taken into the darkness of sin that engulfs the hearts and lives of those who are not following Him. That's the condition behind having this Light—that we follow Him. If we do not follow Him, we will not have this light, this truth, this eternal life.

Physical light is necessary for physical life. The Earth would certainly change very rapidly if there were no longer any sunlight. Plants will never move away from the light—they are said to be positively phototropic, drawn to the light. In the same way, spiritual light is necessary for spiritual life. The believer will always tend toward spiritual things; therefore, the true light. The unbeliever always does the opposite (John 1:5; 3:19–20) because light exposes his evil, and he hates the light. Indeed, no man can come into the true spiritual light of Jesus Christ unless he is enabled (John 6:37).

The followers of Christ will never walk in darkness, which is a reference to the assurance of salvation we enjoy. As the moon has no light of its own, reflecting the light of the sun, so are believers to reflect the Light of Christ so that all can see it in us. The Light is evident to others by the good deeds we do in faith and through the power of the Holy Spirit. The emphasis here is maintaining a credible and obvious witness in the world, a witness that shows us to be faithful, God-honouring, trustworthy, sincere, earnest, and honest in all that we do.

John 1 also says, "6 There was a man sent from God whose name was John. 7 He came as a witness to testify concerning that light, so that through him all might believe. 8 He himself was not the light; he came only as a witness to the light. 9 The true light that gives light to everyone was coming into the world. 10 He was in the world, and though the world was made through him, the world did not recognize him. 11 He came to that which was his own, but his own did not receive him. 12 Yet to all who did receive him, to those who believed in his name, he gave the right to become children of God— 13 children born not of natural descent, nor of human decision or a husband's will, but born of God. 14 The Word became flesh and made his dwelling among us. We have seen his glory, the glory of the one and only Son, who came from the Father, full of grace and truth. 15 (John testified concerning him. He cried out, saying, "This is the one I spoke about when I said, 'He who comes after me has surpassed me because he was before me.'") 16 Out of his fullness we have all received grace in place of grace already given. 17 For the law was given through Moses; grace and truth came through Jesus Christ. 18 No one has ever seen God, but the one and only Son, who is himself God and is in closest relationship with the Father, has made him known."

To pierce the darkness is to bring light into darkness, which means bringing Jesus into a state of blindness, confusion, anger, doubt or violence. For light dispels darkness! Darkness is never greater than the light, for the light of Christ illuminates and shines brightly for all eternity. Genesis 1 says, "2 Now the earth was formless and empty, darkness was over the surface of the deep, and the Spirit of God was hovering over the waters. 3 And God said, "Let there be light," and there was light. 4 God saw that the light was good, and he separated the light from the darkness."

2 Corinthians 6 says, "14 Do not be unequally yoked together with unbelievers. For what fellowship has righteousness with lawlessness? And what communion has light with darkness? 15 And what accord has Christ with Belial? Or what part has a believer with an unbeliever? 16 And what agreement has the temple of God with idols?" Light and dark cannot coexist. Just so, we cannot walk in light or in darkness. As Christians, we must walk

by the true Light so that all may see that in such Light there is true hope and joy.

1 John 2 says, "15 Do not love the world or the things in the world. If anyone loves the world, the love of the Father is not in him. 16 For all that is in the world—the lust of the flesh, the lust of the eyes, and the pride of life—is not of the Father but is of the world. 17 And the world is passing away, and the lust of it; but he who does the will of God abides forever." The things of this world brings darkness, for the devil is the temporary ruler of this earth (2 Corinthians 4:4). The phrase "god of this world" (or "god of this age") indicates that Satan is the major influence on the ideals, opinions, goals, hopes and views of the majority of people. His influence also encompasses the world's philosophies, education, and commerce. The thoughts, ideas, speculations and false religions of the world are under his control and have sprung from his lies and deceptions. Yet, his time has been determined by God, for the devil is no god but a fallen angel. Yet for those under his sway, he leads them into darkness, for he only comes to steal, to destroy and to kill (John 10:10).

Psalm 18 says, "28 You, Lord, keep my lamp burning; my God turns my darkness into light." In God is our victory. Psalm 23 says, "4 Even though I walk through the darkest valley, I will fear no evil, for you are with me; your rod and your staff, they comfort me." As believers, we do not have to fear the dark, no matter the demons or the wickedness that lurk, for God is always greater. God's light brings us comfort, hope, strength, and joy. God is love, and the light leads us home.

Proverbs 4 says, "18 The path of the righteous is like the morning sun, shining ever brighter till the full light of day. 19 But the way of the wicked is like deep darkness; they do not know what makes them stumble." To pierce the darkness is simply about declaring Jesus so that the morning sun, or in better words, the glorious SON (Jesus) shines upon people. For while we are in the dark, we shall stumble through life, yet by the Light we see, perceive and we find our way to green pastures and quiet rivers (Psalm 23:2). God's word is a lamp for our feet and a light for our path (Psalm 119:105) because it provides moral and spiritual guidance in a world of immorality, decadence and apostasy.

To pierce the darkness is about declaring the Gospel, and honouring God in our conduct, speech, faith and love. As the demon-possessed man at the tombs ran to Jesus, so people shall run to the light to escape the dark. But they first need to see the Light and know what the Light is. By declaring the Truth of God, the Light shall shine and the darkness shall be pierced. Jesus is the deliverance from darkness, and in His light, we shall not stumble.

# Covenant-keeping warriors shake the gates of hell

We need to understand that those who truly uphold the Covenant of God pose a huge danger to the spiritual realm. Those who lead Covenant lives, meaning upholding, honouring, respecting and revering the Covenant with God, are seated in the heavenly places and move in the authority and power of a mighty and glorious God.

They are a huge danger and threat to the kingdom of darkness, for they change the spiritual atmosphere and take back territories! The effectiveness of such an end-time remnant depends on how much we are going to commit to the spiritual principles of God's Covenant.

An end-time remnant with a passion for the Covenant and to lead a Covenant-honouring life will, by God's power, fulfil the Great Commission, be a witness to the end-time great revival harvest to bring in the end-time harvest. Such a remnant will indeed be dangerous to the kingdom of darkness, for a remnant who upholds the Covenant and the unity among the brethren will indeed move in God's authority and power.

God is raising an end-time remnant who will again honour and respect the covenant, for the revival is here. He is calling people who will again understand the importance of God's Covenant and the importance of the Body of Christ to walk in covenant agreement with each other.

A covenant in the ancient world was similar to what we in the modern world would call a contract, treaty, or will. Each covenant established the basis of a relationship, conditions for that relationship, promises and conditions of the relationship and consequences if those conditions were unmet. One of the most familiar examples of a covenant for us is marriage.

Covenant comes from the Latin origin (con venire), meaning a coming together. It presupposes two or more parties who come together to make a contract, agreeing on promises, stipulations, privileges, and responsibilities. The biblical words most often translated "covenant" are berit in the Old Testament and diatheke in the New Testament. The preferred meaning of this Old Testament word is bond; a covenant refers to two or more parties bound together. The New Testament word for covenant has usually been translated as covenant, but testimony and testament have also been used.

Covenant relationships are found throughout the Bible. There are personal covenants between two individuals (e.g., David and Jonathan in 1 Samuel 23), political covenants between two kings or nations (e.g., King Solomon and King Hiram in 1 Kings 5), legal covenants with a nation (such as the laws about freeing Hebrew slaves), and so forth. Entering into covenants was a major part of what it meant to live in the ancient Near East. So God partnered with humans through a structure they already understood.

God created man in His own image and likeness for a purpose—to offer man eternal life as children in His family (Hebrews 2:10). Instead, humans chose disobedience and death. It is only through the promise made to Abraham that salvation can come, and man can be saved. People must repent and turn away from sin and accept Christ's sacrifice on their behalf, and then these eternal offers from God can be theirs. This renewed biblical covenant is based on the same laws but has the benefit of the help of the Holy Spirit and better promises. This New Covenant supersedes the Old Covenant and brings us to a point of evaluating our own lives in the light of God's law, which is holy, just and good. Only in this way can we receive the promise of eternal life, which God has made possible for all mankind through Jesus Christ.

Jesus perfectly succeeded at every point where humanity failed. He is the guarantor and mediator of the new and better covenant (Hebrews 7:22, 9:15). Now, people from every nation, tribe, and tongue who trust Jesus can become a part of God's covenant family. In the new covenant, we receive the forgiveness of sins and God's empowering Spirit to lead the lost to Christ. Because of Jesus, we can live righteously and partner with Him as He renews the hearts of the broken. The New Covenant is the promise that God will forgive sin and restore fellowship with those whose hearts are turned toward Him.

Under the New Covenant, we are allowed to receive salvation as a gift (Ephesians 2:8–9). Our responsibility is to exercise faith in Christ, the One who fulfilled the Law on our behalf and brought an end to the Law's sacrifices through His sacrificial death. Through the life-giving Holy Spirit who lives in all believers (Romans 8:9–11), we share in the inheritance of Christ and enjoy a permanent, unbroken relationship with God (Hebrews 9:15). We also have a responsibility to obey Him, follow His ways, will and truth. He remains God, and we are God's spiritual children. We do not dictate the terms of the Covenant, for God is the author and mediator of the Covenant.

Yet, we live in times where believers want to tell God what to do, and they want to dictate how they want to live, and what to believe in. We are then in violation of the Covenant, and we walk the dangerous road of rebellion!

How can believers be a danger to the kingdom of darkness if they walk in the dark and do not honour their King, His ways, truth and will? How can we truly pierce the darkness and set the captives free when we walk in rebellion and violate the covenant because of our pride? Make no mistake, dictating to God how we want to live is pride in action.

Yet such pride is rebellion against God. 1 Samuel 15:23 (NIV) says, "For rebellion is like the sin of divination, and arrogance like the evil of idolatry." If we walk in rebellion, we might as well be practitioners of divination, or in other words, sorcery! Since the kingdom of darkness is a system of the occult (sorcery), how then can we destroy demonic strongholds and tear down anything that exalts itself against God?

John 8:12 says, "Then Jesus spoke to them again, saying, "I am the light of the world. He who follows Me shall not walk in darkness, but have the light of life." And also "John 12:46 I have come as a light into the world, that whoever believes in Me should not abide in darkness." By walking in the light, meaning walking in holiness and purity, we uphold the Covenant. By walking in righteousness and seeking the Kingdom above all, we uphold the Covenant. If we engage in the dark and its deeds, which are the ways of the world and the devil, we then violate the Covenant? How can we then be effective warriors for God?

1 John 2 says, "15 Do not love the world or the things in the world. If anyone loves the world, the love of the Father is not in him. 16 For all that is in the world—the lust of the flesh, the lust of the eyes, and the pride of life—is not of the Father but is of the world. 17 And the world is passing away, and the lust of it; but he who does the will of God abides forever."

If we love God, we must love the Covenant, meaning to obey, follow and yield to the Spirit. Then we shall move in God's glorious power and by His authority. We cannot be engaged in the spiritual war if we continuously violate the Covenant, for then we mock God. We cannot live in the dark and the light, for then we are neither hold nor cold for the Kingdom. We then play a dangerous game, and such a game within the spiritual realm takes no prisoners.

Remember, Christians are united with Jesus Christ in His resurrected life (Colossians 2:12; Romans 6:4). The apostle Paul prays for the Ephesians to understand "the incredible greatness of God's power for us who believe him. This is the same mighty power that raised Christ from the dead and seated him in the place of honor at God's right hand in the heavenly realms" (Ephesians 1:19–20, NLT). A little later, in Ephesians 2:4–10, Paul explains that the greatness of God's incredible power toward believers is rivalled by the magnitude of His love, mercy, and grace.

Before salvation, we were spiritually dead in our sins because our "sinful nature was not yet cut away," but then God made us "alive with Christ, for he forgave all our sins" (Colossians 2:13, NLT; see also 1 Corinthians 15:22). Our transgression no longer separates us from God (Colossians 1:21–22; Romans 8:38–39) because we now share in the life of Christ (Romans 8:11). Since Christ is seated "at God's right hand in the heavenly realms," so too are we in a spiritual sense. Since we have been "raised to new life with Christ," we can now set our sights "on the realities of heaven, where Christ sits in the place of honor at God's right hand" (Colossians 3:1, NLT). Physically, we still live in the natural world. But God, by His great power, and because of His immense love, mercy, and grace, raised us from our spiritually dead status to new life in Christ. We now sit in heavenly places.

To sit in heavenly places is more than a figure of speech. It is a spiritual reality for the believer. Because of our union with Christ, we reap the benefit of His position of divine authority (see Psalm 110:1; cf. Acts 2:34–35). He is our Head and our Representative. Peter taught, "Now Christ has gone to heaven. He is seated in the place of honor next to God, and all the angels and authorities and powers accept his authority" (1 Peter 3:22, NLT; see also Philippians 2:9–11). The gates of hell will not overcome the church (Matthew 16:18; see also 1 John 2:13) because we are more than conquerors through Christ (Romans 8:37; see also 1 John 5:4–5) who gives us the victory (1 Corinthians 15:57).

Our spiritual seat in the heavenly realms is a position of high honor. We have been given the royal privilege of being enthroned with the Son and will one day partake of His glory. If we let this spiritual truth sink in, it will change the way we think and live. Because we are seated with Christ in heavenly places, our position in heaven is secure, but we must never forget that we don't deserve our place there. We did nothing to earn it, but God graces us with it anyway (Ephesians 2:8; 4:7; 2 Corinthians 3:5).

As we sit in heavenly places while still living on earth, we have access through Jesus Christ to all of heaven's privileges and spiritual blessings (Ephesians 1:3–14). The power of God that raised Jesus from the dead is available and working on our behalf as we walk in this world (Ephesians 1:18–19; Acts 17:28; 1 John 4:9). We have the whole armor of God at our disposal to help us "stand against the devil's schemes" and stand firm "against the rulers, against the authorities, against the powers of this dark world and against the spiritual forces of evil in the heavenly realms" (Ephesians 6:11–12).

Yet, it is important to remember that if we truly want to operate in power and authority based on such a position, we need to uphold the Covenant. We need to remember that we need to remain (abide) in Christ to be seated in such a place. It is because of the Covenant that we enjoy such a seat of honour. Do we truly think we can move in God's authority and power, based on such a position, if we violate the Covenant and choose not to 'live' Christ? Today, some believers do not follow God's truth, who are not even filled by the Spirit of God, and who do not even know the Word of God. How can we then operate from such a spiritual position

– ruling and reigning in partnership even now with Christ – if we choose to live in the dark and walk in the light? We mock the Covenant and find ourselves at the mercy of a ruthless predator who loves it when people rebel against God and who walk in pride.

Considering to what lengths God went to achieve His master plan through the covenant, surely He then deserves all our attention, devotion and love? The Lord reminds us He is always to be our first love. As the Father called Israel to love Him as their First Love, still today He deserves all our honour and praise. He is a jealous God, and when He speaks, we should listen and we should obey. The greatest commandment in Matthew 22 is clear: "37 Jesus said to him, "'You shall love the Lord your God with all your heart, with all your soul, and with all your mind.' 38 This is the first and great commandment." Exodus 20:3 says, "You shall have no other gods before Me." We are called to love God above all else. He is called to be our first love.

Of the greatest commandment, we read in Mark 12 (NIV): "28 One of the teachers of the law came and heard them debating. Noticing that Jesus had given them a good answer, he asked him, "Of all the commandments, which is the most important?" 29 "The most important one," answered Jesus, "is this: 'Hear, O Israel: The Lord our God, the Lord is one. 30 Love the Lord your God with all your heart and with all your soul and with all your mind and with all your strength.'

What Jesus said in Mark 12 is what Moses said in "Deuteronomy 6: 4 Hear, O Israel: The Lord our God is one Lord: 5 And thou shalt love the Lord thy God with all thine heart, and with all thy soul, and with all thy might." God doesn't change. Of Israel under the Old Covenant, He called them to serve and love Him with all their strength. Of the disciples under the New Covenant, the same applies.

We are called to lead a life that upholds the Covenant of God, all day and every day. And then we shall shake the gates of hell, for we then move in His power and authority. We uphold the Covenant by serving God with all our strength. Do we serve and love God with all our strength? For if we do, then we must make every effort, day and night, to obey God, to follow Him, to love Him, and to serve Him. Then and only then do we uphold the Covenant, and we can drive back the darkness. We must do so with every ounce of our strength, with every ounce of conviction, and there must be no room, none whatsoever, for the world to steal our love for God, or our devotion, loyalty and faithfulness. To love God with all our strength (might) is to constantly seek His will, His ways and truth. It calls for us to pay attention to God, to be serious about Him above everything else and to love Him as our First Love.

We read in "Matthew 22: 36 "Teacher, which is the great commandment in the law?" 37 Jesus said to him, "'You shall love the Lord your God with all your heart, with all your soul, and with all your mind.' 38 This is the first and great commandment." It is that simple. We must love God WITH ALL OUR HEART. Not part of it. Not proportionally. In totality. We must be consumed by a love for God, for He must be our first love. Our heart must beat for God in the morning, in the afternoon, in the evening, yes, every second of the day! Our hearts must yearn for God, for God is glorious and wonderful.

James 4 says, "4 Do you not know that friendship with the world is enmity with God? Whoever therefore wants to be a friend of the world makes himself an enemy of God. 5 Or do you think that the Scripture says in vain, "The Spirit who dwells in us yearns jealously"?" God is jealous of our love. He wants our hearts. He wants our affection, attention and devotion. There is nothing greater for your heart to beat for God and for God to live in your hearts through the indwelling presence of the Holy Spirit. In Revelation 3:20 we read of how Jesus stands at the door and knocks, for yes, He seeks to make His home in every heart.

In Psalm 91, written by Moses, we read the following: "14 Because he set his love on Me, therefore I will save him; I will set him [securely] on high, because he knows My name [he confidently trusts and relies on Me, knowing I will never abandon him, no, never]. 15 "He will call upon Me, and I will answer him; I will be with him in trouble; I will rescue him and honor him. 16 "With a long life I will satisfy him and I will let him see My salvation." May we set our hearts upon the Lord, and love Him above all else, lest we fall into the trap of idolatry, and may we behold Him as Moses beheld Him.

God is our Life, our Hope and our Strength. Praise Him. Love Him. Obey Him, Seek Him. Know Him. Ecclesiastes 3:11 says, "He has made everything beautiful in its time. He has also set eternity in the human heart; yet no one can fathom what God has done from beginning to end." Our God is mighty and awesome! He desires for us to fellowship with Him, to share our hearts with Him and to yield our life unto His loving embrace.

Yes, there is a cry from the Lord for believers to again take Him seriously and to fear Him. Yes, fear Him! This is something hardly preached on anymore, yet the beginning of wisdom is to fear God. There is a cry from God for believers to once again seek holiness and purity. There is a cry from God for believers to once again hunger for God and to put the world aside once and for all. There is a cry for obedience - complete and utter obedience and to seek after the perfect will without argument or making excuses. For sadly, a deep complacency has set into the church like rot - a complacency of disobeying God as if He can be toyed with or be mocked. It is complacency in engaging in idolatry and not considering how we provoke God to jealousy.

We have to be reminded that God is always the same and He never changes. He is still the Almighty, and His Truth forever stands the time. Yet, more than ever, we have become nonchalant when it comes to dealing with God. Have we truly forgotten who He is? Do we truly love Him? Are we still madly in love with God? Is He our all and everything, all the time? Is He truly our first love? The commandment not to commit adultery also highlights the importance of not committing spiritual adultery, for this then violates the first two commandments of the 10 commandments! For spiritual adultery is idolatry, meaning we do not regard God as our first love.

Spiritual adultery is unfaithfulness to God. It violates the covenant. It is having an undue fondness for the things of the world or casting your prayer or worship upon another, including a so-called god. Spiritual adultery is analogous to the unfaithfulness of one's spouse: "'But like a woman faithless to her lover, even so, have you been faithless to me, O house of Israel,' says the LORD" (Jeremiah 3:20; see also Isaiah 1:21; 57:8; Ezekiel 16:30).

The Bible tells us that people who choose to be friends with the world are "adulterous people" having "enmity against God" (James 4:4–5). The world, after all, is under the sway of Satan's control (John 12:31; Ephesians 2:2; 1 John 5:19). The world system, with its contrived and deceitful scheme of phoney values, worthless pursuits, and unnatural affections, is designed to lure us away from a pure relationship with God. Spiritual adultery, then, is the forsaking of God's love and the embracing of the world's values and desires (Romans 8:7–8; 2 Timothy 4:10; 1 John 2:15–17). It is not to honour God as your first love.

Therefore in the New Testament, James defines spiritual adultery as claiming to love God while cultivating friendship with the world (James 4:4–5). The person who commits spiritual adultery professes to be a Christian yet finds his real love and pleasure in the things that Satan offers. For believers, the love of the world and the love of God are direct opposites. Believers committing spiritual adultery may claim to love the Lord, but, in reality, they are captivated by the pleasures of this world, its influence, comforts, financial security, and so-called freedoms.

Jesus said, "No one can serve two masters. Either you will hate the one and love the other, or you will be devoted to the one and despise the other" (Matthew 6:24). The Bible exhorts us, "Do not love the world or anything in the world. If anyone loves the world, love for the Father is not in them. For everything in the world—the lust of the flesh, the lust of the eyes, and the pride of life—comes not from the Father but from the world" (1 John 2:15–16). Yes, we must love God above all else. To avoid spiritual adultery, "set your hearts on things above, where Christ is, seated at the right hand of God. Set your affection on things above, not on things on the earth" (Colossians 3:2, KJV).

We read in "Jeremiah 31: 33 But this is the covenant that I will make with the house of Israel after those days, says the Lord: I will put My law in their minds, and write it on their hearts; and I will be their God, and they shall be My people." So when we therefore truly follow God, and remain under the Covenant, then our hearts should be beating only for God. We will then adore and worship God alone and no one else. After all, if we truly follow Him and seek Him as our highest treasure, then His Law – His truths and commandments – should be written on our hearts!

Sadly, if we look at the church today, and especially the heart of the church, do we truly still love God as our first love, or do we covet and seek after other things? Remember, idolatry is anything loved more than God, wanted more than God, desired more than God, treasured more than God or enjoyed more than God. Paul says in Romans 1:25 that "they exchanged the truth about God for a lie and worshipped and served the creature" — anything that is created — "rather than the Creator." Romans 1 deals specifically with God's wrath. Idolatry is therefore when we turn away from God and exchange His love, His presence, His worth, His value and His greatness for another treasure or desire. This is idolatry, and this invites wrath.

Exodus 20 (NKJV) says, "4 You shall not make for yourself a carved image—any likeness of anything that is in heaven above, or that is in the earth beneath, or that is in the water under the earth; 5 you shall not bow down to them nor serve them. For I, the Lord your God, am a jealous God, visiting the iniquity of the fathers upon the children to the third and fourth generations of those who hate Me."

God is jealous when someone gives another something that rightly belongs to Him. It is not that God is jealous or envious because someone has something He wants or needs. In these verses, God is speaking of people making idols and bowing down and worshipping those idols instead of giving God the worship that belongs to Him alone. God is possessive of the worship and service that belong to Him. It is a sin (as God points out in this commandment) to worship or serve anything other than God. It is a sin when we desire, or we are envious, or we are jealous of someone because he has something that we do not have.

It is a different use of the word "jealous" when God says He is jealous. What He is jealous of belongs to Him; worship and service belong to Him alone and are to be given to Him alone. And in this jealousy, God shall unleash vengeance and judgment on the unrighteous, as spelt out in the Book of Revelation and Romans 1 for they have not honoured Him not as the living and only God. God's jealousy is appropriate, for He is God and there is none like Him. He deserves all our praise and honour. Matthew 6 in the Lord's Prayer says "For Yours is the kingdom and the power and the glory forever. Amen.]' Jesus underlines the superior nature of God, and because God is above all and anything, all praise, worship and adoration belong to Him alone.

God is jealous of His people because He created all of us. He is jealous of His Kingdom, His Truth, and His Name. He is God - the one true living Deity that has made it all. There is no other god. There are only imposters and pretenders. Satan is the greatest imposter, trying to claim God's throne. God made this earth, He gave us all life, and He will bring about the New Jerusalem. God is a jealous God, yet we try to exploit and manipulate Him, we play with His Name, we play with His Truth and Word, we mock Him, we mock His Spirit, and we mock Jesus with our sins and idolatry. We run after man and gods [demons], we destroy this planet, we destroy each other and we trample on love.

God is a jealous God, but we have made Him cheap, we have made His Covenant cheap, we have made His Kingdom cheap and we have denied His excellence and glory, all for the sake of our kingdoms. God is a jealous God, but we think we can make the rules, bend the rules, change the rules and we strive to reign and rule like gods. He is all-powerful, yet we dare to command Him what to do, how to do it and when to do it! We are His creation, yet we are on this planet pretending He is our creation and thus our little pet. We constantly provoke Him to jealousy. Yet, He is mighty, glorious and powerful, He breathes life and is life. He is light. He is Truth. There is no other, He parts the seas. He makes our heartbeat every second of the day. His grace and mercy have allowed us the opportunity at eternal life.

At the burning bush, the Lord said to Moses, "I AM." There is none like God. No rival. No equal. He made all. All things are upheld by a mighty God. So He deserves all the thanks from mankind, thus His creation, yet we would rather choose to serve other 'gods', or ourselves. So daily this entire world is provoking God to jealousy, for as His creation, we rebel against Him.

Revelation 4 also demonstrates the honour and the glory due to I AM: "8 And the four living creatures, each one of them having six wings, are full of eyes all over and within [underneath their wings]; and day and night they never stop saying, "Holy, holy, holy [is the] Lord God, the Almighty [the Omnipotent, the Ruler of all], who was and who is and who is to come [the unchanging, eternal God]." 9 Whenever the living creatures give glory and honor and thanksgiving to Him who sits on the throne, to Him who lives forever and ever, 10 the twenty-four elders fall down before Him who sits on the throne, and they worship Him who lives forever and ever; and they throw down their crowns before the throne, saying,"

When giving the Ten Commandments in Exodus 20 (which is part of the Covenant made with Moses), God warns that He is a jealous God, who does not tolerate rivals. He wants a committed love relationship with us, and He is not prepared to share our affections with any other. He will not tolerate what might be called an "open relationship" in today's terms – he is strictly monogamous. When the people of Israel (or any of his beloved, including you and I) spend too much time and attention with another, allow our hearts to go astray, or prioritise something or someone else ahead of him, there is a righteous response of jealous anger. And why shouldn't God be angry? And such anger and being provoked to jealousy goes against our romantic view of God. He has given everything for us and to us, and our hearts should belong to Him.

Our entire life should be devoted to God, and we should be jealous of anything that steals our devotion and adoration reserved for God. We should be passionate about guarding our devotion, and be careful of anything that robs our attention of God. Yes, we must revere the Covenant, and walk by its spiritual truth. We serve god not because of duty, but because we have a Covenant with God. By that Covenant we are in partnership with God. By the Covenant, God works with His children to establish His Kingdom, and to destroy the demonic strongholds and darkness in the hearts of man.

We cannot serve man and God. We cannot serve the kingdoms of the world and the Kingdom of Heaven. If we do, we bow before two altars. If we do so, we burn with God's fire and profane fire. It is time again that we return to the Covenant by committing our very lives again to the Lord so that there is a cry in our hearts we will serve no other God and that He is our First Love and He is our Master and Lord! There is only the Covenant with one spiritual master that should be in place – and that is with God. We must love a mighty covenant-making God, for by the covenant of the Lamb we have life and life in abundance.

Yes, there is power in upholding, revering, and honouring the Covenant! There is even greater power when the Body of Christ is truly united in purpose and truth by the same Spirit and the same faith. For a people who are united with God in Covenant, upholding and honouring its principles, and who are also united with each other in covenant (standing in agreement to serve God, to serve each other, and to uphold God's truth by the Spirit), and indeed incredibly dangerous to the darkness of darkness. Together, they operate out of the exalted spiritual position, and together in unity they exert God's authority and power in accordance with God's will and Word. In unity, they move by the Spirit of God, and they become an incredibly powerful force to shine God's light in a dark world.

James 5 speaks of how the effectual fervent prayer of a righteous man availeth much. Therefore, there is greater power in such prayer to establish God's Kingdom and to see the captives set free. Now, what if we have more than one such person praying, and they are in covenant agreement, and they uphold the Covenant as sealed by the Blood of the Lamb? Oh yes, great power will be unleashed! Power to shatter strongholds, to shake the gates of hell, to pierce the darkness, to see the lost saved, and those spiritually slumbering revived!

Of this reality, we read in Acts 2 when the first church gathered and grew: "42 And they continued steadfastly in the apostles' doctrine and fellowship, in the breaking of bread, and in prayers. 43 Then fear came upon every soul, and many wonders and signs were done through the apostles. 44 Now all who believed were together, and had all things in common, 45 and sold their possessions and goods, and divided them among all, as anyone had need. 46 So continuing daily with one accord in the temple, and breaking bread from house to house, they ate their food with gladness and simplicity of heart, 47 praising God and having favour with all the people. And the Lord added to the church daily those who were being saved."

Take note, here we find a people upholding and honouring the Covenant. They continued steadfastly in the apostles' doctrine. We read how they broke bread (communion), which speaks of honouring and respecting the price paid by Jesus. But they were also in covenant agreement and unity with each other. It speaks of fellowship, having things in common, and selling their possessions and goods. They did daily with one accord in the temple.

Because they were a people upholding the Covenant, and who enjoyed a covenant unity among each other, the church grew! Understand, in those days when the church grew, it meant people were truly being saved, and so the devil was losing the battle! It wasn't about church growth for the sake of boosting someone's ministry or status, but it was all about God and seeking people revived. They were actively engaged in a spiritual war, setting the captives free. Growth speaks of revival.

Because they honoured the covenant with God and each other, we read of how many wonders and signs were done through the apostles. This speaks of activated and manifested power. It is the reality of Mark 16, where Jesus said that signs, wonders and miracles will follow those who believe. There's power in the Covenant, for the Covenant has been sealed by the Blood of Jesus. There is power in the Blood to see people saved, redeemed, restored, and delivered.

We do not see vital church growth and such manifested power of God anymore across the Church globally because corporately, as the Church, we do not uphold the Covenant. The people of God are also hardly walking in covenant agreement with each other. We violate God's covenant because of our idolatry, living for the self, building our kingdoms, and we constantly flirt and even engage in sin and iniquity. Among ourselves, we fight, bicker, and argue, and we find ourselves incredibly divided. Such division is often caused because we hold onto the flesh and we are ruled by traditions, religion and the ways of man. It is because we walk in the dark, and so the work of the flesh divides. It leaves the church spiritually paralysed, immobilised and demilitarised.

Oh yes, there is great power in the Covenant, yet if the church wants to be truly effective in the end of days by fulfilling the Great Commission, we need to return to the solemn and sacred duty of upholding the Covenant.

We also need to forge greater unity among the brethren, as we see in Acts 2. In corporate unity, reflecting covenant agreement, and honouring God's Covenant, the church will indeed make a massive impact to see the world swept away by God's revival.

A return to the Upper Room in the end-times

More than ever, there is a need for the church to return to the Upper Room. The Lord has laid it strongly on my heart that it is time for the Church to rediscover the importance of the Upper Room in our spiritual walk. But then we need to understand what the Upper Room is, and what it truly means. For it was more than the place where the Holy Spirit was poured out. Yes, so much more.

We all know what happened in the Upper Room. We all know the story of "Acts 2: 1 And suddenly there came a sound from heaven, as of a rushing mighty wind, and it filled the whole house where they were sitting. 3 Then there appeared to them divided tongues, as of fire, and one sat upon each of them. 4 And they were all filled with the Holy Spirit and began to speak with other tongues, as the Spirit gave them utterance."

Another translation is as follows: Complete Jewish Bible (CJB): 1 The festival of Shavu'ot arrived, and the believers all gathered together in one place. 2 Suddenly there came a sound from the sky like the roar of a violent wind, and it filled the whole house where they were sitting. 3 Then they saw what looked like tongues of fire, which separated and came to rest on each one of them. 4 They were all filled with the Ruach HaKodesh and began to talk in different languages, as the Spirit enabled them to speak.

Oh yes, there in the room, after waiting as instructed by Jesus for the power from on high, 10 days taking into consideration the 40 days before Ascension after the resurrection, the disciples were equipped and empowered by the very presence of God, filling them and enabling them to be witnesses unto the ends of the earth!

Glory to God. Yes, there was a wind, for the Spirit is the Ruach Elohim – the very breath of God. Of those born in the Holy Spirit, it says, "John 3:8: The wind blows wherever it pleases. You hear its sound, but you cannot tell where it comes from or where it is going. So it is with everyone born of the Spirit."

Indeed, of the breath of God, we read in Ezekiel 37 regarding the prophecy of the dead bones. For the life-giving Spirt of the Living God descended upon the disciples, fulfilling the promise of John 16 verse 7: But I tell you the truth, it is to your advantage that I go away; for if I do not go away, the [a]Helper (Comforter, Advocate, Intercessor—Counselor, Strengthener, Standby) will not come to you; but if I go, I will send Him (the Holy Spirit) to you [to be in close fellowship with you].

Glory to God! And we know what happened beyond the Upper Room. We know of the first sermon that touched the lives of 3000. We know that Acts 4:3 says, "and with great power the apostles gave witness to the resurrection of the Lord Jesus". In Acts 5 we read: "12 And through the hands of the apostles many signs and wonders were done among the people. And they were all with one accord in Solomon's Porch. 13 Yet none of the rest dared join them, but the people esteemed them highly. 14 And believers were increasingly added to the Lord, multitudes of both men and women, 15 so that they brought the sick out into the streets and laid them on beds and couches, that at least the shadow of Peter passing by might fall on some of them. 16 Also a multitude gathered from the surrounding cities to Jerusalem, bringing sick people and those who were tormented by unclean spirits, and they were all healed".

Yes, great was the impact of the believers. Great was the witnessing of the Lord, and so the harvest grew. Why? Because of the Upper Room. Yes, because of the Holy Spirit! They were touched by God, for God is the all-consuming fire. The Upper Room, also known as the Cenacle, is located in the southern part of the Old City of Jerusalem on Mount Zion and is perhaps best known as the traditional site of the Last Supper since the fourth century AD. It was not just the place where the disciples were filled by the Holy Spirit, but it was the place of intimate fellowship with God Himself!

We read in Luke 22: 7 Then came the Day of Unleavened Bread, when the Passover must be killed. 8 And He sent Peter and John, saying, "Go and prepare the Passover for us, that we may eat." 9 So they said to Him, "Where do You want us to prepare?" 10 And He said to them, "Behold, when you have entered the city, a man will meet you carrying a pitcher of water; follow him into the house which he enters. 11 Then you shall say to the master of the house, 'The Teacher says to you, "Where is the guest room where I may eat the Passover with My disciples?" ' 12 Then he will show you a large, furnished upper room; there make ready." 13 So they went and found it just as He had said to them, and they prepared the Passover.

Jesus thus set the scene, not man, for it was not going to be any room, but a room chosen by God. He chose Peter and John, two of his loved disciples, for an important assignment. The Lord had set apart a place not only for the Last Supper but also for Pentecost. A place for fellowship, just as God had set Moses aside on Mount Sinai for 40 days. According to tradition, this room would become the place where the apostles stayed when they were in Jerusalem. The Cenacle is also where Jesus washed his disciples' feet (John 13:1–20), which symbolises the ministry of loving service. It is where the concept of a loving friendship with Jesus was introduced, as outlined in John's Last Supper discourses (John 14—16), and gave the apostles a glimpse into the beautiful prayer life of Jesus, sometimes known as the "high priestly prayer," recorded in John 17.

It is the place where the disciples gathered in fear after the death of Jesus. We read in John 20: New King James Version (NKJV): 19 Then, the same day at evening, being the first day of the week, when the doors were shut where the disciples were assembled, for fear of the Jews, Jesus came and stood in the midst, and said to them, "Peace be with you." 20 When He had said this, He showed them His hands and His side. Then the disciples were glad when they saw the Lord. 21 So Jesus said to them again, "Peace to you! As the Father has sent Me, I also send you." 22 And when He had said this, He breathed on them, and said to them, "Receive the Holy Spirit. 23 If you forgive the sins of any, they are forgiven them; if you retain the sins of any, they are retained."

Just as the Spirit descended upon Jesus at the baptism and rested upon Him in Power for the work of His earthly ministry, so also the disciples were regenerated and indwelt by the Spirit of the resurrected Christ before Pentecost. But at Pentecost, the Spirit was poured out upon them in power, because Christ had ascended to the throne of God and received all authority and power. Yes, in the Upper Room, what Jesus started by breathing upon them, the Spirit comes to completion with the outpouring of the Ruach Elohim! So we, therefore, find the Risen Lord breathing on them the Holy Spirit "on the evening of that first day of the week" (John 20:19). It is from there that the apostles went forth with boldness, sharing the Good News. All in the power of God, and to the glory of God!

And so by tradition, this is the same room where Jesus appeared, both before and after the resurrection. It was here that the Risen One made visible His wounds to see and touch, and the room where the faith of Thomas emerged. We read of this in John 20: 24 Now Thomas, called the Twin, one of the twelve, was not with them when Jesus came. 25 The other disciples, therefore, said to him, "We have seen the Lord." So he said to them, "Unless I see in His hands the print of the nails, and put my finger into the print of the nails, and put my hand into His side, I will not believe." 26 And after eight days His disciples were again inside, and Thomas with them. Jesus came, the doors being shut, and stood in the midst, and said, "Peace to you!" 27 Then He said to Thomas, "Reach your finger here, and look at My hands; and reach your hand here, and put it into My side. Do not be unbelieving, but believing."

It was therefore not just the room where the Spirit was breathed upon them, but also the room from which, filled with the power of the Holy Spirit, the apostles would ultimately leave to change the world—your world and mine. It is a room where all doubt vanished and the disciples were bolstered in their hope and faith to change the world! This was not a room of fear, but conviction in the greatness of God.

We read in Psalm 104:30: "Send forth your spirit, they are created, and you renew the face of the earth." The fruits of Jesus's life and ministry, as witnessed in the precious moments in the Upper Room documented in Scripture, continue in and through the Church up to today. In this humble space, the most important room in all of Christendom, Jesus set a remarkable precedent of faith and service, and so we are given a new understanding of God's love and the revolutionary power of the Holy Spirit was unleashed.

Indeed, it is the Upper Room where the disciples were truly moulded to be followers of Jesus. They had learned from the Master. They had spent time with God, with each other, and so they learned of fellowship, of unity, of truth, of humanity, of love, of hope and redemption. Yes, so much happened in the Upper Room for it was here that Jesus also told of Judas's betrayal and Peter's denial (John 13:21–30, 36–38). The humanity of each apostle is vibrantly portrayed in the Upper Room, giving us a glimpse into our hearts and nature, as well as into the unrelenting love of Jesus Christ for his followers.

We also read in Acts 1, before the ascension of Jesus thus during the 40 days after His resurrection: Acts 1: 1 The former account I made, O Theophilus, of all that Jesus began both to do and teach, 2 until the day in which He was taken up, after He through the Holy Spirit had given commandments to the apostles whom He had chosen, 3 to whom He also presented Himself alive after His suffering by many infallible proofs, being seen by them during forty days and speaking of the things pertaining to the kingdom of God. 4 And being assembled together with them, He commanded them not to depart from Jerusalem, but to wait for the Promise of the Father, "which," He said, "you have heard from Me; 5 for John truly baptized with water, but you shall be baptized with the Holy Spirit not many days from now." 6 Therefore, when they had come together, they asked Him, saying, "Lord, will You at this time restore the kingdom to Israel?" 7 And He said to them, "It is not for you to know times or seasons which the Father has put in His own authority. 8 But you shall receive power when the Holy Spirit has come upon you; and you shall bewitnesses to Me in Jerusalem, and in all Judea and Samaria, and to the end of the earth."

Take note of the following.... "speaking of the things pertaining to the kingdom of God". So by all accounts, the Lord spoke to them about the Kingdom, probably many things not recorded before ascending to the Father. We can only imagine the teaching they received, and how their faith was bolstered! For them, Matthew 6 would have become a reality where Jesus taught to first seek His Kingdom and righteousness. And yes, Moses was on that mountain for 40 days, learning and knowing God, and so it is not by accident that the Lord has also set apart 40 special days after His resurrection to equip His followers for their great work that waited for them. And much of that fellowship would have taken place in the Upper Room! There in the Upper Room, the Holy Spirit came in glory to take over the work of the Son.

Yes, in the Upper Room, the disciples had to make room for God in His Totality as the Trinity! They had to make room for His divinity, presence, and glory, and so they learned and grew spiritually and in the knowledge of His fullness. Yes, in the Upper Room, the disciples understood once and for all that Jesus is the Resurrection and the Life. They had fellowship with the Risen Lord – the Alpha and the Omega, not just at the Last Supper but even beyond the cross and the tomb. For them, they would have understood more clearly the significance of the Last Supper, where they learned about the cup and the bread. They would have understood the power of the Blood and that Jesus is the hope of glory!

And yes, by all accounts, the disciples simply replicated what they had experienced in the Upper Room once they were led out in the world under the power of the Holy Spirit. We read of this in "Acts 2: 43 A sense of awe was felt by everyone, and many wonders and signs (attesting miracles) were taking place through the apostles. 44 And all those who had believed [in Jesus as Saviour] were together and had all things in common [considering their possessions to belong to the group as a whole]. 45 And they began selling their property and possessions and were sharing the proceeds with all [the other believers], as anyone had need. 46 Day after day, they met in the temple [area] continuing with one mind, and breaking bread in various private homes. They were eating their meals together with joy and generous hearts, 47 praising God continually, and having favor with all the people. And the Lord kept adding to their number daily those who were being saved."

And also Acts 4: 32 Now the company of believers was of one heart and soul, and not one [of them] claimed that anything belonging to him was [exclusively] his own, but everything was common property and for the use of all. 33 And with great ability and power the apostles were continuously testifying to the resurrection of the Lord Jesus, and great grace [God's remarkable lovingkindness and favor and goodwill] rested richly upon them all. 34 There was not a needy person among them, because those who were owners of land or houses were selling them, and bringing the proceeds of the sales 35 and placing the money down at the apostles' feet. Then it was distributed to each as anyone had need.

The disciples simply replicated and put into motion what they had learned in the Upper Room! And what had they learned? Yes, what it means to be the true church (ecclesia), and they learned of the Kingdom, and of being a servant.

The Upper Room was also a place of prayer. It says in Acts 1 (following the Ascension): 12 Then the disciples returned to Jerusalem from the mount called Olivet (Olive Grove), which is near Jerusalem, [only] a Sabbath day's journey (less than one mile) away. 13 When they had entered the city, they went upstairs to the upper room where they were staying [indefinitely]; that is, Peter, and John and [his brother] James, and Andrew, Philip and Thomas, Bartholomew (Nathanael) and Matthew, James the son of Alphaeus, and Simon the Zealot, and Judas (Thaddaeus) the son of James. 14 All these with one mind and one purpose were continually devoting themselves to prayer, [waiting together] along with the women, and Mary the mother of Jesus, and with His brothers.

Take note, it says the disciples devoted themselves to prayer. It was therefore a place of unified prayer, supplication and seeking God's will. Paul would echo the importance of prayer in Ephesians 6: 18 With all prayer and petition pray [with specific requests] at all times [on every occasion and in every season] in the Spirit, and with this in view, stay alert with all perseverance and petition [interceding in prayer] for all God's people.

To return to the Upper Room is for the Church to return to deep prayer life, but also a united prayer life with other disciples. A life of seeking God, seeking His will, and praying as the Spirit leads. Unity is so important for the Church, for in the Upper Room the disciples learned of fellowship, of unity, of sharing, of caring, and the power of God's love. In the Upper Room, they spoke for the first time in other languages, and they knew beyond a doubt that God would be with them as witnesses unto the ends of the earth. No wonder Jesus had to set aside a special place because He needed to prepare those who were set aside for the Kingdom!

So why is the Upper Room so important? Simple. In the upper room, the church – consisting of Spirit-filled disciples - was ACTIVATED in Power and then MOBILISED to be witnesses unto the ends of the world, thus fulfilling the Great Commission. Yes, the Church was mobilised, for the Church was the disciples, and the Church today is still the living and breathing disciples! The Upper Room as the building and the room were not the Church, but only served as the Ark that housed for a season and a time the disciples who were about to be ignited with fire by the Ruach Elohim! The true Church left the building to be the Church, for they were activated and empowered to be mobilized. And this is a process of moving, being active and serving the Kingdom.

Yes, they left the Upper Room! They did not call people to join them in the building, but the Church went into the crowd to bring Jesus to a world dying and in need of a true Saviour!

And so the first sermon touched the lives of 3000 people, simply because the disciples were now moving in Kingdom power, and they were focused only upon Jesus and His Kingdom and the lost who needed the King of kings! The disciples were equipped and trained one last time, then activated and then they went. Thus, they FOLLOWED first and then out of the door of the Upper Room into the world (literally among the crowd) to preach and teach.

The Church went from that Upper Room, yes, they left what was comfortable and safe, and they embraced a hostile world with the Good News of hope and glory! It says in "Mark 16: 15 And He said to them, "Go into all the world and preach the gospel to every creature. 16 He who believes and is baptized will be saved; but he who does not believe will be condemned. 17 And these signs will follow those who believe: In My name they will cast out demons; they will speak with new tongues; 18 they will take up serpents; and if they drink anything deadly, it will by no means hurt them; they will lay hands on the sick, and they will recover."

Glory to God! The disciples, as the Church, were now activated and mobilised, and yes, signs and wonders of God's power followed them! These disciples were not running after the signs and wonders, but they walked in the Truth of God, filled by the Spirit, and so as they went, mobilised, the Kingdom of God manifested in the world. The disciples were on fire for the Lord, for they understood they were called to be the Church and they were called to be the fulfilment of Mark 16 and Matthew 28. In Acts 3, we read how a lame man was healed, and in Acts 2, we read in verse 43 how "many wonders and signs were done through the apostles" and how the "Lord added to the church daily those who were being saved."

Was God's intention to fill a building when it says adding to the church? No, he was adding followers to the disciples who were willing to preach and teach the Kingdom, thus those who were willing to be also empowered and mobilised! Suddenly, the living Church was growing for God is a God of Life, and suddenly, the Church was truly alive with hope, expectation, and with purpose and intent! The disciples were following the blueprint of Jesus of making disciples, and so the Church, activated and mobilised, was now making a huge impact in the world. Why? Not because of clever sermons, or interesting services or because of the coffee and cake, no, because they were following Jesus in the Spirit of the Living God, and they were not willing to back down, to be slowed down or to compromise. The active Church was empowered to be a powerful testimony of God's grace and mercy!

So when the Lord speaks of returning to the Upper Room, this is, therefore, a time for the Church to again be ACTIVATED (a return to the Spirit, to the Kingdom, to the Truth) for the Church to be mobilised to fulfil the Great Commission! Now is the time to move, to follow God's blueprint of discipleship, and to be again filled with Kingdom purpose and intent! Now is the time to be the true active Church, empowered in the fullness of the knowledge of Jesus!

For it is time to again follow and go as commanded by the Lord! Yes, in the Upper Room was the activation and the mobilisation by the Spirit, just as Jesus was activated by the Spirit and then mobilised for three-plus years in His ministry on earth! How we need as the Church of Spirit-filled disciples to be reactivated to go into this world preaching and teaching only the Truth of God and nothing else, for only the Truth of God sets man free in the liberty of the grace of a living God.

In Daniel 6, we read: 10 Now when Daniel knew that the writing was signed, he went home. And in his upper room, with his windows open toward Jerusalem, he knelt down on his knees three times that day, and prayed and gave thanks before his God, as was his custom since early days.

The Upper Room thus ties in back to the Old Testament, even when Daniel would seek the Lord in this sanctuary. Just as the disciples truly walked and talked with God, just so Daniel found his strength in his time with God in the Upper Room. Daniel connected to God just as the disciples connected with God in the Upper Room, first with Jesus and then with the Holy Spirit.

It was in the Upper Room in 1 Kings 17 where Elijah revived the widow's son. We read 19 And he said to her, "Give me your son." So he took him out of her arms and carried him to the upper room where he was staying, and laid him on his own bed. 20 Then he cried out to the Lord and said, "O Lord my God, have You also brought tragedy on the widow with whom I lodge, by killing her son?" 21 And he stretched himself out on the child three times, and cried out to the Lord and said, "O Lord my God, I pray, let this child's soul come back to him." 22 Then the Lord heard the voice of Elijah; and the soul of the child came back to him, and he revived. 23 And Elijah took the child and brought him down from the upper room into the house, and gave him to his mother. And Elijah said, "See, your son lives!"

You see, the disciples learned in the Upper Room of the God who gives life, not just physically but spiritually. They walked and talked with the Lord who is the Resurrection and Life, and in the upper room, the prophet moved in such life and power when God restored the son to live. Yes, there is life in the Upper Room, for God is life, and we are called to walk in resurrected life and power!

So for us to return to the Upper Room is really to return as disciples to God and His Kingdom, to reconnect, and to learn again about fellowship. It is for us to learn again about unity as children of God, of caring, and sharing. It is about worshipping and fellowshipping with the Risen Lord. In the Upper Room of our spiritual experience, we need to return to the true path of God and once again submit and yield to His presence. It is about connecting to the God of power and life.

How we need to make room again for God, and so dwell and abide in Him. It is a call to return to love, to hope, to the power from on high, and to be a vessel on fire for God. It is a return to the

Covenant, to the power of the Blood, a return to our humanity as children of God, and a return to faith beyond doubt and a return to walking in His Glory when beyond the doors the world is dying spiritually.

May we indeed return to the Upper Room of our faith, our relationship and our walk with Jesus – the Lamb who was slain yet returns as the victorious King! May we indeed walk in the indwelling power of the Spirit to walk in the Lord's will, to be sanctified and to know the Truth of the Kingdom?

Yes, it is time to return to where the Church truly began, for as the Church we have lost our way beyond the Upper Room we have strayed from the course and the Master. May we return with weeping and joy and may the Church keep moving, keep moving in the power of God, so that the world may see the manifestation of His Kingdom, of His Love and the reality of His Glory.

From the Upper Room revival flowed. In simple terms, it is about coming alive. It is being awakened from sleep, from a comatose state and even from death. Lazarus was revived by Jesus, when after four days, he emerged from the tomb. At the time, Jesus said He is the Resurrection and the Life (John 11:25). True life, and not artificial life, comes from God and God alone.

To be revived can be defined as restoring to life, or consciousness, or to regain life or strength. In Ephesians 3, we read: "14 For this reason I bow my knees to the Father of our Lord Jesus Christ, 15 from whom the whole family in heaven and earth is named, 16 that He would grant you, according to the riches of His glory, to be strengthened with might through His Spirit in the inner man." It is by the Holy Spirit that we are truly revived. It is by the Holy Spirit we are reborn (John 3), and we are strengthened to come alive.

In 1 Corinthians 2, we read "16 For who has known the mind of the Lord that he may instruct Him?" But we have the mind of

Christ." As we are reborn of God, our minds are quickened, and out of such quickening, we become conscious of the reality of God. John 3 speaks about 'seeing the Kingdom of God' when we are reborn. In the Spirit of God, we became intimately aware of God's presence and His Kingdom. We are, therefore, conscious and thus no longer 'asleep' in the depravity of this world. To be conscious means alert, awake, and you are aware of what is happening around you.

In Ephesians 5, we read: "13 But all things that are exposed are made manifest by the light, for whatever makes manifest is light. 14 Therefore He says: "Awake, you who sleep, arise from the dead, and Christ will give you light."

In our fallen ways, we are spiritually disconnected from God and we are not conscious of His ways or Kingdom. We are thus slumbering in our spiritual deadness. Yet in Christ, we now walk in the light of our awakening and the light of our renewal. Indeed, in Christ, we became awake to righteousness (Corinthians 15:34). We rejoice in God's work of redemption and restoration, which brings 1 Peter 2:9 to reality: "9 But you are a chosen generation, a royal priesthood, a holy nation, His own special people, that you may proclaim the praises of Him who called you out of darkness into His marvelous light."

1 Thessalonians 5 says: "5 You are all sons of light and sons of the day. We are not of the night nor of darkness. 6 Therefore let us not sleep, as others do, but let us watch and be sober. 7 For those who sleep, sleep at night, and those who get drunk are drunk at night. 8 But let us who are of the day be sober, putting on the breastplate of faith and love, and as a helmet the hope of salvation." Only in Christ do we come to a point of being sober, meaning we walk in the clarity of mind, of thought, intention and will. We are no longer confused, but our gaze is certain and our focus is upon the eternal Kingdom.

A lot has been written about revival. A lot has been spoken about it. There have been several noticeable revivals over the last couple of hundreds of years, such as the Azusa and the Welsh revivals. Such revivals, including the Great Awakenings in America, have all been characterized by men and women who were hungry for God. They prayed in earnest to God as they sought revival. Yet such a hunger, such a thirst and such a longing is the work of the Holy Spirit. For it is by the Holy Spirit we are convicted of our fallen ways and by the Spirit of God, we are awakened to the truth that we desperately need Jesus.

It should also be noted, and this is of great importance, that revival is not external but internal. Revival is not something that just suddenly externally comes upon the church, but as we will explore, it should be the natural yet supernatural outflow of a disciple, thus a product of true and real discipleship. Thus, revival is actually the product of fulfilling the Great Commission!

In John 7 we read "37 On the last day, that great day of the feast, Jesus stood and cried out, saying, "If anyone thirsts, let him come to Me and drink. 38 He who believes in Me, as the Scripture has said, out of his heart will flow rivers of living water." 39 But this He spoke concerning the Spirit, whom those believing in Him would receive; for the Holy Spirit was not yet given, because Jesus was not yet glorified." It is by such waters of life that we truly come alive! For only by the Spirit of God do we know true life and such life has a name – Jesus. For Jesus is the Resurrection and the Life. And by the Spirit of God, we come alive in His Glory, in His Hope and strength! For it is the work of the Spirit to awaken us to the reality of Jesus, to His Truth, to His Way and the Covenant of Grace. By the Spirit, we are awakened to the glorious nature of God who loves us, who has redeemed us and who brings us to a point of life when we are once dead in our transgressions (Ephesians 2:1).

To be reborn speaks of life! The entire process of birth after all is about life. In a biological sense, birth is seen as the start of life as a physically separate being. In a spiritual sense, when we are reborn we celebrate the start of life as a spiritual being reconnected to the Creator! Birth is life, and God gives us physical and spiritual life. In John 3 Jesus speaks about the process of being reborn, and we take note that religion cannot facilitate such a process. One can truly only be reborn by the Spirit of God. So the only way for us to come alive, thus revived, is by the Spirit of the Lord. It is without a doubt the Holy Spirit is ever-present when it comes to a believer being reborn. The reality, therefore, is that there is no revival without the Holy Spirit. You cannot try and produce a revival out of one's strength, imagination or effort. No programme will produce a sustainable and life-sustaining revival without the Holy Spirit.

The Bible provides a blueprint for everything when it comes to our spiritual walk. This includes discipleship and revival. Directly following the Pentecost, we read in Acts 2 how 3000 people were moved by one sermon to follow Christ. Why? Because the Spirit of God was speaking through Peter. God was present. God was moving, and He was the focal point of Pentecost, not man. We read in Acts 2 the following: 40 And with many other words he testified and exhorted them, saying, "Be saved from this [l]perverse generation." 41 Then those who gladly received his word were baptized; and that day about three thousand souls were added to them. 42 And they continued steadfastly in the apostles' [n]doctrine and fellowship, in the breaking of bread, and in prayers. 43 Then fear came upon every soul, and many wonders and signs were done through the apostles. 44 Now all who believed were together, and had all things in common, 45 and sold their possessions and goods, and divided them among all, as anyone had need. 46 So continuing daily with one accord in the temple, and breaking bread from house to house, they ate their food with gladness and simplicity of heart, 47 praising God and having favor with all the people. And the Lord added to the church daily those who were being saved." Acts 2 is a revival in its purest form! Revival produces unity among the brethren, and it produces hope, love and above all, a people who are Christ-focused and Christ-oriented.

Thus, one of the greatest revivals in church history is directly after Pentecost! Why? Because the Spirit of God initiated the revival. Those in the Upper Room were filled with holy fire. They were filled with the holy presence of God. They were fearless, bold and unapologetic. In the power of the Holy Spirit, they truly came alive and were ready in the power of God to be the light and the salt unto a broken world. If we truly want revival in the church, we need to yield again to the Spirit and begin to obey. We need to be filled again with holy fire, with a holy conviction and a holy purpose! If not, we will continue to have dead churches and believers who are spiritually self-destructing.

Consider the life-generating power of the Holy Spirit in the fact that on the Day of Pentecost 3000 lives found Jesus. Compare that to the 3000 lost in the Old Testament because of the rebellion against God at Mount Sinai. At the mountain, where God gave the Law 50 days after the first Passover, the people decided to worship a golden calf. And so they died. At Pentecost – 50 days after the Passover - the law of the Spirit of life in Christ Jesus has made us free from the law of sin and death (Romans 8:2). So powerful was the Spirit of God on that day that the 3000 who were lost to the Kingdom were redeemed by the regenerating work of the Spirit by the 3000 who believed in the new way of Christ! Talk about revival. Talk about the Spirit giving life, hope and strength!

The power of the Holy Spirit to regenerate and to bring to life is perfectly illustrated in "Ezekiel 37: 1 The hand of the Lord came upon me and brought me out in the Spirit of the Lord, and set me down in the midst of the valley; and it was full of bones. 2 Then He caused me to pass by them all around, and behold, there were very many in the open valley; and indeed they were very dry. 3 And He said to me, "Son of man, can these bones live?" So I answered, "O Lord God, You know." 4 Again He said to me, "Prophesy to these bones, and say to them, 'O dry bones, hear the word of the Lord! 5 Thus says the Lord God to these bones: "Surely I will cause breath to enter into you, and you shall live. 6 I will put sinews on you and bring flesh upon you, cover you with skin and put breath in you; and you shall live. Then you shall know that I am the Lord."'"

We also learn in verse 11 that the bones are the whole house of Israel. We also read "12 Therefore prophesy and say to them, 'Thus says the Lord God: "Behold, O My people, I will open your graves and cause you to come up from your graves, and bring you into the land of Israel. 13 Then you shall know that I am the Lord, when I have opened your graves, O My people, and brought you up from your graves. 14 I will put My Spirit in you, and you shall live, and I will place you in your own land. Then you shall know that I, the Lord, have spoken it and performed it," says the Lord.'"

Glory to God! There is only life by the Spirit of God! There is only revival by the Spirit of God! The church these days is filled with dry bones. It is filled with dry religion, dry programmes, dry believers and dry agendas. For as we have read, where the Spirit of God is, there are living waters. There is also liberty in the Spirit. Nothing can be dry where the water flows! Nothing is yoked, broken, or in bondage where the Spirit of God moves. Nothing can be dry where the Spirit flows to bring the dead bones to life. How we need the Spirit back in the church, for in our power and strength there will be no awakening or revival! This is the truth of "Zechariah 4:6: So he answered and said to me: "This is the word of the Lord to Zerubbabel: 'Not by might nor by power, but by My Spirit,' Says the Lord of hosts."

We read in 2 Kings 13 of the following account: "20 Then Elisha died, and they buried him. And the raiding bands from Moab invaded the land in the spring of the year. 21 So it was, as they were burying a man, that suddenly they spied a band of raiders; and they put the man in the tomb of Elisha; and when the man was let down and touched the bones of Elisha, he revived and stood on his feet."

Elisha was the successor of Elijah in the office of the prophet in Israel (1 Kings 19:16, 19–21; 2 Kings 5:8). He was called to follow Elijah in 1 Kings 19:19, and he spent the next several years as the prophet's protégé until Elijah was taken into heaven. At that time, Elisha began his ministry, which lasted about 60 years, spanning the reigns of kings Jehoram, Jehu, Jehoahaz, and Joash.

Elisha stepped into his calling when Elijah put his cloak around Elisha—a sign that Elijah's responsibilities would fall on Elisha. This is after Elijah fled from Queen Jezebel following a mighty display of God's power against the prophets of Baal and a return of the rain after a long drought. Elijah, refreshed by an angel and prepared for a forty-day journey to Mount Horeb, was told by God that there were 7 000 remaining who had not bowed to Baal. Elijah found Elisha, who was ploughing with a pair of oxen at the time. Elisha left his old life and followed Elijah as his servant (true discipleship). Elisha thus completely removed himself from his former life—essentially hosting a celebration and leaving himself no option to return to his oxen.

Elijah was of course a prophet filled with God's presence. And God's presence is life and resurrection. Such power and presence rested upon Elisha as well. Remember, the Holy Spirit was always present from the beginning of the foundation of the world, but became only available to all believers after Pentecost. Yet without a doubt, both these prophets operated by the Holy Spirit, for it is only by the Spirit of God that God's power is activated and becomes manifested.

Remember, Elisha asked for a double portion of Elijah's spirit. Does it mean he was going to have more of the Holy Spirit than Elijah? We need to realise that you can't get more of the Holy Spirit than you have right now. When you received the Holy Spirit, you received Him in His fullness.

It's not a matter of more of Him, it's a matter of how much more of you He can get. He fills only what is yielded to Him. The idea of a double portion in the Bible is one of a double blessing. It was typically used in the Old Testament to refer to the birthright or the inheritance received by the oldest son. For example, Deuteronomy 21:17 says, "He shall acknowledge the firstborn, the son of the unloved, by giving him a double portion of all that he has, for he is the firstfruits of his strength. The right of the firstborn is his."

The request by Elisha for a double portion of Elijah's spirit in 2 Kings 2 referred likewise to being doubly blessed in his life and ministry. And by all accounts, more miracles were accounted to Elisha than Elijah. The power of the Holy Spirit was the same on both prophets, but the power manifested in a greater manner in the life of Elisha because of what he asked. And who performed these miracles through the prophet Elisha? Remember, Elisha pursued Elijah through several (See 2 Kings 2:1-15).

So to return to 2 Kings 13, we find that man was revived when he simply touched the bones of Elisha. Just as the Spirit could revive the dead bones of Israel in Ezekiel 37, just so we see how the prophet was so saturated by the Spirit of God that resurrected power and life was still present in his bones! And by such power of the Holy Spirit, the man was let down in the tomb was revived. Glory to God. The Holy Spirit can revive anything. We must just be a people saturated with the Holy Spirit so that the dead may be revived, the broken may be revived and the dry bones restored! When you invite the anointing of the Spirit of God by desire, God will surely visit you and flow through you by His Spirit as He wills and He wills to move in you more than you can imagine. We must just be willing to surrender and die unto the Lord to live in Christ.

In Acts 1 we read "8 But you shall receive power when the Holy Spirit has come upon you; and you shall be witnesses to Me in Jerusalem, and in all Judea and Samaria, and to the end of the earth." Only by the Spirit of God is there life and growth and hope! By His power we become alive and we can shine His light in a dark world. In His power, we become true disciples, ready and willing to declare the Gospel. True disciples like Elisha willing to follow the Master.

In Ezekiel 37 the Lord spoke about how He will put breath in the dry bones and they shall live ... "then you shall know that I am the Lord." The Spirit of God hovering over the waters in some translations of Genesis 1:2 comes from the Hebrew phrase Ruach Elohim, which has alternately been interpreted as a great wind. Rûach has the meanings "wind, spirit, breath," and Elohim can mean "great" as well as "god". And what happened on Pentecost in the Upper Room? "2 And suddenly there came a sound from heaven, as of a rushing mighty wind, and it filled the whole house where they were sitting. 3 Then there appeared to them divided tongues, as of fire, and one sat upon each of them. 4 And they were all filled with the Holy Spirit and began to speak with other tongues, as the Spirit gave them utterance."

Oh yes, how we need to come alive again in the power of the Holy Spirit to be true representatives of God on this earth. How we need the wind of the Spirit to blow again through our churches, our hearts and our lives! How we need to again seek the Spirit of God to lead us in all truth, in power, in boldness, in God's beauty and strength! God has spoken prophetically how the Church needs to get back to the Upper Room. This means we need to reconnect with the Spirit. For directly after the rushing wind there was revival. And such revival continued and flowed like a mighty river beyond the Upper Room and into the streets of Jerusalem and still today to the outer reaches of the world. The revival in the Upper Room was sustained and gained momentum for it was the Holy Spirit that was birthing the church. In Acts 2 it says that the Lord added to the church daily those who were being saved. Yes, God was in control, thus the Spirit, and not man. To 'add' speaks of divine intervention. Thus pure revival! How we need to yield and submit again to the Lord and just connect with the Spirit of God.

Indeed, how we need the Spirit of God to breathe life into us! How we need the Holy Spirit to shake our worlds so that we become alive from our spiritual apathy to be on fire for God! How we need the Holy Spirit to be filled with conviction and a certainty that God is faithful and true. How we need the holy fire of God to burn in our bones so that the dry bones may live and the spiritually dead and lost and forgotten may be revived.

In Matthew 3, John the Baptist said: "11 I indeed baptize you with water unto repentance, but He who is coming after me is mightier than I, whose sandals I am not worthy to carry. He will baptize you with the Holy Spirit and fire." Glory to God. How we need the fire of the Spirit in our churches again! For such fire rested like tongues upon the first disciples. And such disciples had no great wealth or influence yet changed the world. They had a lasting impact because the Spirit of God dwelled within them, radically transforming them into the image of the Kingdom. They were truly on fire for God, infused with the Holy Spirit. Yes, we do not need more programmes or agendas in churches, but we just need the Holy Spirit to lead us as Elijah and Elisha were led in power.

For Paul wrote in "1 Corinthians 2: 1 And I, brethren, when I came to you, did not come with excellence of speech or of wisdom declaring to you the testimony of God. 2 For I determined not to know anything among you except Jesus Christ and Him crucified. 3 I was with you in weakness, in fear, and in much trembling. 4 And my speech and my preaching were not with persuasive words of [b]human wisdom, but in demonstration of the Spirit and of power, 5 that your faith should not be in the wisdom of men but in the power of God." Paul on the Road to Damascus was reborn when he met Jesus. And from that day he moved in the power of the Holy Spirit (Acts 1:8), fulfilling the Great Commission by declaring the Good News far and wide. Revival truly followed Paul, for Paul was following Christ in Spirit and truth. Paul had crucified his flesh and was now regenerated by the Spirit of God. For the water of life inside of him was manifesting wherever Paul ministered by the grace and power of God.

For it says in Mark 16 that signs and wonders follow those who believe in Christ. Yes, revival must follow the disciple, for the disciple follows the author of life! For as we follow Christ, we walk in His life and Spirit, and by such life and Spirit, the lost shall know that God still redeems and saves the broken, the lost and the forgotten!

We need to remember no one else can save us. God sent Jesus, His one and only Son, to earth so that He could make a way for our salvation (John 3:16). After living a perfect life, Jesus was crucified, bearing the punishment for our sins upon Himself. He was resurrected from the dead three days later, conquering death. When we place our faith in Jesus and His sacrifice, we are saved and filled with the Holy Spirit. The Holy Spirit within us is what enables us to live out the spiritual rebirth that has taken place: "But I say, walk by the Spirit, and you will not gratify the desires of the flesh" (Galatians 5:16). Yet it is also the Spirit that wakens us up from our slumber through divine conviction. Those legitimately born again are indwelt by the Holy Spirit (John 3:5). What does it mean to have the Holy Spirit living within us? Fundamentally, it means that the Holy Spirit is communicating a conviction about Christ's moral beauty to the eyes and ears of our hearts.

Thus we need to understand very clearly it is by the Spirit of God that we are ultimately made alive to be united with Christ. John 6:63 says: "It is the Spirit who gives life; the flesh is no help at all." So the new birth — and the new life that comes with it — is the work of the Holy Spirit. The Holy Spirit is our direct connection to God and enables us to remain free from the power of sin. When we are spiritually reborn, we walk anew with the Holy Spirit as our guide and companion (John 6:63; Romans 8:14). The Spirit's presence in our life is the seal of our salvation (Ephesians 1:13–14). Through Christ's sacrifice and the continual presence of the Holy Spirit within us, we can walk with God in the freedom that comes from spiritual rebirth. It is written in Romans 6: (New King James Version): 11 Likewise you also, reckon yourselves to be dead indeed to sin, but alive to God in Christ Jesus our Lord." As our physical life comes from our parents, so life has to come from our spiritual Father – as we are birthed miraculously in the physical, so is our spiritual birth a miracle and one that will forever astound and amaze us.

You can also call the Spirit's work a process of regeneration. Another word for regeneration is "rebirth," from which we get the concept of being "born again." Again, the classic proof text for this can be found in John's gospel: "I tell you the truth, no one can see the kingdom of God unless he is born again" (John 3:3). We need to understand that the Holy Spirit, who is God Himself as part of the Trinity, is the source of new life. Moses told the Israelites before entering the Promised Land that "The Lord your God will circumcise your hearts and the hearts of your descendants, so that you may love him with all your heart and with all your soul, and live" (Deuteronomy 30:6). This circumcision of the heart is the work of God's Spirit and can be accomplished only by Him.

Right in the beginning, the world was dark and void of life. We read that the Holy Spirit hovered. Yes, He was first mentioned as part of the Trinity. Only when the Father spoke, "Let there be light" did the Holy Spirit move and bring about life. Yes, the Father spoke, and so the Spirit was activated to bring about life, and so the earth was rebirthed. If we are talking about the Holy Spirit being the conceiver of life, consider "Matthew 1:20 But while he thought on these things, behold, the angel of the Lord appeared unto him in a dream, saying, Joseph, thou son of David, fear not to take unto thee Mary thy wife: for that which is conceived in her is of the Holy Ghost." Yes, the Lord Jesus was conceived and brought to life by the Spirit of the living Lord! Indeed, Jesus said He is the Life and He gives Life in abundance, but remember the Lord is ONE, and so Jesus, while on earth, was operating and functioning in the life-giving power of the Holy Spirit! After all, Jesus was baptised by the Holy Spirit.

We read of such conception in "Luke 1: 29 But when she saw him, she was troubled at his saying, and considered what manner of greeting this was. 30 Then the angel said to her, "Do not be afraid, Mary, for you have found favor with God. 31 And behold, you will conceive in your womb and bring forth a Son, and shall call His name Jesus. 32 He will be great, and will be called the Son of the Highest; and the Lord God will give Him the throne of His father David. 33 And He will reign over the house of Jacob forever, and of His kingdom there will be no end." 34 Then Mary said to the angel, "How can this be, since I do not know a man?" 35 And the angel answered and said to her, "The Holy Spirit will come upon you, and the power of the Highest will overshadow you; therefore, also, that Holy One who is to be born will be called the Son of God."

How we need the church to be overshadowed again by the Spirit of God. How we need the Holy Spirit to conceive divine life within the believer and the church in such perilous times. How we need the Spirit of God to set our hearts on fire for God and the lost! In Luke 1 we read "41 And it happened, when Elizabeth heard the greeting of Mary, that the babe leaped in her womb; and Elizabeth was filled with the Holy Spirit." There is such beauty where the Spirit is present at the conception of our rebirth. And we need to tell the world of Jesus so that all may know the beauty of such conception and John 3:16. By the Spirit of God, we are reborn and brought to life to the glory of God.

In all three Synoptic gospels, Jesus concludes a conversation about the contrast between his teaching and practice and that of the Pharisees (and John the Baptist) by means of a parable about wine and wineskins (Matthew 9:16-17, Mark 2.21–22, Luke 5.36–39). As we are made alive and renewed by the Blood of the Lamb and by the Spirit of God, we can now walk in the divine presence of God (the new wine) via the infilling of the Holy Spirit. Yet we need to make sure that we do not revert to the old wineskin, meaning our old lives. We are made new, called to lead a holy life in the power of the Holy Spirit, and called to tell people of Jesus so that they may be revived and renewed as well.

And such beautiful 'wine' was indeed poured out on Pentecost to empower the disciples to become new wineskins, thus revived. And by the new 'wine' to lead a broken world to Jesus, who still to this very day offers all those who believe a new life of hope. We play a part in revival by fulfilling the Great Commission, yet we can only do so in the power of the Holy Spirit. If we truly want to see the church revived and impact people in this world, we need the 'new wine' of the Spirit more than ever! For revival flowed from the Upper Room, and will again flow from a people who seek to walk with God as worshippers in spirit and truth.

And it is very important to take note that to be a worshipper in spirit and truth implies a balance between walking in the passion and the fire of the Holy Spirit but also being grounded solidly in the Word (Logos of God). We cannot be merely just spiritual without the Word of God, for then the fire will rage without being counterbalanced by God's Truth. And we cannot be merely grounded in the Word and become so intellectual that we fail to move in the liberty and the freedom of the Spirit of God.

As disciples of God, we are called not just to be revived, but to revive others. And such revival should burn in the bones of the disciple that serves God as a worshipper in spirit and truth. Just as we are called to be disciples, we must also disciple others. For the Spirit was poured out so that we may be revived, but also by the power of the Spirit, revive others by sharing the Gospel, thus fulfilling the Great Commission.

As mentioned at the beginning of this article, revival is not external. Right now, a lot of people in churches are crying out for revival. They are crying out that God will pour out revival on the church so that the nations can be revived. What happens when a disciple is reborn? Yes, such a disciple is revived. What is a disciple supposed to do? Yes, fulfil the Great Commission. Revival is thus the product of a believer coming alive and walking in such resurrected power of God, and by such power to bring revival by declaring the Gospel and seeing others reborn in the Spirit of God to the glory of Jesus.

And how is a disciple supposed to bring revival? Simple. Through discipleship! If a disciple truly fulfils the Great Commission and denies the self to take up the cross, then such a disciple should be walking in the power of the Holy Spirit. And by such power, the disciple will lead others to Christ, and they shall be reborn in Spirit. Thus, discipleship is supposed to deliver revival!

And through discipleship, a town or city is won for Christ, and in that victory, revival spreads like wildfire.

While the church is crying out for revival, what we fail to realise is the ONE who revives us has already been poured out on Pentecost. Churches are waiting for some kind of external event to spark a revival. Yet God is waiting for the church to again reconnect with the Spirit of God that regenerates and brings the church to life! At the tomb of Lazarus, Jesus said He is the Resurrection and the Life. The church, in general, is struggling to walk in revival power and to see revival spread across towns and cities simply because the church has failed to be revived, thus be a church reborn in the Spirit of God!

It says in "John 6:63 It is the Spirit who gives life; the flesh profits nothing. The words that I speak to you are spirit, and they are life." Thus, we are called to speak Jesus to the world as worshippers in spirit and truth, for then we shall speak life! And such life is the essence of revival! For such life brings to life the dry bones, the entombed, the broken, the defeated and the hapless and hopeless. Indeed, the Word of God is also living and active (Hebrews 4:12) and, when quickened by the Holy Spirit, has dynamic power to impart spiritual life to us. For in God is our life. He is our refreshing and revival. So as a disciple, we are called to abide in God, thus abide in life, and speak life so that the lost may be found and be revived! For Jesus is the hope of glory, and as we live by His Word and Truth, we shall live and we declare He is the Resurrection and Life so that others may live and be discipled.

By the Spirit of God, we are reborn and we now become true epistles of Christ as what Paul wrote about in "2 Corinthians 3: 1 Do we begin again to commend ourselves? Or do we need, as some others, epistles of commendation to you or letters of commendation from you? 2 You are our epistle written in our hearts, known and read by all men; 3 clearly you are an epistle of

Christ, ministered by us, written not with ink but by the Spirit of the living God, not on tablets of stone but on tablets of flesh, that is, of the heart. 4 And we have such trust through Christ toward God. 5 Not that we are sufficient of ourselves to think of anything as being from ourselves, but our sufficiency is from God, 6 who also made us sufficient as ministers of the new covenant, not of the letter but of the Spirit; for the letter kills, but the Spirit gives life."

In John 14 we read: 15 "If you love Me, keep My commandments. 16 And I will pray the Father, and He will give you another Helper, that He may abide with you forever— 17 the Spirit of truth, whom the world cannot receive, because it neither sees Him nor knows Him; but you know Him, for He dwells with you and will be in you. 18 I will not leave you orphans; I will come to you."

Take note, we are not left to be orphans! Jesus will return for His children, but in the meantime, the resurrected indwelling power of God resides in the believers who follow the Lord. Romans 8 declares: "4 For as many as are led by the Spirit of God, these are sons of God. 15 For you did not receive the spirit of bondage again to fear, but you received the Spirit of adoption by whom we cry out, "Abba, Father." 16 The Spirit Himself bears witness with our spirit that we are children of God, 17 and if children, then heirs—heirs of God and joint heirs with Christ, if indeed we suffer with Him, that we may also be glorified together." By the glorious sanctifying and regenerating work of the Holy Spirit, we become alive, and we are adopted into the royal priesthood of sons and daughters of the Most High God. God has not rejected or forsaken us, but by the Holy Spirit, we become alive to the Kingdom, to His Presence as our Father and to the love of the Son – Jesus Christ. We do not need to fear for God is with us, in us and always victorious.

John 7:38 declares: "Whoever believes in me, as Scripture has said, rivers of living water will flow from within them." You see, the living waters don't flow from the outside to the inside, but from the inside to the outside! As we are revived and reborn in the glorious resurrected power of God, we become vessels of Glory, and within us, the new wine will flow, and the rivers of life will flow from us. And the purpose of the new wine and the living waters is so that others may be touched by God, may know God and be filled by God's glory. This is revival. It is thus the living waters within a disciple flowing from the inner to the outer to touch the dry bones of those who have withered under the onslaughts of this world.

The entire Book of Acts speaks of revival. Yet it is also the account of the disciples fulfilling the Great Commission. Revival flowed from the disciples. A revival was the result of the disciples acting in obedience to God. A revival was a product of disciples moving in the living power of God. Just as signs and wonders are supposed to follow those who believe (Mark 16), revival follows those who follow Christ. This happened in the Book of Acts, for it is a powerful account of God's power, glory and mercy. And it all happened because of Spirit-filled disciples seeking God, seeking His Truth and seeking His Way (Acts 2).

We must thus pray for God to truly revive us internally, which calls for submission and yielding to God. For then, as disciples, as we seek God and worship Him in the liberty of the Spirit, we shall know revival first and foremost. And then we can take revival to the world. How can a church truly revive towns or cities of people without being revived itself? May His life truly burn in our bones, and may the world see the life of God within us!

The end-time remnant sings the song of the Lamb

Revelation 5:9 (NKJV): And they sang a new song, saying: "You are worthy to take the scroll, And to open its seals; For You were slain, and have redeemed us to God by Your blood out of every tribe and tongue and people and nation.

The end-time remnant will be known for worship, for deep faith and trust in God. Their lives will be a song of victory and hope. I was reminded of the song that Moses and Miriam sang. It was a song of joy, of giving God Glory for His deliverance, His provision and His greatness. In Deuteronomy 32, we read: "For I proclaim the name of the Lord: Ascribe greatness to our God. 4 He is the Rock, His work is perfect; for all His ways are justice, a God of truth and without injustice; Righteous and upright is He."

Exodus 15 NKJV says, "1 Then Moses and the children of Israel sang this song to the Lord, and spoke, saying: "I will sing to the Lord, For He has triumphed gloriously! The horse and its rider He has thrown into the sea! 2 The Lord is my strength and song, And He has become my salvation; He is my God, and I will praise Him; My father's God, and I will exalt Him. 3 The Lord is a man of war; The Lord is His name. 4 Pharaoh's chariots and his army He has cast into the sea; His chosen captains also are drowned in the Red Sea. 5 The depths have covered them; They sank to the bottom like a stone. "Your right hand, O Lord, has become glorious in power; Your right hand, O Lord, has dashed the enemy in pieces. 7 And in the greatness of Your excellence You have overthrown those who rose against You; You sent forth Your wrath; It consumed them like stubble. 8 And with the blast of Your nostrils The waters were gathered together; The floods stood upright like a heap; The depths congealed in the heart of the sea."

We also find in the same chapter the Song of Miriam: "20 Then Miriam the prophetess, the sister of Aaron, took the timbrel in her hand; and all the women went out after her with timbrels and with dances. 21 And Miriam answered them: "Sing to the Lord, For He has triumphed gloriously! The horse and its rider He has thrown into the sea!"

In Psalm 33:3 David declares "sing to Him a new song; Play skillfully with a shout of joy." He also writes in "Psalm 40:3 He has put a new song in my mouth— Praise to our God; Many will see it and fear, And will trust in the Lord." Throughout Psalms we find the reference to the song to glorify God, to glorify His greatness and goodness. It says for example in "chapter 96: 1 Oh, sing to the Lord a new song! Sing to the Lord, all the earth." And also "Psalm 98:1 Oh, sing to the Lord a new song! For He has done marvelous things; His right hand and His holy arm have gained Him the victory." And also "Psalm 144:9 I will sing a new song to You, O God; On a harp of ten strings I will sing praises to You" and "Psalm 149:1 [Praise to God for His Salvation and Judgment] Praise the Lord! Sing to the Lord a new song, And His praise in the assembly of saints."

Even the prophet Isaiah wrote in "chapter 42:10 [Praise to the Lord]: Sing to the Lord a new song, And His praise from the ends of the earth, You who go down to the sea, and all that is in it, You coastlands and you inhabitants of them!" A song was present in the heart of David, in the heart of the prophets like Moses and Isaiah, because despite the difficulties, despite the troubles, despite the storms, they knew they served a mighty and glorious God. They did not give up hope, and so they praised Him, they honoured

Him, and they worshipped Him. In Him, they found peace and joy. And in such a song is remembrance, and in such a song of internal trust and faith, we lift up His Name, and we refuse to lose sight of His majesty.

Indeed, the song within them – that state of praise and exaltation that comes from the inner, deep belief in the greatness of God – did not die. Moses, Isaiah and David endured much strife, yet they did not let the song die. Within their heart, within their spirit, and within their life, they continued to 'sing a song' to the Lord. They kept believing, they kept following, and they kept abiding, for they knew God is all-powerful, almighty, glorious and magnificent. They refused for the song to die, for they refused for life and its troubles and woes to steal their joy and their hope and belief in the goodness of God.

Remember the story of Paul and Silas in Acts 16? They were imprisoned for doing the work of the Lord, yes they suffered, yet the song did not die. And so we read: "5 But at midnight Paul and Silas were praying and singing hymns to God, and the prisoners were listening to them." Glory to God! The song did not die! Their hope, belief and trust in God were alive. And what happened when they had faith and worshipped? We read: "26 Suddenly there was a great earthquake so that the foundations of the prison were shaken; and immediately all the doors were opened and everyone's chains were loosed." And yes, the jailer was saved, because the song did not die. When we lift up God in our song, in our word, in deed, in conduct and in thought, we lift up His greatness and darkness is shaken and fear loosens its grip.

In Acts, we read of how the disciples continually met and broke bread, and it says in verse 47 that they praised God, and so they found favour with all the people. The result of their loyalty and hope? It says the Lord added to the church daily those who were being saved. Indeed, the song did not die with the first disciples, no matter the threat of persecution, ridicule or rejection. They praised the Lord for God is good, great and mighty! God is faithful and true.

In Revelation 15, we read: "3 They sing the song of Moses, the servant of God, and the song of the Lamb, saying: 'Great and marvelous are Your works, Lord God Almighty! Just and true are Your ways, O King of the saints!" This passage speaks of those who "have the victory over the beast, over his image and over his mark and over the number of his name, standing on the sea of glass, having harps of God." And what are they doing? Yes, they are not just singing the song of Jesus, but also of Moses! Oh yes, Moses is not our Saviour, but he did point to the Saviour who would liberate us from our bondage and yokes. Moses, like Jesus, was also a mediator between man and God.

Significantly, those who overcame clearly show us the importance of connecting the Old and the New, for the song of Jesus would not be possible if it were not for the song of Moses! For Jesus was born out of the tribe of Judah. He was born a Jew, in a land promised to Abraham and Moses and Joshua. And so we need to understand the entire and rich history of Israel, how God positioned Israel in history for a greater purpose and His relationship with Israel for mankind to reach the climactic point in history for Jesus' divine arrival in a small town. Jesus' birth at a certain time and place was significant and not random, yet we need to understand the Old Testament completely and fully to comprehend God's incredible plan of salvation. The Old Testament is not archaic or obsolete. It holds a wealth of knowledge, insight and wisdom for those willing to learn and understand.

We read in "Ephesians 2: 19 Now, therefore, you are no longer strangers and foreigners, but fellow citizens with the saints and members of the household of God, 20 having been built on the foundation of the apostles and prophets, Jesus Christ Himself being the chief cornerstone, 21 in whom the whole building, being fitted together, grows into a holy temple in the Lord, 22 in whom you also are being built together for a dwelling place of God in the Spirit." The foundation consists of the prophets of the Old Testament along with the apostles of the New Testament. It is ONE foundation, formed by the same tapestry woven by God from Genesis right throughout thousands of years of Israel's history to the town of Bethlehem, setting the stage for the birth of the church in Jerusalem at the outpouring of the Holy Spirit. Jesus has always been the capstone, for He was the Lamb slain from the foundation of the world, and this same Lamb that will return as the Lion of Judah is glorified in Revelation at the end of all time in chapter 1: "And when I turned I saw seven golden lampstands, 13 and among the lampstands was someone like a son of man, dressed in a robe reaching down to his feet and with a golden sash around his chest."

The end-time remnant, therefore, serves the God of the Old and the New Testament, for it is one God and one complete story of God's redemption. It is the story of God's grafting the Gentiles into the vine of the Jewish people. It is the story of God's master plan to save both the Jewish and Gentile people. We can never separate the Old from the New. We can never be a remnant without understanding, appreciating and respecting the complete story as waved by God. Therefore, the end-time remnant sings the song of Moses and of the Lamb, for it glorifies God who is the Redeemer and Deliverer of the Jews and Gentiles. Without Israel, there is no Christ born to be the Messiah of the world! In the Old Testament, we discover the heart of God, as it reveals, unravels and exposes God's greatness, His beauty and unfathomable grace and mercy. The end-time remnant is not just stuck in the New, but walks the ancient of paths (Jeremiah 6:16) for they discern, comprehend, and value God who is the alpha and the omega, therefore, the author and finisher of our faith!

The end-time remnant will not let the song die in their heart. No matter what, the remnant is called to keep hoping and keep believing. In all things give the Lord praise and honour. In all things keep your eye upon Him, for He still parts the sea and He still raises the dead, heals the sick and He still makes a way where there is no way. He is our hope of glory, our deliverer, our hope, our strength, our healer, our fortress, our redeemer and our provider! Yes, sing your song, for our God is not dead. He is alive, He is real, and He knows all and sees all. Trust. Hold onto hope and fight the good fight of faith. And may our song join the song of all those who have ever walked the road of the Kingdom. "Hebrews 12: Therefore we also, since we are surrounded by so great a cloud of witnesses, let us lay aside every weight, and the sin which so easily ensnares us, and let us run with endurance the race that is set before us, 2 looking unto Jesus, the author and finisher of our faith, who for the joy that was set before Him endured the cross, despising the shame, and has sat down at the right hand of the throne of God."

Prophetic utterance and vision:

I SAW AN ARMY ARISING with a SONG on their lips. I saw this army singing, dressed in the armour of God, and they are singing the praises of God in a time and hour of NOW and they are lifting their voices to heaven (high praises on their lips). They are declaring the authority, the glory and the power of God! For the Lord says such an army is now arising with the authority and praise and worship upon their lips, and they are singing the song of the Lamb, they are declaring the song of Moses, they are declaring the victory song, for they shall not go quietly into the night. This is the song of victory, this is the song of glory, this is the song of deliverance, for as they sing, says the Lord, let the heavens hear and the oceans roar and the mountains quake and the enemy tremble. Watch as the Goliaths and the Absaloms fall, and watch as the empires crumble, but watch also for God to arise!

For only they who know the Lord and His heart, voice and Kingdom shall know the song and they sing it and declare the victory of God. The enemy shall run, shall flee, for sing says the Lord, sing and declare and stand up and arise in My truth and Spirit and let the heavens know and let the heavens declare the song of the Lamb! Let us know the victory that Moses knew, for it is the victory of now and let us know that the battle belongs to our God!

Yes, they are coming over the mountains, in the valleys, taking their place on the towers and watchtowers and at the city gates. They are coming and they are declaring the song of the Lord... a song placed in their hearts, on their lips, and by such glory and praise the gates of hell shall tremble and quake and shatter and move. Sing says the Lord and declare My truth and glory and do not be silent!

Revelation 14: 1 Then I looked, and behold, a Lamb standing on Mount Zion, and with Him one hundred and forty-four thousand, having His Father's name written on their foreheads. 2 And I heard a voice from heaven, like the voice of many waters, and like the voice of loud thunder. And I heard the sound of harpists playing their harps. 3 They sang as it were a new song before the throne, before the four living creatures, and the elders; and no one could learn that song except the hundred and forty-four thousand who were redeemed from the earth. 4 These are the ones who were not defiled with women, for they are virgins. These are the ones who follow the Lamb wherever He goes. These were redeemed from among men, being firstfruits to God and to the Lamb. 5 And in their mouth was found no deceit, for they are without fault before the throne of God.

And yes, there is an arising, and it is coming. They come with banners, trumpets, and shofars. And the heavens will know the song of the Lord for the Bride. Yes, the Bride knows the song! No one else knows it but only the Bride.

End-time lovers of God's wisdom

There is no excuse for ignorance. The saying goes that 'ignorance is bliss', yet with the Lord and with His Kingdom, such reasoning is mere folly and not wisdom at all. It says in "Hosea 4:6: My people are destroyed from lack of knowledge. because you have rejected knowledge, I also reject you as my priests; because you have ignored the law of your God, I also will ignore your children." Take note, the people were not destroyed because of idolatry or iniquity, but because they rejected God's ways, thus His Truth. And if we reject His Truth, we ultimately reject God's order and God Himself. Therefore, there is great danger in ignorance.

Thus, a lack of knowledge speaks of ignorance. The definition of ignorance is that it is a lack of knowledge or information. In Hosea 4, the people were warned that they were being destroyed because they rejected the Lord's knowledge. The Holy Spirit according to Isaiah 11 is the Spirit of knowledge, wisdom and understanding. The Spirit was poured out to lead and guide us in all truth; therefore, there is no excuse for ignorance. We are called to walk in God's Wisdom, and not the wisdom or the knowledge of this world. And we must be careful not to interpret the truth according to the wisdom formed or shaped by our own perceptions, ideas and education. Indeed, the wisdom that is from above is first pure, then peaceable, gentle, and easy to be entreated, full of mercy and good fruits, without partiality, and without hypocrisy (James 3:17).

But the Lord placed it on my heart there are things we teach, preach, advocate, proclaim, encourage and embrace as being a truth, or there are truths of the Lord that we oppose, merely because we lack understanding and we lack knowledge, thus we walk in ignorance. If we fail to walk in the complete truth of God and remain not seeking the right path, therefore not repenting, then we have rejected the truth. The spiritual realm is complex, and not everything is at times so clear-cut and simple. The prophets understand the reality of the complexities. Thus we need to totally and utterly submit to the Lord for our guidance on the path of truth, lest we do not walk in deception and thus deceive others.

Ignorance is dangerous, for if we lack true understanding, knowledge and wisdom, we shall not be able to guard the gates and the enemy shall come in to destroy, to kill and to steal. Ignorance destroys wisdom, which leads us to the fear of the Lord, and thus to walk a path of holiness and purity unto the Lord. This is not a trivial matter.

We live in a world of great foolishness. To suffer not fools gladly means to refuse to deal with or tolerate ignorant people or behaviour. The expression comes from the New Testament (2 Corinthians 11:19), where Paul sarcastically says, "For ye suffer fools gladly, seeing ye yourselves are wise." To suffer not fools gladly means to refuse to deal with or tolerate ignorant people or behaviour. The expression comes from the New Testament (2 Corinthians 11:19), where Paul sarcastically says, "For ye suffer fools gladly, seeing ye yourselves are wise."

As Christians we are called not to suffer fools gladly, meaning we are not supposed to entertain anything foolish. We are called to walk in wisdom, to hold onto God's truth and to avoid all things foolishness or futile. We do find a lot of foolishness in churches because you have to wonder where is the spiritual maturity in the Body of Christ. There is a lack of character. Lack of wisdom. Lack of discernment. Lack of truth. Lack of values. We have become so self-centred and so self-conscious that we have lost sight of the Kingdom of God. We are so embroiled in the carnal and fleshly temptations and desires we have lost sight and touch with the fiery touch of the Holy Spirit.

Psalm 14 says, "1 The fool has said in his heart, "There is no God." It such times we live, where more and more people are turning away from God, embracing secularism, materialism, nihilism, and spiritualism. It is indeed foolish to claim there is no God. For we then shun all hope and life! If such is our attitude, then it absurd and indeed very foolish!

Do we find the saints are stable, walking in the truth and keeping the course? How can we when it seems so many saints do not know the Word of God? The Word of God is the light and the lamp unto our path. It guides, leads, teaches and shows us the right way to travel, and this is the Way of God. Do we truly know the Word as taught by the Spirit of God from Genesis to Revelation, or do we know in part or according to our perceptions? Indeed, because of the lack of understanding of the Word, which brings forth wisdom and counsel, there is a lot of deception that bewilders and spiritually corrupts. Spiritual maturity breeds discernment, yet when we remain 'children' in the spirit we can easily be deceived, manipulated, exploited and led astray.

Yes, in churches there is a lot of foolishness, along with plenty of fables and demonic teachings! Traditions and the temptations of fame and fortune have caused plenty of distractions and confusion regarding the Truth and Knowledge of the Kingdom. 2 Peter 2 says "1 But there were also false prophets among the people, even as there will be false teachers among you, who will secretly bring in destructive heresies, even denying the Lord who bought them, and bring on themselves swift destruction. 2 And many will follow their destructive ways, because of whom the way of truth will be blasphemed. 3 By covetousness they will exploit you with deceptive words; for a long time their judgment has not been idle, and their destruction does not slumber."

Do we find the saints speaking the truth in love? 1 Thessalonians 2:10 says that "with all unrighteous deception among those who perish, because they did not receive the love of the truth, that they might be saved." Here is the reality – the Church has lost its love for the Truth! Yet the Truth of the Lord, according to John 8:32, sets us free. Jesus is the Truth. So if we lose our love for the Truth, have we not lost our love for our First Love? To the church in Ephesus, in Revelation 2, we read: "4 Nevertheless I have this against you, that you have left your first love. 5 Remember therefore from where you have fallen; repent and do the first works, or else I will come to you quickly and remove your lampstand from its place—unless you repent."

If we forsake the truth of God, we embrace foolishness. Is God not ALL wisdom? From the beginning when there was no beginning, at the end when there is no end? How then do we reason with Him, or try to logically determine His ways, for indeed is His ways and thoughts not so much higher than ours? We may walk by Spirit, yet He is the Lord. Period. Let us remember how God answered Job in Job 40: 2 "Will the one who contends with the Almighty correct him? Let him who accuses God answer him!" 3 Then Job answered the Lord: 4 "I am unworthy—how can I reply to you? I put my hand over my mouth. 5 I spoke once, but I have no answer— twice, but I will say no more." 6 Then the Lord spoke to Job out of the storm: 7 "Brace yourself like a man; I will question you, and you shall answer me. 8 "Would you discredit my justice? Would you condemn me to justify yourself? 9 Do you have an arm like God's, and can your voice thunder like his? 10 Then adorn yourself with glory and splendour, and clothe yourself in honor and majesty."

The famous opening lines from Charles Dickens' seminal novel on the French Revolution goes as follows: "It was the best of times, it was the worst of times, it was the age of wisdom, it was the age of foolishness, it was the epoch of belief, it was the epoch of incredulity, it was the season of Light, it was the season of Darkness, it was the spring of hope, it was the winter of despair, we had everything before us, we had nothing before us, we were all going direct to Heaven, we were all going direct the other way."

Indeed, this describes our perilous times, for some, the days are great, and for some it is not. We are indeed living in times of great darkness and in great light. Times of great wisdom and in great foolishness. We are indeed living in times of hope, but also despair. We are indeed living in times where it seems everyone wants to go to heaven, but many, it seems, are heading the wrong way.

This is what I know, in such strange, weird and perilous times of deception, danger, apostasy, threats and ridicule, that those who remain with God, and those who walk with God, shall indeed know wisdom, the true light, the true way and true hope. Beyond His Presence, we are shrouded by darkness, by violent storms of disbelief and a deafening silence of our immoral failures. This may indeed be a time of great belief, but also of great rejection, and the only One who remains true is the Great I AM. Glory to God. Great may be the revolution in man's heart, but God still calms the waters, feeds the hungry, quells the spiritual thirst and redeems the broken, the lost and the forgotten! Incredible times indeed, but know God above all. Yes, know Him.

By the Spirit of God, we walk in humility, in the will of God, in His Presence and according to His purposes and truths. Beyond the Spirit, we end up on a path of the flesh or engage in demonic creatures that seek to seduce and manipulate us. More than ever we live in the reality of 2 Thessalonians 2, which refers to the great falling away or rebellion or in other words. The Greek word translated "rebellion" or "falling away" in verse 3 of the Scripture is apostasia, from which we get the English word apostasy. It refers to a general defection from the true God, the Bible, and the Christian faith. Every age has its defectors, but the falling away at the end times will be complete and worldwide within the church first. The apostasy is also referred to in the KJV as the "falling away," while the NIV and ESV call it "the rebellion." And that's what an apostasy is: a rebellion, an abandonment of the truth. The end times will include a wholesale rejection of God's revelation, a further "falling away" of an already fallen world.

Apostasy means "a defiance of an established system or authority; a rebellion; an abandonment or breach of faith." In the context of 2 Thessalonians, this refers to the rebellion within the church, for the simple reason the world cannot fall away from the faith when you are not in the position of faith.

Who can argue that we have not already seen an abandonment of the Truth of the Lord? The church has been totally engulfed by moral relativism, humanism and secularism as it continues to be also moulded, influenced and shaped by religious and traditional perspectives and outlooks.

Paul sets the stage when it comes to wisdom versus foolishness in "1 Corinthians 1: 18 For the message of the cross is foolishness to those who are perishing, but to us who are being saved it is the power of God. 19 For it is written: "I will destroy the wisdom of the wise, and bring to nothing the understanding of the prudent." 20 Where is the wise? Where is the scribe? Where is the [h]disputer of this age? Has not God made foolish the wisdom of this world? 21 For since, in the wisdom of God, the world through wisdom did not know God, it pleased God through the foolishness of the message preached to save those who believe. 22 For Jews request a sign, and Greeks seek after wisdom; 23 but we preach Christ crucified, to the Jews a stumbling block and to the Greeks foolishness, 24 but to those who are called, both Jews and Greeks, Christ the power of God and the wisdom of God. 25 Because the foolishness of God is wiser than men, and the weakness of God is stronger than men."

James also writes about foolishness and wisdom in chapter 3: "13 Who is wise and understanding among you? Let him show by good conduct that his works are done in the meekness of wisdom. 14 But if you have bitter envy and self-seeking in your hearts, do not boast and lie against the truth. 15 This wisdom does not descend from above, but is earthly, sensual, demonic. 16 For where envy and self-seeking exist, confusion and every evil thing are there. 17 But the wisdom that is from above is first pure, then peaceable, gentle, willing to yield, full of mercy and good fruits, without partiality and without hypocrisy. 18 Now the fruit of righteousness is sown in peace by those who make peace."

According to James, foolishness is earthly, sensual, and demonic. The church has embraced foolishness, for it has embraced the earthly, sensual and demonic! We are called to walk in wisdom, which is only possible when we are led by the Spirit of God.

Anything that is not built upon God is of no value. It cannot last and its deceptive nature shall be revealed. God likens such deceptive work as 'plastered it with untempered mortar', which means not brought to a proper consistency or hardness. It is, therefore, brittle and will crumble easily. It is weak, destructible and fallible. Such is the nature of foolishness, and to embark on foolish endeavours and plans. This is unlike the foundation of God that stands the test of time as revealed in "Matthew 7: 24 Therefore whoever hears these sayings of Mine, and does them, I will liken him to a wise man who built his house on the rock: 25 and the rain descended, the floods came, and the winds blew and beat on that house; and it did not fall, for it was founded on the rock. 26 "But everyone who hears these sayings of Mine, and does not do them, will be like a foolish man who built his house on the sand: 27 and the rain descended, the floods came, and the winds blew and beat on that house; and it fell. And great was its fall."

God's word against the false prophets in Israel was also underlined in "Ezekiel 22: 27 Her princes in her midst are like wolves tearing the prey, to shed blood, to destroy people, and to get dishonest gain. 28 Her prophets plastered them with untempered mortar, seeing false visions, and divining lies for them, saying, 'Thus says the Lord God,' when the Lord had not spoken." Still today, nothing has changed. The false prophetic movement with its lies and deceptions only produces false visions. It holds no value and its foundation is but weak. It causes destruction and division.

In 1 Corinthians 3 we read "2 Now if anyone builds on this foundation with gold, silver, precious stones, wood, hay, straw, 13 each one's work will become clear; for the Day will declare it, because it will be revealed by fire; and the fire will test each one's work, of what sort it is. 14 If anyone's work which he has built on it endures, he will receive a reward. 15 If anyone's work is burned, he will suffer loss; but he himself will be saved, yet so as through fire." Truly, we cannot fool God. He knows who is building on the true Rock of Jesus and who is building with untempered mortar. He knows who is true to the real foundation and who seeks to build another. We may be fooling people, which is happening in churches, but it will not stand against the fire of God. God will always be against false words and visions, which many times are nothing more than divination. It causes people to believe in a false foundation and to build upon such a weak foundation.

Only when we move in God's will, in His Spirit and truth, can we remain standing on the true foundation and uphold it. Anything else is foolishness and dangerous. The false prophetic movement is right now continuing to present a different foundation of truth, and many are embracing it and trusting their lives to it. Yet when the storms come and when the fire of God falls as on Mount Carmel, then such a foundation is found wanting. Just so the work of the Pharisees and Sadducees, who held onto the Law, was found wanting.

May we seek the right path of wisdom, which is the narrow way. May we shun foolishness and embrace the truth of God. For the devil wants a world to walk in foolish ways, for it leads us away from God, the truth, His kingdom and true love and hope. James 4:7 says, "Therefore submit to God. Resist the devil and he will flee from you." May we then resist foolishness, which is the same as resisting the devil! For yes, a foolish world will attack and rebel against God, so a wise church is called to bring the foolish to the cross, where wisdom and understanding flourish.

God is warning the church against being ignorant, for then we run the risk of looking foolish! Sometimes our arrogance and pride also fuel ignorance. After all, we would love to be right, but to be right doesn't always mean we are walking in the truth. This is the time, more than ever, of "Galatians 6: 4 But let each one examine his own work, and then he will have rejoicing in himself alone, and not in another. 5 For each one shall bear his own load. Indeed, we need to make sure in our walk with God that we do not walk in ignorance, for this is dangerous to our spiritual condition."

Job 36: "5 Behold, God is mighty, but despises no one; He is mighty in strength of understanding. 6 He does not preserve the life of the wicked, but gives justice to the oppressed. 7 He does not withdraw His eyes from the righteous; But they are on the throne with kings, For He has seated them forever, and they are exalted. 8 And if they are bound in fetters, Held in the cords of affliction, 9 Then He tells them their work and their transgressions— That they have acted defiantly. 10 He also opens their ear to instruction, and commands that they turn from iniquity. 11 If they obey and serve Him, they shall spend their days in prosperity, and their years in pleasures. 12 But if they do not obey, they shall perish by the sword, And they shall die without knowledge.

It is made clear in Job 36 that a lack of knowledge does lead to our demise, and such ignorance comes from a lack of obeying God. Jesus said if we love Him, we shall obey Him. He has called us according to the Great Commission to proclaim all that He has taught. By the way, when it comes to Job, remember how Job's friends came to him with all kinds of ill advice? This is because they were ignorant of the truth and the spiritual reality of things. The Lord is very serious that we need to start walking in wisdom, in true knowledge and understanding, lest we fall into the pit and trap of ignorance!

"Proverbs 5: 22 The iniquities of the wicked ensnare him, and he is held fast in the cords of his sin. 23 He dies for lack of discipline, and because of his great folly he is led astray." Indeed, our ignorance shall lead us astray if we wish to remain folly! For such ignorance will ensnare us, and bring about spiritual confusion. And so we are reminded of Psalm 1: Blessed is the man who walks not in the counsel of the ungodly, Nor stands in the path of sinners, Nor sits in the seat of the scornful; 2 But his delight is in the law of the Lord, And in His law, he meditates day and night. If we, therefore, remain in the Lord, in His Word, led by the Spirit, we shall then surely not be led astray down the path of ignorance's folly.

Paul acknowledges his ignorance in 1 Timothy 1:13 when he writes: "Although I was formerly a blasphemer, a persecutor, and an insolent man; but I obtained mercy because I did it ignorantly in unbelief." Yes, Paul was ignorant, but it was because he was an unbeliever. Here we find Paul calling himself a blasphemer for he turned away from the truth of God. Let us remember on the road to Damascus Paul was still an unbeliever, for he was not yet following Jesus. So he was still blinded by ignorance and folly. Yet, surely a child of God who is supposed to walk in spirit and truth must and should not be ignored or walk in spiritual darkness. A child of God has no excuse to claim ignorance!

Ephesians 5: 15 See then that you walk circumspectly, not as fools but as wise, 16 redeeming the time, because the days are evil. 17 Therefore do not be unwise but understand what the will of the Lord is.

Therefore, more than ever we as children of God need to seek the Lord, and we need to cry out for wisdom, and we need to walk in discernment and knowledge! Ignorance holds great danger, for only the Truth of the Lord sets free. Ignorance breeds religion, traditionalism and legalism. Ignorance enslaves and ensnares. Paul writes of the spiritual gifts in 1 Corinthians 12 and begins by saying in verse 1: Now concerning spiritual gifts, brethren, I do not want you to be ignorant. Paul wants the believer to fully grasp and understand the work of the Holy Spirit, to thus be equipped by such knowledge and understanding so that WE ARE NOT IGNORANT. Believers, we can no longer be ignorant. It is time for us to mature and to grow in maturity, thus in knowledge and wisdom.

Take note of what Paul says in "2 Corinthians 2: 10 Now whom you forgive anything, I also forgive. For if indeed I have forgiven anything, I have forgiven that one for your sakes in the presence of Christ, 11 lest Satan should take advantage of us; for we are not ignorant of his devices."

Considering the book of Jude, and then we realise this is a day and time where ignorance has no place in the heart or mind of any believer. We need to be sober, and alert and seek the Lord to walk in His Truth all the time. And then at the same time, not be in danger of rebelling against God by rejecting His truth by exchanging it with our own version of the truth.

One fears the church is caught up in all kinds of apostasy, deceptions, idolatry, strife and spiritual adultery, simply because we remain ignorant in our ways and remain oblivious and ignorant to how the devil has come to steal, destroy and kill right amid the church! For the influences of the devil have caught the church off-guard because of ignorance, which has resulted in 2 Timothy 2:23 (Amplified): But have nothing to do with foolish and ignorant speculations [useless disputes over unedifying, stupid controversies], since you know that they produce strife and give birth to quarrels.

Take note of what Paul says in "1 Thessalonians 4 (AMP): 1 Finally, believers, we ask and admonish you in the Lord Jesus, that you follow the instruction that you received from us about how you ought to walk and please God (just as you are actually doing) and that you excel even more and more [pursuing a life of purpose and living in a way that expresses gratitude to God for your salvation]. 2 For you know what commandments and precepts we gave you by the authority of the Lord Jesus. 3 For this is the will of God, that you be sanctified [separated and set apart from sin]: that you abstain and back away from sexual immorality; 4 that each of you know how to control his own body in holiness and honor [being available for God's purpose and separated from things profane], 5 not [to be used] in lustful passion, like the Gentiles who do not know God and are ignorant of His will."

Do we truly know the ways of God or are we still ignorant of His Will? Do we truly know His Truth, and can we truly seek His Kingdom and His Righteousness above all else? Indeed, it is time to be set apart, sanctified from this world and ignorance, so that we may walk in the Glory and to Glory of our Lord.

As a last thought, we consider "Ephesians 3: 8 To me, who am less than the least of all the saints, this grace was given, that I should preach among the Gentiles the unsearchable riches of

Christ, 9 and to make all see what is the fellowship of the mystery, which from the beginning of the ages has been hidden in God who created all things through Jesus Christ; 10 to the intent that now the manifold wisdom of God might be made known by the church to the principalities and powers in the heavenly places, 11 according to the eternal purpose which He accomplished in Christ Jesus our Lord, 12 in whom we have boldness and access with confidence through faith in Him."

It should be our heart's cry, our intention, our yearning, our journey to understand, to perceive and to know the manifold wisdom of God, so that we do not walk in ignorance, till we all come to the unity of the faith and the knowledge of the Son of God, to a perfect man, to the measure of the stature of the fullness of Christ (Ephesians 4: 13). Then we shall walk as a people who understand the reality of "2 Corinthians 10: 4 For the weapons of our warfare are not carnal but mighty in God for pulling down strongholds, 5 casting down arguments and every high thing that exalts itself against the knowledge of God, bringing every thought into captivity to the obedience of Christ, 6 and being ready to punish all disobedience when your obedience is fulfilled." We must walk sober and alert, in the fullness of God, so that in His wisdom and truth we may rise against all things counterfeit.

Beware the folly of ignorance

There is no excuse for ignorance. The saying goes that 'ignorance is bliss', yet with the Lord and with His Kingdom, such reasoning is mere folly and not wisdom at all.

It says in Hosea 4:6: My people are destroyed from lack of knowledge. "Because you have rejected knowledge, I also reject you as my priests; because you have ignored the law of your God, I also will ignore your children. Take note, the people were not destroyed because of idolatry or iniquity, but because they rejected God's ways, thus His Truth. And if we reject His Truth, we ultimately reject God's order and God Himself. Therefore, there is great danger in ignorance.

Thus, a lack of knowledge speaks of ignorance. The definition of ignorance is that it is a lack of knowledge or information. In Hosea 4, the people were warned that they were being destroyed because they rejected the Lord's knowledge.

The Holy Spirit, according to Isaiah 11, is the Spirit of knowledge, wisdom and understanding. The Spirit was poured out to lead and guide us in all truth; therefore, there is no excuse for ignorance. We are called to walk in God's Wisdom, and not the wisdom or the knowledge of this world. And we must be careful not to interpret the truth according to the wisdom formed or shaped by our own perceptions, ideas and education. Indeed, the wisdom that is from above is first pure, then peaceable, gentle, and easy to be intreated, full of mercy and good fruits, without partiality, and without hypocrisy (James 3:17).

But the Lord placed it on my heart that there are things we teach, preach, advocate, proclaim, encourage and embrace as being a truth, or there are truths of the Lord that we oppose, merely because we lack understanding and we lack knowledge, thus we walk in ignorance.

If we fail to walk in the complete truth of God and remain not seeking the right path, therefore not repenting, then we have rejected the truth. The spiritual realm is complex, and not everything is at times so clear-cut and simple. The prophets understand the reality of the complexities. We need to totally and utterly submit to the Lord for our guidance on the path of truth, lest we walk in deception and thus deceive others.

Ignorance is dangerous, for if we lack true understanding, knowledge and wisdom, we shall not be able to guard the gates and the enemy shall come in to destroy, to kill and to steal. Ignorance destroys wisdom, which leads us to the fear of the Lord, and thus to walk a path of holiness and purity unto the Lord.

This is not a trivial matter, for if we preach not the entire truth of the Gospel, we then are accursed (Galatians 1:9) and we thus embrace and teach and preach a curse. Even worse, we run the risk of mocking, rebelling against Him for not walking in His Truth (and rebellion is like the sin of witchcraft) and we are in danger of blaspheming against the Holy Spirit. And so it says in Galatians 6: 7 Do not be deceived, God is not mocked; for whatever a man sows, that he will also reap.

And also "Mark 3: New King James Version: 28 "Assuredly, I say to you, all sins will be forgiven the sons of men, and whatever blasphemies they may utter; 29 but he who blasphemes against the Holy Spirit never has forgiveness, but is subject to eternal condemnation"— 30 because they said, "He has an unclean spirit."

To blaspheme the Holy Spirit is to demonise the work of the Spirit, or to call the work of the Spirit unclean, or even the work of man. Today, in churches, there is still great ignorance regarding the move and work of the Holy Spirit. And because of our ignorance, despite our best intentions, we can even blaspheme against the Spirit of the Lord. We do so by rejecting the Truth of the Lord, and such Truth the Holy Spirit has come to lead us in, according to John 16. The Spirit of the Lord has been poured out to lead us in all truth, so if we reject.

This is all important, since our mouth, our mind, our eyes, and our ears are all gates. So we need to be careful what we allow inside our spirit and soul, and we need to be

God is warning the church against being ignorant, for sometimes our arrogance and prides also fuels ignorance. After all, we would love to be right, but to be right doesn't always mean we are walking in the truth. This is the time more than ever of Galatians 6: 4 But let each one examine his own work, and then he will have rejoicing in himself alone, and not in another. 5 For each one shall bear his own load. Indeed, we need to make sure in our walk with God that we do not walk in ignorance, for this is dangerous to our spiritual condition.

Job 36: "5 Behold, God is mighty, but despises no one; He is mighty in strength of understanding. 6 He does not preserve the life of the wicked, But gives justice to the oppressed. 7 He does not withdraw His eyes from the righteous; But they are on the throne with kings, For He has seated them forever, And they are exalted. 8 And if they are bound in fetters, Held in the cords of affliction, 9 Then He tells them their work and their transgressions— That they have acted defiantly. 10 He also opens their ear to instruction, and commands that they turn from iniquity. 11 If they obey and serve Him, they shall spend their days in prosperity, And their years in pleasures. 12 But if they do not obey, they shall perish by the sword, and they shall die without knowledge.

It is made clear in Job 36 that a lack of knowledge does lead to our demise, and such ignorance comes from a lack of obeying God. Jesus said if we love Him, we shall obey Him. He has called us according to the Great Commission to proclaim all that He has taught. By the way, when it comes to Job, remember how Job's friends gave him all kinds of ill advice? This is because they were ignorant of the truth and the spiritual reality of things.

The Lord is very serious that we need to start walking in wisdom, in true knowledge and understanding, lest we fall into the pit and trap of ignorance!

Proverbs 5: 22 The iniquities of the wicked ensnare him, and he is held fast in the cords of his sin. 23 He dies for lack of discipline, and because of his great folly he is led astray. Indeed, our ignorance shall lead us astray if we wish to remain folly! For such ignorance will ensnare us, and bring about spiritual confusion. And so we are reminded of Psalm 1: Blessed is the man who walks not in the counsel of the ungodly, Nor stands in the path of sinners, Nor sits in the seat of the scornful; 2 But his delight is in the law of the Lord, And in His law, he meditates day and night. If we, therefore, remain in the Lord, in His Word, led by the Spirit, we shall then surely not be led astray down the path of ignorance's folly.

Paul acknowledges his ignorance in 1 Timothy 1:13 when he writes: Although I was formerly a blasphemer, a persecutor, and an insolent man; but I obtained mercy because I did it ignorantly in unbelief. Yes, Paul was ignorant, but it was because he was an unbeliever. Here we find Paul calling himself a blasphemer, for he turned away from the truth of God. Let us remember that on the road to Damascus, Paul was still an unbeliever, for he was not yet following Jesus. So he was still blinded by ignorance and folly. Yet, surely a child of God who is supposed to walk in spirit and truth must and should not be ignored or walk in spiritual darkness. A child of God has no excuse to claim ignorance!

Ephesians 5: 15 See then that you walk circumspectly, not as fools but as wise, 16 redeeming the time, because the days are evil. 17 Therefore do not be unwise but understand what the will of the Lord is.

Therefore, we as children of God need to seek the Lord, and we need to cry out for wisdom, and we need to walk in discernment and knowledge! Ignorance holds great danger, for only the Truth of the Lord sets free. Ignorance breeds religion, traditionalism and legalism. Ignorance enslaves and ensnares.

We cannot guard the gates while walking in ignorance.

Paul writes of the spiritual gifts in 1 Corinthians 12 and begins by saying in verse 1: Now concerning spiritual gifts, brethren, I do not want you to be ignorant ... Paul wants the believer to fully grasp and understand the work of the Holy Spirit, to thus be equipped by such knowledge and understanding so that WE ARE NOT IGNORANT. Believers, we can no longer be ignorant. It is time for us to mature and to grow in maturity, thus in knowledge and wisdom.

1 Corinthians 14: 37 If anyone thinks himself to be a prophet or spiritual, let him acknowledge that the things which I write to you are the commandments of the Lord. 38 But if anyone is ignorant, let him be ignorant.... His words echo what the Lord said in "Revelation 22: 11 He who is unjust, let him be unjust still; he who is filthy, let him be filthy still; he who is righteous, let him be righteous still; he who is holy, let him be holy still." The time is upon us to choose ... choose to serve God in fullness, and in the knowledge of God, thus not being led astray by ignorance, or we will choose the path of ignorance and so go astray and lead others astray.

Take note of what Paul says in "2 Corinthians 2: 10 Now whom you forgive anything, I also forgive. For if indeed I have forgiven anything, I have forgiven that one for your sakes in the presence of

Christ, 11 lest Satan should take advantage of us; for we are not ignorant of his devices."

Considering the book of Jude, and then we realise this is a day and time where ignorance has no place in the heart or mind of any believer. We need to be sober, and alert and seek the Lord to walk in His Truth all the time. And then at the same time, not be in danger of rebelling against God by rejecting His truth by exchanging it with our own version of the truth.

One fears the church is caught up in all kinds of apostasy, deceptions, idolatry, strife and spiritual adultery, simply because we remain ignorant in our ways and therefore remain oblivious and ignorant to how the devil has come to steal, destroy and kill right amid the church! For the influences of the devil have caught the church off-guard because of ignorance, which has resulted in 2 Timothy 2:23 (Amplified): But have nothing to do with foolish and ignorant speculations [useless disputes over unedifying, stupid controversies], since you know that they produce strife and give birth to quarrels.

Yes, in our ignorance, we have allowed division and strife to tear the church apart! We have allowed for idolatry and apostasy to cripple the Church, because we remain ignorant of the truth, the spiritual realm, the Kingdom of God and yes, the ways of the devil. It is time to wake up and to rise from our slumber to know what truth is and to proclaim such truth, for the truth of the Lord sets free (John 8). And so we are again reminded of "1 Corinthians 15: 34 Be sober-minded [be sensible, wake up from your spiritual stupor] as you ought, and stop sinning; for some [of you] not know God [you are disgracefully ignorant of Him, and ignore His truths]."

Take note of what Paul says in "1 Thessalonians 4 (AMP): 1 Finally, believers, we ask and admonish you in the Lord Jesus, that you follow the instruction that you received from us about how you ought to walk and please God (just as you are actually doing) and that you excel even more and more [pursuing a life of purpose and living in a way that expresses gratitude to God for your salvation]. 2 For you know what commandments and precepts we gave you by the authority of the Lord Jesus. 3 For this is the will of God, that you be sanctified [separated and set apart from sin]: that you abstain and back away from sexual immorality; 4 that each of you know how to control his own body in holiness and honor [being available for God's purpose and separated from things profane], 5 not [to be used] in lustful passion, like the Gentiles who do not know God and are ignorant of His will."

Do we truly know the ways of God, or are we still ignorant of His Will? Do we truly know His Truth, and can we truly seek His Kingdom and His Righteousness above all else? Indeed, it is time to be set apart, sanctified from this world and ignorance, so that we may walk in the Glory and to Glory of our Lord.

As a last thought, we consider "Ephesians 3: 8 To me, who am less than the least of all the saints, this grace was given, that I should preach among the Gentiles the unsearchable riches of Christ, 9 and to make all see what is the fellowship of the mystery, which from the beginning of the ages has been hidden in God who created all things through Jesus Christ; 10 to the intent that now the manifold wisdom of God might be made known by the church to the principalities and powers in the heavenly places, 11 according to the eternal purpose which He accomplished in Christ Jesus our Lord, 12 in whom we have boldness and access with confidence through faith in Him."

It should be our heart's cry, our intention, our yearning, our journey to understand, to perceive and to know the manifold wisdom of God, so that we do not walk in ignorance, till we all come to the unity of the faith and the knowledge of the Son of

God, to a perfect man, to the measure of the stature of the fullness of Christ (Ephesians 4: 13).

Then we shall walk as a people who understand the reality of "2 Corinthians 10: 4 For the weapons of our warfare are not carnal but mighty in God for pulling down strongholds, 5 casting down arguments and every high thing that exalts itself against the knowledge of God, bringing every thought into captivity to the obedience of Christ, 6 and being ready to punish all disobedience when your obedience is fulfilled."

We must walk sober and alert, in the fullness of God, so that in His wisdom and truth we may rise against all things counterfeit.

End-time servants of preservation

The Lord is expressly placing in my spirit the need for believers to persevere in their faith and to persevere in the truth of the Kingdom. Many are falling away from the truth of the Kingdom.

And many are falling away from the true Way and from the Faith. They are not persevering in the Kingdom and in the will of the Lord. Some have abandoned their calling, others their post as watchmen, and some have simply turned away from the true Way.

Believers, this is a matter of utmost and great urgency. It is a matter that we need to take hold of and take note of, for many are falling away from the truth and the faith says the Lord. Some have stepped away from the light, welcoming the spiritual darkness, and some have chosen to forsake the Truth for riches and wealth as offered by the world and the devil. It says in "1 Timothy 4:16 Pay close attention to yourself [concentrate on your personal development] and to your teaching; persevere in these things [hold to them], for as you do this you will ensure salvation both for yourself and for those who hear you."

Please, take note that Paul urges the believer to persevere in paying close attention to oneself (therefore one's conduct, behaviour, speech, moral fortitude, spiritual growth) and also to the teaching. This is the teaching that has been established by our Lord Jesus, which is still today taught to us by the Holy Spirit (John 16), and that was taught and upheld by the apostles.

Proverbs 4:23 says: Guard your heart with all diligence. Paul writes in "2 Corinthians 13: 5 Examine yourselves, whether ye be in the faith; prove your own selves." There should be within us a similar cry that David cries when he said in "Psalm 26 verse 2: Examine me, O Lord, and prove me; try my reins and my heart". After all, we know it says in Jeremiah 17:9 9 The heart is deceitful above all things, and desperately wicked: who can know it? So we need to persevere. We need to work out our salvation with fear and trembling. We need to continue abiding and resting in the Lord.

We must constantly walk in such a manner that will glorify the Lord and stay the course, no matter the storms, the days of anguish and the days of trials and tribulations. For again the Lord reminds us His grace is sufficient for us. To Timothy, Paul said in "1 Timothy 4: 12 Let no one despise your youth, but be an example to the believers in word, in conduct, in love, in spirit, in faith, in purity."

To persevere means to continue being an example in word, in conduct, in love, in spirit, in faith and in purity. This demands an intentional willingness to surrender to the work of the Lord and to remain true to the ways of the Kingdom. In 1 Thessalonians 5, we read: "19 Quench not the Spirit. 20 Despise not prophesyings. 21 Prove all things; hold fast that which is good. 22 Abstain from all appearance of evil." Yes, we must hold our ground! We must continue to turn away from evil, from blasphemy, from the evil of the world and remain shining the light of Jesus.

Also, take note of the following Scriptures:

2 Thessalonians 2:15 So then, brethren, stand firm and hold to the traditions which you were taught, whether by word of mouth or by letter from us.

Philippians 1:27 Only conduct yourselves in a manner worthy of the gospel of Christ, so that whether I come and see you or remain absent, I will hear of you that you are standing firm in one spirit, with one mind striving together for the faith of the gospel;

Yet, of such teaching and of such spiritual maturity and moral strength in the Lord we are departing, and thus are falling deeper into apostasy and heresy. For we have not persevered. To the church in Galatia Paul writes in "Galatians 1: 6 I marvel that ye are so soon removed from him that called you into the grace of Christ unto another gospel: 7 Which is not another; but there be some that trouble you, and would pervert the gospel of Christ. 8 But though we, or an angel from heaven, preach any other gospel unto you than that which we have preached unto you, let him be accursed."

What happened to the church of Galatia is happening so easily in our time and age! A time where we are so easily removed from the faith and the truth because we choose a different path, or because we have given up the good fight of faith. Yes, we live in such times, where we even pervert grace for gain, needs and wants. Take note, Paul speaks about perverting, which is an action of distorting or corrupting the original course, meaning, or state of the Kingdom.

To persevere speaks about continuing in a course of action even in the face of difficulty or with little or no indication of success. It speaks of an action, thus a process of always striving. It speaks of seeking the Kingdom of God and His Righteousness above all, no matter the cost, strife or battles or suffering. To persevere means striving to continue seeking God's Kingdom, His Will and His Kingdom even when it seems things are stagnant, not moving forward, or when there is great opposition or resistance. It means continuing to shine your light, contesting for the Gospel, standing for the Truth, standing for the Faith and never compromising, surrendering or backing down.

Yet despite all the trials and tribulations that we may face, and despite the times of not understanding or trying to make sense of God's will, we need to PERSEVERE by paying close attention to ourselves and to the teachings of the Kingdom. We need to constantly guard our hearts, our minds and our spirit against the dangers of deception, of hopelessness, of despair, of discouragement and of carnality. Jesus went into the wilderness and despite the harsh conditions, He persevered. Yes, despite the temptations thrown against him by the devil, our Lord stood firm. The devil promised the Lord all kinds of greatness and even temporary satisfaction, yet Jesus persevered. He kept true to the teaching, for He spoke about "it is written", and He kept his life pure and true. The devil wanted to derail our Lord's journey that would eventually end at the cross because He knew once Jesus arrived at Golgotha then the Blood would be spilled for all mankind to be saved who calls upon the Name above all names.

Elijah nearly gave up following the confrontation of Mount Carmel, yet he persevered. Moses persevered, leading the people through the wilderness. King David persevered by always loving the Lord, and Noah held the course by building the ark. So persevere! Yes our Lord persevered, He endured, and held fast to the truth, to His Father and to the Kingdom. In the Garden, He could have given up, but He found peace and strength in the will of His Father. And so He persevered and died on the cross for our sins, but then was raised again for death to lose its sting!

2 Peter 1: 5 But also for this very reason, giving all diligence, add to your faith virtue, to virtue knowledge, 6 to knowledge self-control, to self-control [d]perseverance, to perseverance godliness, 7 to godliness brotherly kindness, and to brotherly kindness love. 8 For if these things are yours and abound, you will be neither barren nor unfruitful in the knowledge of our Lord Jesus Christ. 9 For he who lacks these things is shortsighted, even to blindness, and has forgotten that he was cleansed from his old sins.

Yes, believers we need to persevere! This is a virtue we need to cultivate. It means intentionally and with purpose standing our ground. We need to stand fast, but this is exactly what is not happening in the churches. The truth is being discarded, and many believers are no longer paying close attention to themselves. They have abandoned the gates of the soul, and so the churches are filled with carnality and worldly truths and values.

Indeed we live in the days of Acts 20 where Paul writes: 5 "And indeed, now I know that you all, among whom I have gone preaching the kingdom of God, will see my face no more. 26 Therefore I testify to you this day that I am innocent of the blood of all men. 27 For I have not shunned to declare to you the whole counsel of God. 28 Therefore take heed to yourselves and to all the flock, among which the Holy Spirit has made you overseers, to shepherd the church of God which He purchased with His own blood. 29 For I know this, that after my departure savage wolves will come in among you, not sparing the flock. 30 Also from among yourselves men will rise up, speaking perverse things, to draw away the disciples after themselves. 31 Therefore watch, and remember that for three years I did not cease to warn everyone night and day with tears.

Paul speaks here about taking "heed to yourselves and to all the flock". He speaks about how he was a watchman on the walls, warning against the wolves in sheep's clothing. He makes it abundantly clear He persevered, and he held the course. He makes the remarkable statement: "I have not shunned to declare to you the whole counsel of God". Yes, Paul persevered! He persevered despite the hardships, suffering and persecutions (2 Corinthians 11). He warns about those who speak perverse things (take note, by those among the believers), as he also mentioned about the dangers of seduction and deception in 1 Timothy 4, 2 Timothy 3 and 2 Timothy 4. Peter also spoke of the false teachers and prophets in 2 Peter 2, while Jude issued similar warnings.

There are many wolves in sheep's clothing in churches these days, drawing the flock away. It was spoken about thousands of years ago, and the wolves are growing hungry and thirsty as they feed upon carnality, feeding the flock such deception while the true believers starve in search for the true word and the true way. Indeed, such days are upon us of apostasy, where the church has become a place of smoke and mirrors, mirroring the world, drowning in greed and lust, and where the Truth of God is drowned out by the emotionalism and the hype for self-exaltation.

It is written in "Matthew 10:22: And you will be hated by everyone because of [your association with] My name, but it is the one who has patiently persevered and endured to the end who will be saved." Believers, we need to persevere! We need to stand fast by holding onto the truth, by searching our hearts and testing all things. We need to guard against the wolves in sheep's clothing, and the false teachers and the false prophets. We need to guard against the fables, the myths and the heresies. We must guard against the streams of false doctrines, and the slide into greater apostasy as the church caters for the carnal, the temporary and the flesh.

Yes, in this lifetime much will be done to distract the believer to abandon the path of the Lord. We shall face trials and tribulations. We shall face suffering. We shall face persecution. We shall constantly be surrounded by our enemies, by deception and by spiritual darkness, but we need to persevere and stand our ground (Ephesians 6). Even when we are betrayed and rejected, then stand! It is written in "James 1:12 Blessed [happy, spiritually prosperous, favoured by God] is the man who is steadfast under trial and perseveres when tempted; for when he has passed the test and been approved, he will receive the [victor's] crown of life which the Lord has promised to those who love Him."

Of our Lord and Saviour in Isaiah 42:4 we read "He will not be disheartened or crushed [in spirit]; [He will persevere] until He has established justice on the earth; and the coastlands will wait expectantly for His law" The prophet in this passage of Scripture it seems launched out yet further into the prophecy of the Messiah and his kingdom under the type of Cyrus. Still, we find a prophecy of the Messiah's coming with meekness, and yet with power, to do the Redeemer's work (verse 1-4), His commission opened, which he received from the Father (verse 5-9), the joy and rejoicing with which the glad tidings of this should be received (verse 10-12) and the wonderful success of the gospel, for the overthrow of the devil's kingdom (verse 13-17). Even of the servant of the Father – Jesus Christ the Son of God – it was spoken that He will endure and persevere "until He has established justice on the earth".

Yes, our Lord persevered here on earth and by His Blood – despite the hardship, the rejection and the betrayal – there is justice for all. After all, we are saved and redeemed by the cleansing Blood of the Lamb slain for the world. Of such justice we read of the work of the Holy Spirit in John 16: 8 And when He has come, He will convict the world of sin, and of righteousness, and of judgment: 9 of sin, because they do not believe in Me; 10 of righteousness, because I go to My Father and you see Me no more; 11 of judgment, because the ruler of this world is judged.

Revelation 3:10 Because you have kept the word of My endurance [My command to persevere], I will keep you [safe] from the hour of trial, that hour which is about to come on the whole [inhabited] world, to test those who live on the earth.

Believers, we need to persevere. The Lord is laying it on my heart we are too easily giving up on the fight. Too easily we are succumbing to the pressures, to the hardship, to the suffering and the persecution. Too easily we are allowing ourselves to be swayed by another doctrine, and we allow ourselves to be led astray by the wolves and we allow ourselves too easily to be seduced by the deception and the falseness. We need to persist, stand strong, persevere, and hold fast to the Glory of the Lord. We need to stand guard against taking too easily offended, bitter, or full of anger and hate. We need to test ourselves, examine our hearts and stand true!

John 16:33 says: "These things I have spoken unto you, that in me ye might have peace. In the world ye shall have tribulation: but be of good cheer; I have overcome the world." Let us hold fast to the truth, let us continue to resist the devil, resist the streams of apostasy, resist the call of carnality and depravity, and let us continue in the teachings of our Lord Jesus. Let us guard our hearts and remain true to the way of our Lord Jesus. Yes, let us persevere by remaining true to the course, true to the path, true to the way, for it is about our Lord and His Kingdom, and not about our selfish desires and needs. It is not about popularity, about our riches or wealth or fame, but it is all about Jesus, who is the hope of glory.

We read in "Hebrews 12:1: Therefore we also, since we are surrounded by so great a cloud of witnesses, let us lay aside every weight, and the sin which so easily ensnares us, and let us run with endurance the race that is set before us" and also "1 Corinthians 9:24 [Striving for a Crown] Do you not know that those who run in a race all run, but one receives the prize? Run in such a way that you may obtain it." Paul ran the race, and he persevered. He ran the race until he was being poured out as a drink offering (2 Timothy 4:6). So let us also like Paul press on and persevere.

We read in "Philippians 3: 12 Not that I have already attained, or am already perfected; but I press on, that I may lay hold of that for which Christ Jesus has also laid hold of me. 13 Brethren, I do not count myself to have apprehended; but one thing I do, forgetting those things which are behind and reaching forward to those things which are ahead, 14 I press toward the goal for the prize of the upward call of God in Christ Jesus. So press on and hold the course in the love, in the hope, in the grace and in the glory of the Lord!"

We read in "2 Timothy 2: You therefore, my son, be strong in the grace that is in Christ Jesus. And the things that you have heard from me among many witnesses, commit these to faithful men who will be able to teach others also. You therefore must endure hardship as a good soldier of Jesus Christ." We cannot deny that we live in perilous times. We live in times of persecution, hardships and trials for the believer of God. It is the end of days of great danger and calamity. In certain countries in the world, there are physical persecution still taking place. According to a 2018 Open Doors list, approximately 215 million Christians experience high, very high, or extreme levels of persecution. This means 1 in 12 Christians live where Christianity is "illegal, forbidden, or punished." These are indeed perilous times, and the words of 2 Timothy 2 rings so true.

These not easy times to stand with God and the Truth, yet Paul reminds us to endure such hardship as a good soldier. And if one talks about being a soldier, you have to keep in mind Ephesians 6 where he writes about the armour of God, therefore standing in salvation, in truth, in righteousness, moving in the Spirit of God and faith. The apostle also writes in "1 Corinthians 15:58: Therefore, my beloved brethren, be steadfast, immovable, always abounding in the work of the Lord, knowing that your labor is not in vain in the Lord."

For us to walk in boldness, in faith and confidence in such perilous times, thus not in fear, doubt, anxiety and confusion in the face of persecution, we need to be established in the Word, thus be established in Christ Jesus who is the Word (John 1, 1 John 1). Jesus is the cornerstone of our faith, our hope and life. He is the Rock on which we must build our lives (John 15, Matthew 7:24-27). It says in "1 Peter 5:10: But may the God of all grace, who called us to His eternal glory by Christ Jesus after you have suffered a while, perfect, establish, strengthen, and settle you." The word 'settle' in Greek is 'Themelioo', which means to lay the foundation. We can only be settled in our faith, in our thoughts and in our hope if we are building upon the foundation of Jesus, thus we have to meditate upon Him by meditating upon the Word.

For this reason, it says in "2 Corinthians 1:21: Now He who establishes us with you in Christ and has anointed us is God, 22 who also has sealed us and given us the Spirit in our hearts as a guarantee." Only God can settle us. Only God can grant us peace, soundness and calmness of mind, the prosperity of spirit, soul and body. Yet we must then act upon "Colossians 2: 6 As you therefore have received Christ Jesus the Lord, so walk in Him, 7 rooted and built up in Him and established in the faith, as you have been taught, abounding in it with thanksgiving." We must stay rooted in the Lord, abounding in His glory, for then our faith will also be established, and faith always counters and negates anxiety and fear! Indeed, in Christ we stand upon "2 Thessalonians 3:3 But the Lord is faithful, who will establish you and guard you from the evil one".

Take note of how God will guard us against the evil one, which should give us a great deal of comfort and peace! In such assurance, then surely the peace of God will also stand guard over our hearts and our minds. In the Lord's Prayer, it says in "Matthew 6: 13 But deliver us from the evil one." Yes, the Lord will deliver and guard us, but then we must seek His will, His Kingdom, His Truth, and His Glory as it is in heaven first to be established on earth.

In Acts 4 we read of the resistance to the Gospel as being preached by the disciples. "13 Now when they saw the boldness of Peter and John, and perceived that they were uneducated and untrained men, they marveled. And they realized that they had been with Jesus. 14 And seeing the man who had been healed standing with them, they could say nothing against it. 15 But when they had commanded them to go aside out of the council, they conferred among themselves, 16 saying, "What shall we do to these men? For, indeed, that a notable miracle has been done through them is evident to all who dwell in Jerusalem, and we cannot deny it. 17 But so that it spreads no further among the people, let us severely threaten them, that from now on they speak to no man in this name." 18 So they called them and commanded them not to speak at all nor teach in the name of Jesus. 19 But Peter and John answered and said to them, "Whether it is right in the sight of God to listen to you more than to God, you judge. 20 For we cannot but speak the things which we have seen and heard." 21 So when they had further threatened them, they let them go, finding no way of punishing them, because of the people, since they all glorified God for what had been done. 22 For the man was over forty years old on whom this miracle of healing had been performed. 23 And being let go, they went to their own companions and reported all that the chief priests and elders had said to them. 24 So when they heard that, they raised their voice to God with one accord and said: "Lord, You are God, who made heaven and earth and the sea, and all that is in them, 25 who by the mouth of Your servant David have said: 'Why did the nations rage, and the people plot vain things? 26 The kings of the earth took their stand, and the rulers were gathered together against the Lord and against His Christ.' 27 "For truly against Your holy Servant Jesus, whom You anointed, both Herod and Pontius Pilate, with the Gentiles and the people of Israel, were gathered together 28 to do whatever Your hand and Your purpose determined before to be done. 29 Now, Lord, look on their threats, and grant to Your servants that with all boldness they may speak Your word, 30 by stretching out Your hand to heal, and that signs and wonders may be done through the name of Your holy Servant Jesus." 31 And when they had prayed, the place where they were assembled together was shaken; and they were all filled with the Holy Spirit, and they spoke the word of God with boldness."

The answer to the threats was prayer! In God, we shall overcome. The threats will always exist, but we must endure the hardship and the suffering and continue fighting the good fight. It says in "James 1:2-4: My brethren, count it all joy when you fall into various trials, knowing that the testing of your faith produces patience. But let patience have its perfect work, that you may be perfect and complete, lacking nothing. 12: Blessed is the man who endures temptation; for when he has been approved, he will receive the crown of life which the Lord has promised to those who love Him." Glory to God. We need to embrace and endure the suffering, so that we may grow in completeness in Christ. We need to abide in the Lord, so that we may finish our race to receive the crown of life."

We read in "1 Peter 3: 13 And who is he who will harm you if you become followers of what is good? 14 But even if you should suffer for righteousness' sake, you are blessed. "And do not be afraid of their threats, nor be troubled." 15 But sanctify the Lord God in your hearts, and always be ready to give a defense to everyone who asks you a reason for the hope that is in you, with meekness and fear; 16 having a good conscience, that when they defame you as evildoers, those who revile your good conduct in Christ may be ashamed. 17 For it is better, if it is the will of God, to suffer for doing good than for doing evil. 18 For Christ also suffered once for sins, the just for the unjust, that He might bring us to God, being put to death in the flesh but made alive by the Spirit, 19 by whom also He went and preached to the spirits in prison, 20 who formerly were disobedient, when once the Divine longsuffering waited in the days of Noah, while the ark was being prepared, in which a few, that is, eight souls, were saved through water."

The reality is that in this world we shall be faced with hardship and trials. Paul also wrote the following in "2 Timothy 3:12: Yes, and all who desire to live godly in Christ Jesus will suffer persecution" and "2 Timothy 1:8: Therefore do not be ashamed of the testimony of our Lord, nor of me His prisoner, but share with me in the sufferings for the gospel according to the power of God."

It says in "1 Peter 2: 20 For what credit is it if, when you are beaten for your faults, you take it patiently? But when you do good and suffer, if you take it patiently, this is commendable before God. 21 For to this you were called, because Christ also suffered for us, leaving us an example, that you should follow His steps." Jesus died for us on the cross, and He did suffer. We are called to follow in His footsteps, and so Jesus said in "Luke 9:23: Then he said to them all: "Whoever wants to be my disciple must deny themselves and take up their cross daily and follow me."

In this perilous world, we will face persecution, suffering and demonic attacks, but the greatest challenge is to truly deny oneself and to follow Christ (by picking up the cross). Paul writes in "Colossians 1:24: I now rejoice in my sufferings for you, and fill up in my flesh what is lacking in the afflictions of Christ, for the sake of His body, which is the church." And also "Philippians 3:8: Yet indeed I also count all things loss for the excellence of the knowledge of Christ Jesus my Lord, for whom I have suffered the loss of all things, and count them as rubbish, that I may gain Christ." What is the purpose of enduring trials and hardships? It is simple. To glorify God.

Peter also writes the following:

1 Peter 4: 1 Therefore, since Christ suffered for us in the flesh, arm yourselves also with the same mind, for he who has suffered in the flesh has ceased from sin, 2 that he no longer should live the rest of his time in the flesh for the lusts of men, but for the will of God. 3 For we have spent enough of our past lifetime in doing the will of the Gentiles—when we walked in lewdness, lusts, drunkenness, revelries, drinking parties, and abominable idolatries. 4 In regard to these, they think it strange that you do not run with them in the

same flood of dissipation, speaking evil of you. 5 They will give an account to Him who is ready to judge the living and the dead. 6 For this reason the gospel was preached also to those who are dead, that they might be judged according to men in the flesh, but live according to God in the spirit.

Serving for God's Glory: 7 But the end of all things is at hand; therefore be serious and watchful in your prayers. 8 And above all things have fervent love for one another, for "love will cover a multitude of sins." 9 Be hospitable to one another without grumbling. 10 As each one has received a gift, minister it to one another, as good stewards of the manifold grace of God. 11 If anyone speaks, let him speak as the oracles of God. If anyone ministers, let him do it as with the ability which God supplies, that in all things God may be glorified through Jesus Christ, to whom belong the glory and the dominion forever and ever. Amen.

Suffering for God's Glory: 12 Beloved, do not think it strange concerning the fiery trial which is to try you, as though some strange thing happened to you; 13 but rejoice to the extent that you partake of Christ's sufferings, that when His glory is revealed, you may also be glad with exceeding joy. 14 If you are reproached for the name of Christ, blessed are you, for the Spirit of glory and of God rests upon you. On their part He is blasphemed, but on your part He is glorified. 15 But let none of you suffer as a murderer, a thief, an evildoer, or as a [g]busybody in other people's matters. 16 Yet if anyone suffers as a Christian, let him not be ashamed, but let him glorify God in this matter. 17 For the time has come for judgment to begin at the house of God; and if it begins with us first, what will be the end of those who do not obey the gospel of God? 18 Now "If the righteous one is scarcely saved, where will the ungodly and the sinner appear?" 19 Therefore let those who suffer according to the will of God commit their souls to Him in doing good, as to a faithful Creator.

Paul calls for believers to be edified and encouraged in "Philippians 1: 27 Only let your conduct be worthy of the gospel of Christ, so that whether I come and see you or am absent, I may hear of your affairs, that you stand fast in one spirit, with one mind striving together for the faith of the gospel, 28 and not in any way terrified by your adversaries, which is to them a proof of perdition, but to you of salvation, and that from God. 29 For to you it has been granted on behalf of Christ, not only to believe in Him, but also to suffer for His sake, 30 having the same conflict which you saw in me and now hear is in me." We can, however, take heart during hardship and so we read in "Psalm 108:1: O God, my heart is steadfast; I will sing and give praise, even with my glory."

To overcome the perilous times as a good soldier, we take note of "1 Peter 5: 6 Therefore humble yourselves under the mighty hand of God, that He may exalt you in due time, 7 casting all your care upon Him, for He cares for you. 8 Be sober, be vigilant; because your adversary the devil walks about like a roaring lion, seeking whom he may devour. 9 Resist him, steadfast in the faith, knowing that the same sufferings are experienced by your brotherhood in the world. 10 But may the God of all grace, who called us to His eternal glory by Christ Jesus, after you have suffered a while, perfect, establish, strengthen, and settle you. 11 To Him be the glory and the dominion forever and ever. Amen." Glory to God.

If you look at the life of Apostle Paul, it is absolutely amazing how despite all his hardship and suffering he never found him complaining, or being bitter, or being angry or dejected. In 2 Corinthians 11 we find Paul addressing his credentials compared to the false apostles. He writes for example: "5 For I consider that I am not at all inferior to the most eminent apostles. 6 Even though I am untrained in speech, yet I am not in knowledge."

In 1 Corinthians 2 he writes: "2 And I, brethren, when I came to you, did not come with excellence of speech or of wisdom declaring to you the testimony of God. 2 For I determined not to know anything among you except Jesus Christ and Him crucified. 3 I was with you in weakness, in fear, and in much trembling. 4 And my speech and my preaching were not with persuasive words of [b]human wisdom, but in demonstration of the Spirit and of power, 5 that your faith should not be in the wisdom of men but in the power of God."

In 2 Corinthians 11, we read of his terrible suffering, which was not for self-pity but was actually in defence of his calling. Deuteronomy 25:3 instructs the Israelites that a criminal should receive a maximum of forty lashes as punishment, "not more, lest, if one should go on to beat him with more stripes than these, your brother be degraded in your sight." This caused the Jews to adopt the method of giving a criminal no more than thirty-nine lashes, so that they may not risk breaking this commandment. So Paul received such a severe beating five times! Talk about enduring hardship as a good soldier of Jesus Christ.

And we also know how terrible such a beating can be if we consider how Jesus suffered before His crucifixion. Those who watched the Passion of Christ will know to be beaten in such a manner was not a joke – it was brutal. Remember, Jesus was crucified by the Romans, so there is no reason to believe they would follow a Jewish disciplinary tradition just because Jesus was Jewish. Pontius Pilate ordered Jesus to be flogged but didn't specify a certain number of lashes. We do know that Jesus was not to be killed by the beatings He received because His ultimate death was to come by crucifixion. So, the scourging was a precursor to the crucifixion. It was not supposed to kill Jesus but to torture Him. Yet Jesus was definitely severely beaten, for it says in "Isaiah 50: 6 I turned My back to those who strike Me, and My cheeks to those who pluck out the beard; I did not hide My face from insults and spitting." And also "Isaiah 52: So His appearance was marred more than any man and His form [marred] more than the sons of men."

A Roman flogging (traditionally a scourging) was an excruciating punishment, no matter how many lashes you received. The victim was stripped of his clothes and bound to a post with his hands fastened above him (or sometimes he was thrown to the ground). Guards standing on either side of the victim would incessantly beat him with a whip (flagellum) made out of leather with pieces of lead and bone inserted into its ends. While the Jews only allowed 39 lashes, the Romans had no such limit; many people who received such a beating died as a result. The suffering of Jesus Christ was thus foretold by Isaiah the prophet. A sinless one would come. He would be beaten beyond recognition. But the sins of all of us—our inequities, our sicknesses, and our diseases were laid on Him. It wasn't the Jews who were guilty. It wasn't the Romans. It wasn't anybody. It was God Himself that brought this about. Why? So that you and I could know salvation.

So now consider that even though Paul did not suffer at the hands of the Romans, still five times he received 39 lashes. That is brutal. Yet he continued on his path as a good soldier. And he did it all for the glory of the Kingdom. We also read he was stoned. Stoning, or lapidation, at the time of Paul, was still a method of capital punishment where a group throws stones at a person until the subject dies from blunt trauma.

Can we even imagine such pain and suffering? Beyond the flagellation, Paul was also beaten with rods, and was left shipwrecked (three times), and he also writes about so many dangers he faced from the elements and from man. We also read about his weariness and toil, about his sleeplessness, hunger and thirst. We read of suffering in the cold and from nakedness. Despite all of this, Paul writes: "28 besides the other things, what comes upon me daily: my deep concern for all the churches." Yes, despite all the suffering, and being cold, and hungry, and threatened and facing so many dangers and strife, he was still deeply concerned about the state of the churches!

In perilous times, we are called to endure hardship as good soldiers because it is all about God, His Kingdom and the lost. When we endure suffering, we must not grow bitter. Hebrews 12:15 states: "looking carefully lest anyone fall short of the grace of God; lest any root of bitterness springing up cause trouble, and by this many become defiled." There is great danger in becoming angry at God, or life or at oneself. Paul never becomes bitter or angry. He endured. He triumphed in Christ.

For Paul, the reality of his testing was most likely found in the truth of "Malachi 3:3: He will sit as a refiner and a purifier of silver; He will purify the sons of Levi, and purge them as gold and silver, that they may offer to the Lord an offering in righteousness." Yes, our God is a refiner's fire, and that makes all the difference. A refiner's fire does not destroy indiscriminately like a forest fire. A refiner's fire refines. It purifies. It melts down the bar of silver or gold, separates out the impurities that ruin its value, burns them up, and leaves the silver and gold intact. He is like a refiner's fire. Therefore, purity and holiness will always be a process of cleansing, and it is not always easy. There will always be a proper "fear and trembling" in the process of becoming pure. He is like fire, and fire is serious. You don't fool around with it. Out of the purification comes hope, blessing, and restoration. The furnace of affliction in the family of God is always for refinement, never for destruction. It also says in "Hebrews 12:29: For our God is a consuming fire." God wants to consume all things in our life that prevent a true and deep relationship between us and God, for this will produce a life of life, of peace, of joy and spiritual strength. Paul thus grew stronger and most likely purer in his pursuit of God because of the hardship and suffering! This is a vital lesson for us to also learn.

The truth is, as with Paul, many times we actually go through seasons of purification, and this is done through the purifying fire of God. And this has nothing to do with the devil, or legal ground, or with disobedience. Sometimes God allows us to go through such seasons for a reason. For Peter, it was about how the genuineness of our faith may be found to praise, honour, and glory at the revelation of Jesus Christ.

We may not always know why we go through suffering, or hardships or face trials, but if we hold onto God, then our faith, our character and our pursuit of God become refined. According to 2 Corinthians 11, Paul suffered all kinds of hardships. He was beaten, imprisoned, slept in the cold, did not have food, and faced constant threats. We may wonder why he was so obedient to God, but ultimately God's grace sustained Paul to run his course and finish to the glory of God. Yes, we must persevere in God.

Yes, we are called to overcome, not to merely cope! We overcome by persisting in serving God no matter what. For most people, when it comes to trauma or stress in life, they are simply coping. Coping usually involves adjusting to or tolerating negative events or realities while attempting to maintain your positive self-image and emotional equilibrium. Trauma and stress can even lead to panic attacks, thus an unhealthy fear. Interestingly enough, in the Bible, there is no mention of coping. The reality is, as Christians, we are not called to cope, which means trying to survive, trying to deal with stresses in life and traumatic changes and assaults. We are not called to merely 'hang on' and hope we will survive the storm! Yes, we are human, but God has not called us to merely hope we will make it through the storm. God wants us to thrive, prosper and realise we are more than conquerors. And in

His strength, it is possible, for He is mighty, glorious, loving, our comfort and praise in the stillness of the night and day.

It says in "Romans 8: 31 What then shall we say to these things? If God is for us, who can be against us? 32 He who did not spare His own Son, but delivered Him up for us all, how shall He not with Him also freely give us all things? 33 Who shall bring a charge against God's elect? It is God who justifies. 34 Who is he who condemns? It is Christ who died, and furthermore is also risen, who is even at the right hand of God, who also makes intercession for us. 35 Who shall separate us from the love of Christ? Shall tribulation, or distress, or persecution, or famine, or nakedness, or peril, or sword? 36 As it is written: "For Your sake we are killed all day long; we are accounted as sheep for the slaughter." 37 Yet in all these things we are more than conquerors through Him who loved us."

Paul faced many stresses in life. In light of all of this, Paul writes we are more than conquerors! He knew God was with him. He knew nothing could separate him from the love of Christ. But ultimately, he knew God! He found his strength, comfort, hope and joy in God, and not the world. Paul did not cope; no, he saw himself as more than a conqueror. Psalm 46:1 declares, "God is our refuge and strength, a very present help in trouble". But didn't merely hang on or make it through the storm, he found his hope in the glory of God.

God said to Moses in "Exodus 3: 8 So I have come down to rescue them from the hand of the Egyptians and to bring them up out of that land into a good and spacious land, a land flowing with milk and honey—the home of the Canaanites, Hittites, Amorites, Perizzites, Hivites and Jebusites."

The Lord Himself said He will rescue His people! And yes He still delivers and rescues His people. No wonder David named one of his sons Eliphalet, for the Lord delivers.

We can rejoice, and we can be joyful, for no matter our trouble or woe or trial or tribulation, God still delivers His children and He hears us and He knows of us! Praise His name for He can deliver us out of all situations. There is nothing too hard for God to break through, or to heal, or to help us with to overcome. We are more than conquerors. Our God is the one who still the waves. He parts the waters. He is the Provider. He is the Healer. He is the hope of now and tomorrow. He is our Fortress. He is our Refuge in ever-trying times. He is our song in the morning and our praise in the evening. Yes, we must not be concerned or stressed, and we are not called to merely cope, but to indeed prosper in spirit, soul and body for God Is glorious and He is victory!

For it is written in John 14:1: "Do not let your hearts be troubled." Glory to God. Let us not be troubled. Sadly, so many of God's children have allowed their hearts to become troubled. They have allowed anxiety and fear to overcome them. They have allowed such trouble to blind them to the glory of the Lord, to His majesty, His greatness, His goodness and His mercy. Yes, there are so many storms in this life, so much heartache, betrayal, struggles and battles, BUT DO NOT LET YOUR HEART BE TROUBLED SAYS THE LORD OF HOSTS. The Lord also says in "John 16:33: I have told you these things, so that in Me you may have [perfect] peace. In the world you have tribulation and distress and suffering, but be courageous [be confident, be undaunted, be filled with joy]; I have overcome the world." [My conquest is accomplished, My victory abiding.]

Yes, in this world we will have trouble – it will come in all shapes, sizes and forms. Throughout the entire Scriptures, all the servants of the Lord endured trouble. Just ask Moses, Daniel, David, or the Apostle Paul. Trouble impacts us personally, emotionally, spiritually and psychologically. The troubles wish to break us, shatter us, destroy us, but the Lord cries DO NOT LET

YOUR HEARTS BE TROUBLED! For surely God does not slumber, and He is a jealous God, and He is an all-consuming fire, and His eyes are upon those who seek Him and serve Him. He is our Refuge, our Hope and our Strength.

Psalm 11: For the Lord is [absolutely] righteous, He loves righteousness (virtue, morality, justice); the upright shall see His face.

Yes, we WILL have trouble, but the Lord says to His children LET NOT YOUR HEARTS BE TROUBLED. Why? Because He is the Lord – omnipotent, all-powerful, and He loves His children. He is the Lord of Israel. He is the Great I AM. He is our Peace, our Hope, our Strength. "Deuteronomy 32: 3 I will proclaim the name of the Lord. Oh, praise the greatness of our God! 4 He is the Rock, his works are perfect, and all his ways are just. A faithful God who does no wrong, upright and just is he."

So do not merely cope, but overcome by the word of your testimony and the blood of the Lamb! We need to remain standing strong and committed to God, His truth, Kingdom, and His will. We must continue fighting the good fight, never relenting to do good and always shine our light in the darkness!

End-times lovers of truth

There is a saying that goes that if you don't stand for something, then you might fall for anything. This truth shines like a screaming siren in the night. It is that lighthouse on the seashore that desperately shines its light as we navigate through the storms of life, enduring wave upon wave and storm upon storm. Shall we heed this truth and turn our attention to this frail wonder of how easy we can be lost in the mire of confusion? If so, then we can surely make it to the shore. That lighthouse shines its light; that lighthouse is God.

In this postmodern world of shifting sands and leaders who are but wolves in sheep's clothing, in this world where truth finds itself at the mercy of the brute and the dragon, it has become imperative to urgently find the spiritual truth that grounds us. Mankind also finds itself at the mercy of an existentialist journey, enduring ever-increasing angst over the meaning of life, its purpose, global warming, political upheavals, death and personal loss. However, when done against a background of trying on their own to create the meaning and essence of their lives, as opposed to deities or authorities creating it for them, it poses further challenges to the quest for truth.

Yet here we begin our struggles, and here we begin our journey. Truth. Such a simple word. Such a simple concept, yet so complex with a myriad of connotations. What is the truth? After all, this is the postmodern world of pluralism. This world will simply say your truth and my truth do not need to clash and conflict. My truth is my space, and in my time is the truth. Whatever I deem the truth to be is the truth, for it only applies to me and is therefore beneficial to me. This is pluralism. Fear and loathing, intolerance, supremacy and elitism have driven mankind to this intersection of seeking a contextualised truth rather than a universal one. Yet a contextualised one radically influences our search for meaning and spiritual truths as compared to that of a universal option.

The Hebrew word most used for truth is emeth, which implies certainty and trustworthiness. The truth that we adhere to and fight for must be certain and must be trustworthy. The truth that we seek and the truth we seek to share is not some temporary knowledge, yet it is something eternal and which gives eternal life. It is a truth that abounds with possibilities where the secrets of the supernatural realm are unlocked to be manifested in the natural realm.

We live in a world of mixed generations, consisting of people known as the baby boomers (born out of the 1950s and 1960s), Generation X (1970s and 1980s, X referring to the variable, thus times of constant change) and the New Millennium babies (1980s and 1990s). Each generation, as generations go by, is faced with the challenges of finding truths and answers. Yet, the modern world is one of progression and changing values. As long as man seeks truths in technology and science instead of the divine, then the truth will be hidden among the folds of darkness.

We experience enormous opportunities, yet society is subjected to a constant metamorphosis of state of mind. We live in a world of threat and chaos. Despite all our achievements and efforts to improve ourselves, the world however, has never been as spiritually impoverished as these days. Man believes he has reached enlightenment, as proven by the Age of Enlightenment, yet bloody warfare externally and internally in man over the last three hundred years attests to the fact that man has not reached his enlightenment.

History is a complex saint and a savage beast, exposing humanity's barbarity and intolerance, but also displaying the inherent goodness of God through man and His saving grace. Wars have come and gone, and man has been shaken by natural disasters. Empires and kingdoms have risen and fallen. Leaders and kings have ruled, exploited, set free and changed the times. History does repeat itself, yet man never learns. History is a mirror reflecting a fallen man's way and also the way of a man who has risen spiritually and victoriously in Jesus. History reflects many atrocities and cruelty, but also brilliant days of God's truths breaking forth like daybreak.

Never before has mankind lived in such a false sense of spirituality. Never before has man been so spiritually impoverished, holding on to false comforts and placing his love, faith and hope solely in the perishable. Yet, the deceit of the world tells a sordid tale of fulfilment. The world lives in a state of emotional and intellectual hype. The world lives in a time of smoke and mirrors, being deceived with a false sense of the Lord's power and His hand. These are indeed days of false spirituality and great illusions. The voice of the false prophet and the false teachers have for some time now replaced the true voice of the Father in the hearts and minds of many.

Never before has mankind lived in such deceptive times, being exposed to so much falseness. Yet, mankind remains blind and does not hear, does not perceive or heed the danger, for their knowledge and the false sense of comfort proclaim peace. Ignorance and lack of vision have crippled the world. Mankind systematically believes in his own mortal powers and that they have become more wealthy and knowledgeable than the Lord.

Humanity strives to seek the meaning of life, even looking to the stars, yet so often has placed their trust in vain philosophies or hopeless dreams. This process of seeking and finding answers beyond the realm of the Lord has intensified to a point of great concern. Once again, the events of the last 2500 years have driven man to this point of total spiritual ignorance and blindness.

In Christian circles, from the early struggle between the disciples and Pharisees to the threat of the Gnostics to the birth of Islam and from the struggles of the mystics and scholars, this battle for spiritual truth has been waged. It has been carried forth by the struggle between Catholic and Protestant, between a philosopher and the carrier of the cross.

The Ages of Rationalism and Enlightenment, along with the storms of Romanticism, have opened new doors for alternative truths of enlightenment. Jesus was attacked by the traditionalists for claiming that He was the truth, while the early disciples were constantly under attack for defending the truth against the truth as proclaimed through myths, legends and philosophies of the Romans and Greeks. During the early and high Middle Ages, the monks retreated from the world to find the truth in the monasteries. Philosophers of the ages have sown a theory in terms of the universe, man, destiny, substance and matter, sometimes beyond the realm of divinity. Philosophers, thinkers and scholars who have operated devoid of divinity have prompted mankind to explore a different reality and truth.

The Age of Enlightenment broke away from traditional Church truths, heralding in an era of demystifying society, placing mankind and the individual only under the authority of reason and the senses (empiricism) within the bounds of natural law. The postmodern world has added its weight to the search for truth by insisting that even the universal truths of science and reason within the natural law cannot be absolute or supreme.

The two significant movements in the approach regarding universal and holistic truth have caused a significant ebb and flow in the way society today approaches sensitive subjects like religion. Where the naturalistic approach of the Enlightenment endeavoured to place God under the magnifying glass of science and reason, the postmodern approach holds greater repercussions when it comes to the search for enlightened truth.

The concept and notion of truth are also under enormous pressure from worldly external forces. In the wake of historical events that saw tyrannical governments and oppressive regimes, the postmodern world strongly resists the idea of placing anything in a supreme or elitist category. In our postmodern world, there are no absolutes, for according to the postmodern mindset, we cannot determine the objective reality of this world. History moves in circles and is caught in a constant flux of continuity. The postmodern world of perceptions is similar to the thoughts of the Greek Stoics. Again, these two thoughts are centred on impression and perspective; therefore, reality is determined by the individuals' perception and impression within a cultural context.

Therefore, when we discuss matters of truth, there arises the difficulty of comprehending that in a world of no absolutes, there can be no absolute truth. This is in comparison to the world of the Enlightenment, where truth was determined by science and reason. During this period, God and faith were reduced to deism, meaning a supernatural being that would only intervene through natural laws. Jesus was reduced to a historical figure, and His miracles were defunct and placed under the scrutiny of abstraction. In the Middle Ages, religion and superstition defined truth. Within these parameters, spiritual truth has undergone major and radical transformations.

In the postmodern world, all things about the supernatural or religion are allowed and can be true since there is no longer universalism. Jesus is strongly seen as a historical figure, due to the rather bizarre adventures of the Jesus Seminar, yet the possibilities of miracles and supernatural feats are not totally and utterly dismissed. Jesus has also become a metaphor for our enlightened quest, while sin is but a projection of our misguided or misunderstood needs. Thomas Payne and Erich Fromm attacked religion, and like Karl Marx, felt that God is only a creation or a projection of our perception to make sense of a dualistic world of hate and love.

We live in a global village of interdependence. There are many cultures, and mankind is sensitive about world peace and living in harmony. The last thing this world wants to do is to think about a universal concept of faith, for abuse of power is a stark reminder of man's frailty. Yet, in the wake of the modern secular society, with its emphasis on scientism, rationality and materialism, mankind has been left almost alienated and spiritually bankrupt. No matter how hard mankind has tried to break away from religion, what has been seen in the last couple of decades is actually an increase in spirituality. Without a doubt, mankind feels spiritually homeless and void of divinity.

This quest for spirituality has, however, added a new dimension to the quest for truth. The search for alternative realities and spiritual truths these days falls under the blanket of so-called New Age movements, where studies in cosmology, holism, anthropology and epistemology have come to the forefront. Cosmology simply states that the cosmos is rather a manifestation of God, which is constantly evolving towards perfection. Anthropology discusses the view that human beings are indeed spiritual beings who are created in the image of God and that humanity is part of the greater reality which is God.

In the epistemology school of thought, the emphasis is placed on subjective inner experience as a way of knowing. Epistemology is rather reminiscent of early mystics, as it is argued that a direct experience with God carries more weight than scriptures of the various religions or the dogmas of the church. Absolute authority is therefore vested not in doctrines but in personal experience.

Such a search for spiritual and scientific truth has largely been driven by man's insatiable appetite for knowledge. The great knowledge accumulated by the Hellenic Greeks was for centuries after the birth of Jesus held in the hands of the Arabic nations. It was only after the excursions of a revived Roman Empire during the latter stages of the Middle Ages into the Middle East that knowledge of the Greeks was regained by the West. The spread of knowledge between the East and West was also aided by earlier invasions and trade movements of the Arabs, such as the Saracens and the Moors, into Europe. Before the Renaissance in the West, the Arabs were already more advanced in architecture, literature and other forms of arts, because of their access to the work of the Greek scholars.

A human exploration into knowledge has systematically produced reality and a truth dissociated from divinity, as encapsulated by Nietzsche. Leibniz, Spinoza and Descartes were among the forerunners to introduce a true reality that exists by reason and within natural law, while men like Hume and Lock rather advocated a truth of the senses. The study of divinity has also been treated as a philosophy through the establishment of doctrine and dogma. Yet God is spirit. He cannot be fathomed, understood or manipulated logically or critically. A living, powerful and intimate relationship with our Creator is logically and rationalistically beyond understanding. Faith defies logic and reason because it exists beyond the natural realm.

An absolute world of absolute power has left its scars, for absolute power corrupts, yet maybe the greatest problem in the quest for truth has always been to search for the answer that lies in the absolute and the non-absolute. This does not imply the marriage of faiths or ideas; it simply implies that religion has become absolute because it has been tainted by man, while the possibility of a supreme and true divine faith consists of absolute and non-absolutes. Is this possible? Surely, this then implies we are dealing with the supernatural and the natural, which lends to a situation of absolutes and non-absolutes.

The arguments over spiritual truths and absolutes rage on. Even though such debates may seem complex, the true duel when it comes to secular society as opposed to faith in a personal God is one centred upon the natural and the supernatural. For those who believe in the limitations of the natural world, then everything concerning God and, more specifically, the Bible is seen as mere stories. Therefore, sin is demystified and Jesus is a teacher. For those who believe in the supernatural, then truth takes on a different meaning as God, sin, death and Jesus are no longer confined to natural laws or to history but are also more intrinsically tied in with a realm beyond the senses. In the argument of the naturalist, especially in the postmodern world, absolutes become grey areas.

Truth is contextualised and becomes an impression. In the argument of those who believe in the supernatural, the absolute is clear and so is the truth, for God wants unity with man and therefore sent His son Jesus to act as a Saviour, not just as a teacher. Taking all of this into account, we have an atmosphere for the birth of many truths, gods and spiritual ideas/ideologies. In this millennium, what is punted is that whatever truth we need to get us through the day and will soothe our aching mind from the claws of this world, then that truth shall surely suffice, and no one shall argue with that truth. The truth we seek is then our chosen truth to guide us on our existential journey, as opposed to a universal truth that involves a deity.

The dual over spiritual truth has, for a long time, been debated by scholars, philosophers and those of faith. The world of the naturalist and that of the supernaturalist are two different concepts; therefore, the perspective on truth differs. As one's truth is determined, so do one's beliefs, actions, thoughts, morals and ethics change. Have we considered this? Truth determines our ethics and morals. And if the truth is determined by one's outlook on religion or God, it stands to reason that we have some serious forces at work that dramatically change societies and times.

Philosophers/scholars/lovers of knowledge have therefore prompted man to examine a false truth and false wisdom beyond the realm of the Lord. One of the key spiritual battlefields is for the control of the mind. The child of the Lord won't, in general, be easily swayed by other religions, for the obvious reasons that it denounces the Father, Son and Holy Spirit as the Lord, but rather they could be deceived through subtle forms of reason and logic.

It is written in Daniel 12:4 that many will go to increase knowledge. The angel of the Lord spoke this to Daniel before the end time finally comes. 2500 years later knowledge exalting itself against the Lord has increased rapidly, giving birth to religions, governments, ideologies, philosophies and pagan practices. This knowledge extends into all spheres of life throughout all ages. It is not the knowledge of the Lord or the wisdom of the Spirit. It is not Jesus, who is the true root of Jesse and the offspring of the tribe of Judah. This knowledge exalts man's mind to a place of spiritual rebellion and to become his own god.

We no longer live in a world of universal truths. The accumulation of all philosophical movements after the Middle Ages has surely shot those notions down. The truth lies scattered, almost like a hidden treasure, and we desperately search for it. Christian bookstores overflow with books on all kinds of subjects yet again we have the conundrum: so many books proclaiming so many truths. Preacher upon the preacher, teacher upon the teacher, scholar upon scholar, presenting to the eager listener a truth they want to hear. We live in a supermarket society of choosing what we want. We can choose where we want to shop for clothes, groceries and basically anything else. We also have a choice of what truth we want and where to go to glean it. The world is a wide-open marketplace full of activity.

Consider the enormous barriers of wading between our subjective and objective mindsets. The truth today is subjective, for it serves the individual's needs. Subjective implies nothing universal but rather something personal, which fuels the environment of pluralism. So is the church. It is a marketplace. Whatever is needed will be found. Anything is possible and everything is available to appease our tortured and tormented longing for true peace and meaning. The truth we adhere to and fight for must be certain and must be trustworthy. Do we still find this in a postmodern society? The truth that we seek and the truth we seek to share is surely not some temporary knowledge, yet it is something eternal and which gives eternal life. It is a truth that abounds with possibilities where the secrets of the supernatural realm are unlocked to be manifested in the natural realm.

2 Peter 2 vividly issues a warning of the last day and how false teachers and prophets will open the legal spiritual door for deception, evil deeds, strife and division. Since the ascension of the Lord, the words of Paul and Peter have rung true throughout history, but never before has it borne so much fruit as today. The self has been exalted, which is no surprise, for this is what philosophy has forced a man to explore, in other words, the ego. The Word has warned future generations of great deceptions and even the outcome of such deception. We have been warned about the false prophets, false teachers, false apostles, false philosophies and false religions, yet do we heed?

There are indeed mighty spiritual movements happening today, yet some are false and some are true. The false movement of false security and salvation leads us away from the Lord. Humanity has simply evolved to the point of determining its own gods, creating a world and way of life conducive to satisfying its needs and desires. Yet, this is false, causing an ever-greater spiritual impoverishment and a catastrophic desire to plunge into a state of spiritual darkness and ignorance.

Man's call is not to evolve to a point of self-exalted power and enlightenment to rule, but rather to be reformed and renewed by the Lord to a point of humility and spiritual strength to serve a broken world. In our societies where pain and bitterness are inflicted, we bear witness to a world that seemingly regresses and fails to find its sanity. The world may not be furled in war across all her borders, but the war inside of man, that savagery and that hate, rises predominantly to declare its wish to rule.

In this darkened world, are we then surprised to find how little universal truth remains, shrouded in subjective and conscientious trickery? Humanity has evolved to the point of extreme survival, determining their own lukewarm gods, and creating a world and way of life conducive to satisfying their needs and desires. Yet, this causes an ever-greater spiritual impoverishment and a catastrophic desire to plunge into a state of spiritual darkness and ignorance. It is said in journalism that there are two sides to a story, and in between the two lies the truth. The struggle over the divine truth reflects this approach. Somewhere in between all our dogma and doctrine, formed by reason or by faith, lies the divine truth.

The spiritual fight has always been one of truth versus deception, for the truth sets you free. Such an escalation of conflict between truth and falseness has been in progress since the devil lost his place in heaven. This is a fight for right and wrong. The fight involves our spiritual condition. The saints need to seek, pray and adhere to the truth for the Lord to be restored in the hearts of man. The truth will bolster our condition and set our faith soaring.

We have been given the Kingdom on earth, the Blood of the Son, the wisdom of the Father, and guidance of the Spirit, yet we still prove to be ineffective because of our love for carnal and empty knowledge instead of abiding faithfully in the Lord. Germany was brought to its knees through a united allied front, just so the Father is calling for a united bride to bring down the false strongholds of the mind.

Paul warned the churches in Galatians not to listen to any other gospel but the one preached by him and his fellow apostles. He warned the churches against those preaching a different Jesus, or those preaching a different gospel, such as one that enslaves by adhering only to the Law of Moses. Similar warnings can be issued against the churches as well: whose gospel and truths are we proclaiming, keeping in mind the works of deception?

There is but little unity in the church at the moment. This adds to the complexities of finding the truth. There are so many points of view, arguments and debates raging about what is right and wrong. For centuries, streams of thought have challenged the death, resurrection and ascension of Jesus. Doubt has been placed upon the origin of mankind and against the fall of mankind into sin.

The validity of the Word (if it should be read figuratively, literally, symbolically) has come under fire. Questions have been raised about whether the Old Testament should be ignored (many, however, do regard it as useless information) or if the entire Bible should be pushed aside completely because it was written thousands of years ago. Questions about man's goodness, the truth, the role of society and universal laws have kept man busy with a meaningless search that has not brought him closer to unity with divinity but only being a part of a changing yet repeating history.

For centuries, there has been a dark call for faith and reason to be united. There are calls for the church to get real (simply implying to conform and submit to the wisdom of the world) and that the manifestation of the Holy Spirit is but signs of emotional hype. The Father's nature and purpose and will have been attacked, and so has His Son been mocked. Such blatant attacks are not solely the work of heathens, but also, and at times, the most strongly, those within the folds of the church who have also been horribly deceived. Again, this is all but an attack against the truth.

We are fully aware that we need to wage a battle for truth against pride, racism and ignorance. The pride and arrogance of man have led us to exalt our minds above the Lord's while regarding our wisdom and knowledge as more powerful than His. We have become ultimately demigods and self-righteous kings. It is written in Isaiah 55 that the Lord's ways and thoughts are higher than ours. Shall we forget that the Lord's word is eternal, everlasting and settled in heaven? Shall we forget that Jesus is the truth, the way and life? It may sound simple, but the church, in general, seems to forget who the Master is.

1 Corinthians 1 and 2 make it clear that since the age of man there has been a conflict between the wisdom of the Lord and the wisdom of man. The Lord's wisdom is settled in the divine, supernatural realm. His wisdom is untouchable, infallible, pure, holy and true. Man's wisdom is tainted, twisted, fallible and touchable. Man's wisdom dwells in the natural and sinful realm.

1 Corinthians 1 speaks strongly against the wisdom of man, which is strongly settled in the voice of the philosophers and scholars. Yet, these wise men will be brought low and their wisdom will be shown as foolishness. Such wisdom will not last. Those who wish to walk in the natural, fed by the flesh, can't fathom or understand the supernatural, fed by the spiritual, so the works of the Father, of Jesus Christ and the Holy Spirit, can't be logically,

rationally or through reason be grasped. Faith is a supernatural calling, and only through sheer spiritual beliefs can we stand firm in the Word.

Romans 1 states that because man has, since the beginning of the ages, chosen not to follow the Lord, and therefore, not submitting to His wisdom, he has been given over to become a slave of darkness. Since man has chosen idolatry above the Lord, his wisdom above the Lord's, his ways above the Lord's, and his thoughts above the King's, he has been given over to the dreadful cage of the deprivation of his mind. Is it therefore not surprising that sin is so rampant in every nation and tribe? Is it not surprising how strong the spirit of rebellion is, waging war against what is right?

Let us then consider that the Word of the Lord should be brought into our hearts through the Holy Spirit, digested through a humble and contrite spirit. Let us consider that only when we allow for Scripture to be taught and interpreted by the Spirit, therefore becoming a living and breathing faith, then there will be no room for flesh or man's arrogance to glory. When we allow ourselves to submit to the final and authoritative teachings of the Spirit, then only will Scripture be the vital life force of truth in our soul and spirit. Yet, we act like philosophers and scholars, adapting and adopting truth through our interpretation by means of the flesh and soul. We should submit and yield only to the wisdom of the Lord.

In our times of vain imaginations and distortions of truth, the way the believer should live has never changed. We can only exercise spiritual authority in the spiritual realm as long as we remain constantly and reverently submissive under the only and true Headship of the Lord. Sin remains sin, and our relevance pertains to the measure of love, grace and hope we present to a broken world. This world has fallen into a state of immorality simply because it has moved away from the Lord's truth. Many still say that universal values, or what we've called truth, have only been the personal expressions of those who promoted them. Christianity is apparently guilty of promoting the "herd mentality," where believers are like a herd of animals drifting towards sameness and comfort. Yet the truth of the believer is not founded on opinion or being a personal expression, but is the Word of God. And such a Word eternal, true, real, living and powerful!

Man has sadly crawled away from God, away from the true nature of serving Him, glorifying the Son and being completely and utterly captivated by divinity. In this postmodern world, we have chosen to crawl away from a truth that involves divinity, seeking something in this world alone that will calm our nerves. We, it seems, are returning to mysticism and to contemplative prayer and silence. Why do we seek noise when in silence there is God? Why do we need performance when God seeks truth and honesty? Why do we seek structure and hierarchy, as in the way of the Romans, when God's order still needs to be discovered?

Jesus Himself confounded every scholar, philosopher, ruler and leader. He was God in man, commanding no army, yet He conquered the world. By His death, resurrection and accession, He defied an empire and the Hebrew scholars. Still today, God confounds minds through His work. God sent Jesus to confuse scholars. Miracles, signs and wonders confound logic. Over the last forty years, man has especially sought to reach higher for fame and glory, seeking the answers in the stars and the cosmos. Men have pooled their knowledge together to build empires and cities.

Pushing all things aside and things we have learned, including our enormous pride, we begin to understand truth by embracing God's wisdom. Wisdom will tell us that it is wise to heed God. Wisdom tells us that it is those who seek God who will find Him, and we will find the truth. She tells us that it is wise to heed Him morning and night, seeking not after man's tainted wisdom.

Can truth be re-established here on earth in nations? A universal truth? A binding truth of faith? History has scarred us, yet what if God is the universal truth and the only truth from which all things flow? Shall we shun this because of pride, or is there the possibility of a universal truth beyond religion or man's influence that can bring lasting peace and unity? Like the epistemology school of thought and like the mystics, the probable answer lies in that true and direct and personal contact with divinity, void of man's doctrines and religions. Maybe then, a universal belief in the universal God, and not in man, would bring us to the point of love and recognition. For then, possibly, as mankind, we will stand and prosper ... in truth.

End-time lovers of holiness and purity

Years ago, the Lord spoke in my heart about three key aspects of our spiritual journey: Mortification. Abandonment. Purity. Together, they abbreviate M.A.P. Thus, the map to follow in our pursuit of holiness. For if we pursue such practice of always seeking God, yielding and laying it down for His glory, we shall then pursue holiness, and we shall abide in His glorious presence.

In the end times, we are living in a time of so much depravity, carnality, debauchery, rebellion and immorality that it is critical to cultivate a love for God's holiness! We serve a great God, and so from the majesty of the heavens, ruling all dominion, He is Life, and He shall forever be the One who grants us the physical breath and the spiritual regeneration of hope and glory. We are free because of the greatness of His love. We are called to abandon all unto His care. To seek holiness. To seek purity. And to surrender it all to His Glory.

To abandon speaks of laying down the Self, to lay down our crowns and lay down the pursuit after our own will and desires. To abandon speaks of trusting purely in God, seeking Him, and seeking His will. Matthew 6 is the cry of us those who seek God above all: Thy kingdom come, Thy will be done in earth, as it is in heaven (v 10). For this is also the crux of "Matthew 16:24: Then said Jesus unto his disciples, If any man will come after me, let him deny himself, and take up his cross, and follow me." We are called to walk in holiness. 1 Peter 1 says, "1 6Because it is written, Be ye holy; for I am holy."

Indeed, we may be human and mortal, but the Scriptures are clear: we must seek holiness and be pure. Yes, we must pursue purity, for it is written in "Psalm 24: 3 Who shall ascend into the hill of the Lord? or who shall stand in his holy place? 4 He that hath clean hands, and a pure heart; who hath not lifted up his soul unto vanity, nor sworn deceitfully. 5 He shall receive the blessing from the Lord, and righteousness from the God of his salvation."

As we abandon ourselves in His care, we shall know Truth and Power. Faith is supernatural. Only when we behold Him in true worship, there where we are silent and abandoned to His will, will we know Him and know faith and know love and know the truth. Our faith will again rise when we seek true union with Him. Let not our trust be manifested in things that are constructed upon shifting sands of illusions and delusions. Comprehending the goodness, beauty and power of the Lord will only allow His strength to carry us over shore and sea for all of our days.

Isaiah 55: 6 Seek the Lord while he may be found; call on him while he is near. 7 Let the wicked forsake his way and the evil man his thoughts. Let him turn to the Lord, and he will have mercy on him, and to our God, for he will freely pardon. 8 "For my thoughts are not your thoughts, neither are your ways my ways," declares the Lord. 9 "As the heavens are higher than the earth, so are my ways higher than your ways and my thoughts than your thoughts.

To forsake implies a process of abandoning and deserting. It implies an active and functional activity whereby one chooses voluntarily and with intent to walk the path of righteousness and not the path of evil inclination. And so we must forsake all – this world and its cravings to dwell with God. In God, we find our rest, our hope and strength.

We are called to seek and to call, which indicates a decision that we have to make and no one else can make it for us. We are called to forsake and we are called to turn away and to abandon all that is wicked, evil and not right. We must never forget He is Holy. He is Beauty. He is Purity. He is Love. He is Wisdom. Holy indeed is the Lord, and indeed, we shall bow before the holy Lord who upholds all things. May we pursue holiness, but then we need to abandon all, mortify our old ways and yearn for purity. Romans 8 says, "13 For if ye live after the flesh, ye shall die: but if ye through the Spirit do mortify the deeds of the body, ye shall live."

To mortify conjures up some nasty images and ideas. Mortification refers in Christian theology to the subjective experience of sanctification, thus the objective work of God between justification and glorification. Literally, it means the 'putting to death' of sin in a believer's life, thus the action of subduing one's bodily desires. Throughout Church history, many people have opted for a form of self-mortification, which is when a person punishes himself, often physically.

Based on Romans 8, the Church has for a long time given physical expression to the mortification of the flesh. When the Lord referred me to this Scripture years ago, it was quite an eye-opener, for your first thoughts drift towards self-mortification, which ranges from a number of practices such as self-denial — like not drinking alcohol or even fasting — to hitting one's shoulders and back with a whip or strap.

When Paul speaks about mortification, was it Paul's intention for us to subdue or deaden the bodily appetites by afflicting physical pain? Also, remember, the word mortify is only found in the King James Version and has been omitted among other translations of the Bible. Based on what Paul wrote, the Church, for a long time, especially during the Middle Ages, resorted to severe abstinence or self-inflicted pain or discomfort to mortify his body for spiritual purification. This has led to flagellation, which is the beating or whipping of the skin, most often on the back, and often drawing blood, as a bodily penance to show remorse for sin. It was therefore a supposed imitation of Jesus of Nazareth's suffering and death by crucifixion.

Another form of mortification was the wearing of sackcloth. Old Testament precursors include Zechariah 13:6 and 1 Kings 18:28-29 of suffering for a cause. Although the term 'mortification of the flesh', which is derived from Romans 8:13 and Colossians 3:5 in the Bible, is primarily used in a Christian context, other cultures may have analogous concepts of self-denial; secular practices exist as well. Some forms unique to various Asian cultures are carrying heavy loads and immersion in water.

Those who resorted within Christianity to such extreme means, most likely quoted Paul who wrote, "I chastise my body and bring it into subjection: lest perhaps when I have preached to others I myself should be castaway" (1 Corinthians 9:27); "In my flesh I complete what is lacking in Christ's afflictions, for the sake of his body, that is the Church." (Colossians 1:24).

Through the centuries, some Christians have practised voluntary penances as a way of imitating Jesus who, according to the New Testament, voluntarily accepted the sufferings of his passion and death on the cross at Calvary to redeem humankind. After all, it is true Christ also fasted for 40 days and 40 nights, an example of submission to the first person of the Trinity, God the Father, and as a way of preparing for ministry.

The early Christians also mortified the flesh through martyrdom and through what has been called "confession of the faith", thus joyfully accepting torture. As Christians experienced persecution, they often embraced their fate of suffering due to their love for Christ and the transformation they said they experienced from following him; these individuals became martyrs of the Christian faith. Saint Jerome, a Western church father and biblical scholar who translated the Bible into Latin (the Vulgate), was famous for his severe penances in the desert.

The truth is Paul specifically wrote that to mortify the deeds of the flesh is through the Spirit, not physical punishment. It is a life yielded and submitted to God that leads to a life of holiness and purity, not beating yourself up or starving. It is also a shame that the word mortify has been omitted from so many translations because even though it has led to some strange and weird behaviour within the church, it still expresses how serious it is to seek after the Spirit and not the flesh. The reality is we can only mortify the deeds of the flesh in the Spirit, and not through abstinence or punishment.

Martin Luther, for example, realised this when the great Reformer underwent unexpected enlightenment, a term he used to describe the turning point at which he recognised and expressed the principle of the righteousness of God known as "sola gratia". According to historical records, this realisation occurred in his study in the South Tower of the Augustinian Monastery in Wittenberg. Martin Luther experienced a strong feeling of freedom and release when he found what he had been looking for many years in the following Bible verses: 'The just shall live by faith.'" (Habakkuk 2:4) and also "Romans 1:17For therein is the righteousness of God revealed from faith to faith: as it is written, the just shall live by faith." At that point Luther was trying everything in his power to seem acceptable to God, be it through good works or penance, but only when he truly found God that his life was changed.

And so Paul writes that in order to really mortify, thus be a new creation is through the Holy Spirit. After all, in John 3 we read that only by the Spirit can we be reborn. And still today the work of the Spirit is to change and conform our character so that we 'become' in character and nature and behaviour more like our Lord Jesus Christ. And this can only happen when we allow the Spirit to change us, to renew our minds and hearts so that we can truly bring honour and glory to our Lord God.

We also have to remember there is a difference between Spirit-filled mortification and legal mortification. Gospel mortification is found upon gospel principles, thus walking in the Spirit of God [Romans 8. 13), purifying our hearts by faith (Acts 15:9) and the constraining love of Christ constraining [2 Corinthians 5.14, thus there are certain things which love prevents us from doing].

Legal mortification is from a legal principle, thus adopting worldly motives and intent. This comes in the form for example of seeking the applause and praise of men, as in the Pharisees; from pride of self-righteousness, as in Paul before his conversion; from the fear of hell; from a natural conscience; or for a purpose resting in selfish agenda or desire. For example, someone may perhaps will not drink and swear, but they do this not under the conviction of the Spirit, or because they seek to please the Lord, but because this person is setting up and establishing a righteousness of his own, or to please others or for the sake of his own health and conscience.

Indeed, in God and in His grace alone we can mortify the deeds of the flesh, for it is written in 2 Corinthians 12:9: But he said to me, "My grace is sufficient for you, for my power is made perfect in weakness." Otherwise, our intentions will be based on our own strength and desire, thus set up for failure.

The true believer fights and overcomes with grace's weapons, namely, the Blood of Christ, the Word of God, the promises of the Covenant, and the virtue of Christ's death and cross. In Galatians 6 we read NKJV: "14 But God forbid that I should boast except in the cross of our Lord Jesus Christ, by whom the world has been crucified to me, and I to the world."

It is only by the cross, by the Blood and by our love for the Lord that we must seek holiness and purity. Ultimately, the Spirit leads us to the reality of "Colossians 3 (New King James Version): Not Carnality but Christ: 1 If then you were raised with Christ, seek those things which are above, where Christ is, sitting at the right hand of God. 2 Set your mind on things above, not on things on the earth. 3 For you died, and your life is hidden with Christ in God. 4 When Christ who is our life appears, then you also will appear with Him in glory. 5 Therefore put to death your members which are on the earth: fornication, uncleanness, passion, evil desire, and covetousness, which is idolatry. 6 Because of these things the wrath of God is coming upon the sons of disobedience, 7 in which you yourselves once walked when you lived in them. 8 But now you yourselves are to put off all these: anger, wrath, malice, blasphemy, filthy language out of your mouth. 9 Do not lie to one another, since you have put off the old man with his deeds, 10 and have put on the new man who is renewed in knowledge according to the image of Him who created him, 11 where there is neither Greek nor Jew, circumcised nor uncircumcised, barbarian, Scythian, slave nor free, but Christ is all and in all. 12 Therefore, as the elect of God, holy and beloved, put on tender mercies, kindness, humility, meekness, longsuffering; 13 bearing with one another, and forgiving one another, if anyone has a complaint against another; even as Christ forgave you, so you also must do. 14 But above all these things put on love, which is the bond of perfection. 15 And let the peace of God rule in your hearts, to which also you were called in one body; and be thankful. 16 Let the word of Christ dwell in you richly in all wisdom, teaching and admonishing one another in psalms and hymns and spiritual songs, singing with grace in your hearts to the Lord. 17 And whatever you do in word or deed, do all in the name of the Lord Jesus, giving thanks to God the Father through Him."

Indeed, all that read about in Colossians 3 is only possible in the strength, wisdom, might and counsel of the Holy Spirit. After all, when we talk about the fruits of the Spirit in Galatians 5, it speaks of the fruit of THE Spirit, thus the Holy Spirit, indicating in our own effort and strength we cannot bear any fruit which is truly holy and pure. Only when we yield and submit to the Spirit do we find the Spirit works in us to change and renew us to become more like our Lord.

Galatians 5 makes us realise the importance of a disciple being led by the Spirit, for it speaks of the moral fabric of a disciple: "22 But the fruit of the Spirit is love, joy, peace, longsuffering, kindness, goodness, faithfulness, 23 gentleness, self-control. Against such there is no law. 24 And those who are Christ's have crucified the flesh with its passions and desires. 25 If we live in the Spirit, let us also walk in the Spirit. It is therefore important for the disciple to be baptised in the Spirit, but also to disciple others by showing them how to lead a life under the guidance of the Spirit. For when we are led by the Spirit of the Lord, we walk in the ways, nature and in the glory of the Lord, reflected in our behaviour and character."

Take note of what Paul writes that when we are led by the Spirit of the Lord, we walk in the ways, nature and in the glory of the Lord, reflected in our behaviour and character. Indeed, the glory of the Lord cannot be reflected in our behaviour or character without the glory when we are not led by the Spirit of the Lord. Again, this is the work of the Spirit, to lead us to become more like our Lord Jesus in behaviour and character.

In Romans 7, Paul argues that when the Law was introduced, he became more aware of sin, but the more he became aware of sin through his conscientious approach, the more he became aware of sin in his life and the working of sin that brings about a spiritual death. For he understood that the Law in itself is spiritual, for it highlights the unspiritual nature of sin, and it forces one to realise that if one is still subjected to sin and its working then one in the end remains unspiritual. Colossians 3, the opening Scripture of this chapter, highlights the difference between following Christ and those who are still subjected to the work of sin in one's moral fabric.

Based on his argument, Paul wrote the following in the same chapter: "14 We know that the law is spiritual; but I am unspiritual, sold as a slave to sin. 15 I do not understand what I do. For what I want to do I do not do, but what I hate I do. 16 And if I do what I do not want to do, I agree that the law is good. 17 As it is, it is no longer I myself who do it, but it is sin living in me. 18 For I know that good itself does not dwell in me, that is, in my sinful nature. For I have the desire to do what is good, but I cannot carry it out. 19 For I do not do the good I want to do, but the evil I do not want to do—this I keep on doing. 20 Now if I do what I do not want to do, it is no longer I who do it, but it is sin living in me that does it. 21 So I find this law at work: Although I want to do good, evil is right there with me. 22 For in my inner being I delight in God's law; 23 but I see another law at work in me, waging war against the law of my mind and making me a prisoner of the law of sin at work within me."

Paul understood that while sin was working in him, and while he was becoming aware of sin through the Law, he had become almost wretched in his outlook regarding himself and life for he found the work of sin was so powerful that it kept corrupting him, despite his good intentions of leading a life without sin. This is the power of sin in all our lives – it has a profound effect on our moral character, for it determines how we behave, how we speak, how we act and how we approach life and those we come into contact with.

Paul takes the work of sin in his soul to such extreme by likening it to death, for it puts to death our good intentions of living according to God's laws and teachings. And yet, Paul then comes to the conclusion when he says: "25 Thanks be to God, who delivers me through Jesus Christ our Lord! So then, I myself in my mind am a slave to God's law, but in my sinful nature a slave to the law of sin."

Paul concludes that as long as we allow our sinful nature to rule our lives, we will remain a slave to our sinful nature and therefore morally we will fail to walk in the fullness of God and our character will fall short of God's intent. As long as we remain bound to the sinful nature highlighted in Colossians 3, the work of sin will remain active in our minds and we will remain feeling wretched and despondent.

There is, however, good news. In Romans 8, Paul makes it known that his argument is not yet done but now he tackles the issue of sin in the inner man by focussing on the work of the Holy Spirit. And this is the glorious message that is presented in this chapter - only when we live in subjection and submission to the Holy Spirit and follow the lead of the Spirit, then will we be no longer subjected to a life which is a slave to sin, but we live as children who are under the Spirit. And such children live according to the inner power and liberating glory of the Spirit and are not subject to one's sinful nature.

Therefore, Paul emphasises that in our own effort, we will remain subject to the inner working of sin and our character and our morality will testify to it. It is only when we allow the Spirit of God to work in us that we can lead a life that strives towards holiness and character-pleasing unto the Lord.

As the Law convicted Paul of his sin, just so the Spirit convicts us of the inner working of sin in our lives and where our character needs to be refined. But the difference is that the Law in itself is void of power to strengthen us to counter such sinful work, but the Spirit of God is alive and powerful, always working is us so that we are changed in the image of God.

In Paul's first letter to the Corinthians, he refers to three types of people: the Natural Man, the Spiritual Man, and the Carnal Man. Our spiritual journey is about spiritual maturity, thus growing up from being natural to being spiritual. It is about growing mature in our character so that we become morally mature and more like our Lord.

First of all, what is the Natural Man? The natural man is a person who does not know Christ. They have never been born again by the Holy Spirit and therefore the Spirit does not live within them. Because the Spirit does not live within them, they neither desire spiritual things nor can they understand them. Paul says that the things of God are foolishness to such men. To them, salvation and surrender to Christ are a waste of time. Rather than living for God, they would rather live for self.

The second type of man Paul refers to is the Spiritual Man. Perhaps the most important part of Paul's description of the spiritual man is that he or she 'has the mind of Christ.' To have the mind of Christ does not mean that we reach a level of perfection or infallibility equal to Jesus. Rather it means that Christ shares with us His spiritual wisdom that enables us to see life from a heavenly perspective and therefore make decisions that are wise for both now and eternity. How does someone become a spiritual man? The spiritual man is someone whose life is under the control of God's Spirit. I Corinthians 2 says, "9 However, as it is written: "What no eye has seen, what no ear has heard, and what no human mind has conceived" - the things God has prepared for those who love him - 10 these are the things God has revealed to us by his Spirit. The Spirit searches all things, even the deep things of God. 11 For who knows a person's thoughts except their own spirit within them? In the same way no one knows the thoughts of God except the Spirit of God. 12 What we have received is not the spirit of the world, but the Spirit who is from God, so that we may understand what God has freely given us. Through the indwelling presence of the Holy Spirit, God reveals to us His deep spiritual truths. Such truths include God's plan of salvation as well as how to live the Christian life."

But there is a third type of man Paul describes and he is the 'Carnal Man.' The word 'carnal' means – 'fleshly.' When applied to a Christian, it means someone, who although they are born-again, they are still allowing their flesh to control much of the way they live and think. Paul called the believers at Corinth 'carnal' because they were still acting spiritually immature. Rather than bearing the Spirit's fruit of – love, joy and peace; these believers were yielding to old fleshly emotions such as envy, strife and division.

So we need to submit and yield to the Spirit so that we may grow from carnality to spiritually abide in the Lord. When we consider our moral fabric and our character, we think of John 3: 1 which speaks of being reborn in the Spirit, for only then can we truly live victoriously in our character.

Nicodemus would most likely today fit our ideal opinion of what it means to be a Christian. Looking at his history he is principled, knowledgeable, morally upstanding, courteous, and humble. However, Nicodemus had two big problems despite all of that outward religious appeal. He was blind to the truth and spiritually dead. The man was lost. That is, he did not have a relationship with God through Jesus Christ. As a Pharisee, Nicodemus adhered to strict Jewish codes and laws, so he was certainly religious. But the problem of the lost person is not attitudes, conduct, or even character. We can change and control those through sheer determination, and so often we do. What people really need is a change of condition. We come into this world with a sinful nature that is bent away from God.

Jesus, however, explained to the observant rabbi that all his outward goodness couldn't erase, replace, or change his nature. Instead, every person who desires to serve God must be born again. The Lord promised that if Nicodemus received Him as Saviour, then he would enter into a brand-new life. His old sinful nature would be transformed so that he could have a real relationship with

God. Instead of appearing to be a religious man, Nicodemus would be a true believer.

When we look back over history at all the great movements rooted in humanism and philosophy, we see that indeed man and society cannot be changed through external efforts to make us appear outwardly good.

Throughout history, man has sought to lay down laws of external conduct that would hopefully bring about a just and pure society, for such laws were aimed at producing citizens whose actions are moral and good. But such external laws have failed for only the inner working of the Spirit can change man's fallen nature. God has made man and within man is the DNA of divinity – so man is driven, inherently, to act morally just. For this reason, mankind has tried to establish just societies governed by just laws, but we can only remain true to our inherent needs if we are spiritually reborn.

Numerous external laws and man's noble ideas over thousands of years to turn mankind's old nature into something noble have simply failed. Revolutions, massacres and wars over the last 00 years speak of man not becoming enlightened but remaining inherently lost. The 20th C speaks of an age where mankind, void of God, remains but brutal. The two great wars, the massacres applied by Hitler and Stalin, ethical fighting and the constant dangers of wide destruction caused by nuclear weapons speak of failed external laws. Without God, mankind is left to the reckless and dangerous actions of our old nature.

Man's behaviour and his conduct simply cannot be conformed, be determined by the application of external laws or by appearing good or even religious. Only the internal working of the Spirit that conforms to our spirit and soul will lead to man becoming heavenly civilised. Such internal workings enforced by the Spirit are of a divine and eternal nature. Jesus said it is what is inside a man that makes him unclean. Once a man is reborn spiritually into a new creation, only then will he live just, morally and ethically good.

No one gets into heaven on the strength of good works and kind behaviour. When we stand before God, only our spiritual condition, determined by a true relationship with the Lord, will matter.

And so we read in "Ephesians 4: The New Man: 17 This I say, therefore, and testify in the Lord, that you should no longer walk as the rest of the Gentiles walk, in the futility of their mind, 18 having their understanding darkened, being alienated from the life of God, because of the ignorance that is in them, because of the blindness of their heart; 19 who, being past feeling, have given themselves over to lewdness, to work all uncleanness with greediness. 20 But you have not so learned Christ, 21 if indeed you have heard Him and have been taught by Him, as the truth is in Jesus: 22 that you put off, concerning your former conduct, the old man which grows corrupt according to the deceitful lusts, 23 and be renewed in the spirit of your mind, 24 and that you put on the new man which was created according to God, in true righteousness and holiness. 25 Therefore, putting away lying, " Let each one of you speak truth with his neighbor," for we are members of one another. 26 "Be angry, and do not sin": do not let the sun go down on your wrath, 27 nor give place to the devil. 28 Let him who stole steal no longer, but rather let him labor, working with his hands what is good, that he may have something to give him who has need. 29 Let no corrupt word proceed out of your mouth, but what is good for necessary edification, that it may impart grace to the hearers. 30 And do not grieve the Holy Spirit of God, by whom you were sealed for the day of redemption. 31 Let all bitterness, wrath, anger, clamor, and evil speaking be put away from you, with all malice. 32 And be kind to one another, tenderhearted, forgiving one another, even as God in Christ forgave you."

Romans 12 also expounds on what it means to behave like a Christian: "9 Let love be without hypocrisy. Abhor what is evil. Cling to what is good. 10 Be kindly affectionate to one another with brotherly love, in honor giving preference to one another; 11 not lagging in diligence, fervent in spirit, serving the Lord; 12 rejoicing in hope, patient in tribulation, continuing steadfastly in prayer; 13 distributing to the needs of the saints, given to hospitality. 14 Bless those who persecute you; bless and do not curse. 15 Rejoice with those who rejoice, and weep with those who weep. 16 Be of the same mind toward one another. Do not set your mind on high things, but associate with the humble. Do not be wise in your own opinion. 17 Repay no one evil for evil. Have regard for good things in the sight of all men. 18 If it is possible, as much as depends on you, live peaceably with all men. 19 Beloved, do not avenge yourselves, but rather give place to wrath; for it is written, "Vengeance is Mine, I will repay," says the Lord. 20 Therefore " If your enemy is hungry, feed him; If he is thirsty, give him a drink; For in so doing you will heap coals of fire on his head."

21 Do not be overcome by evil, but overcome evil with good."

Let us then seek the Lord so we may be changed in our spirit, and in our soul, meaning our heart and our mind. The more we submit and yield to the Spirit of the Lord, indeed the more we become like the Lord and the more our minds and hearts become renewed. As mentioned, we in our natural way cannot do this by our own effort, for this Paul discovered. Only when we yield and submit to the Spirit can we be inwardly changed, and not just outwardly appear to be good and just.

In the strength, wisdom and power of the Holy Spirit do we move closer to "Ephesians 3: 14 For this reason I bow my knees to the Father of our Lord Jesus Christ,15 from whom the whole family in heaven and earth is named, 16 that He would grant you, according to the riches of His glory, to be strengthened with might through His Spirit in the inner man, 17 that Christ may dwell in your hearts through faith; that you, being rooted and grounded in love, 18 may be able to comprehend with all the saints what is the width and length and depth and height— 19 to know the love of Christ which passes knowledge; that you may be filled with all the fullness of God.20 Now to Him who is able to do exceedingly abundantly above all that we ask or think, according to the power that works in us, 21 to Him be glory in the church by Christ Jesus to all generations, forever and ever. Amen."

Let us allow the Holy Spirit to work in us so that we changed morally to be just and good. Let us allow the fruit of the Spirit to become manifested in us as we yield and submit to the Lord. For then we shall truly be able to mortify the deeds of the flesh in the pursuit of holiness.

1 Thessalonians 3 says, "12 And may the Lord make you increase and abound in love to one another and to all, just as we do to you, 13 so that He may establish your hearts blameless in holiness before our God and Father at the coming of our Lord Jesus Christ with all His saints." And also "1 Thessalonians 4: 7 For God did not call us to uncleanness, but in holiness."

I believe there are depths that man has not yet discovered of the Lord, yet which we can discover. There are still spiritual depths and levels of God that can be experienced, yet we are holding back. The key that unlocks discovering the deeper depths of the Lord in holiness. It says of holiness - "2 Peter 1:21: for prophecy never came by the will of man, but holy men of God spoke as they were moved by the Holy Spirit." There is power in holiness, because God is holy, and those who walk in holiness walk in the presence of the Almighty. 2 Peter 3 says, "10 But the day of the Lord will come as a thief in the night, in which the heavens will pass away with a great noise, and the elements will melt with fervent heat; both the earth and the works that are in it will be burned up. 11

Therefore, since all these things will be dissolved, what manner of persons ought you to be in holy conduct and godliness, 12 looking for and hastening the coming of the day of God, because of which the heavens will be dissolved, being on fire, and the elements will melt with fervent heat?" Peter admonishes the believer to remain committed to holy conduct and godliness, for this is all that matters on the day that the Lord returns.

Moses had a face-to-face relationship with the Almighty God (Exodus 33:11). Just so, our spiritual walk with God must be blameless and pure so that we can walk in greater levels of intimacy. It says in Ephesians 3:17-19: "And I pray that you, being rooted and established in love, may have power, together with all the saints, to grasp how wide and long and high and deep is the love of Christ, and to know this love that surpasses knowledge – that you may be filled to the measure of all the fullness of God."

This complete fullness can manifest in our lives throughout the day and throughout the year! It is, however, a choice that we have to make if we are going to walk with God in proper respect or not to walk with God on an intimate level. Holiness is also the key that unlocks the anointing. The Lord wants us to manifest His holiness.

Anointing doesn't come as given according to proportions. In God is all the fullness, therefore all the fullness of the anointing. The fullness of the anointing comes by walking in the fullness of God, therefore submitting and obeying and following the Lord.

The Lord doesn't add anointing to us; we need to walk in the anointing by walking in the Presence of God. This is the same with holiness. The day we have been redeemed, we are holy in spirit. We have been made holy by the Blood of Jesus. Just so, in spirit, we are sanctified and justified. Colossians 1 says, "21 And you, who once were alienated and enemies in your mind by wicked works, yet now He has reconciled 22 in the body of His flesh through death, to present you holy, and blameless, and above reproach in His sight—

23 if indeed you continue in the faith, grounded and steadfast, and are not moved away from the hope of the gospel which you heard, which was preached to every creature under heaven, of which I, Paul, became a minister."

1 Corinthians 1 declares, "30 It is because of him that you are in Christ Jesus, who has become for us wisdom from God—that is, our righteousness, holiness and redemption. 31 Therefore, as it is written: "Let the one who boasts boast in the Lord.""

The Lord has therefore given us the full means to walk in manifested holiness, for His grace is sufficient for us to overcome. It says in "Hebrews 12: 1 Therefore, since we are surrounded by such a great cloud of witnesses, let us throw off everything that hinders and the sin that so easily entangles. And let us run with perseverance the race marked out for us, 2 fixing our eyes on Jesus, the pioneer and perfecter of faith. For the joy set before him he endured the cross, scorning its shame, and sat down at the right hand of the throne of God. 3 Consider him who endured such opposition from sinners, so that you will not grow weary and lose heart. 4 In your struggle against sin, you have not yet resisted to the point of shedding your blood." The cloud of witnesses is those who have gone before us and who have fought the good fight of faith and who have overcome the world. The key to victory lies in our relationship with Jesus, who Himself suffered so that we can be free.

The problem is that our soul is still far distant from God. Our mind, heart and will must still come into alignment with God for us to walk in holiness. Therefore, when the Scriptures speak about being holy as God is holy, we have to realise that God says that when we are redeemed we are holy, but now we have to start walking in holiness so that holiness may be manifested in us.

Since we are already holy and righteous in our spirit, the problem then lies in the realm of the soul. The more our minds are renewed, our hearts transformed, and our will becomes submitted, the greater our walk with God and the greater the holiness manifested in us. The closer we draw to God in manifested holiness, the greater the flow of anointing that already exists in all fullness in Jesus.

The problem lies with us ... the more we die, the more we live in the existing state of fullness. To walk in the fullness of the anointing requires a greater sacrifice of the Self. And such a sacrifice leads to holiness and purity. The anointing is the natural flow of God's power upon us and through us. The anointing is the manifestation of God's presence and fullness made alive by the Holy Spirit and empowered by the Blood of Jesus. That awesome flow of power comes upon us and flows through us like pure lightning when we allow ourselves to be conductors for God's power.

We as His vessels must be pure so that His manifested full anointing can flow in and through us. When we lay hands on the believer or the unbeliever, whatever the condition or circumstance, it will then be the anointing that flows from God's throne room, accumulating power from God's presence, flowing onto and through our hands. Where the gifts of the Holy Spirit manifest, there you also find the manifestation of the anointing.

The Holy Spirit is the giver of gifts and is the executor of the almighty power. If we then seek the greater flow of God's gifts, power and presence, we have to surrender all so that we can walk intimately with the Holy Spirit, with our Lord Jesus Christ and with God the Father. We must open our hearts and minds so that the anointing and the power can be set free and so that the presence of the Lord will explode like divine thunder through us.

As we submit to the Spirit, we allow the Spirit of God – our Parakletos – to strengthen and empower us to renew our minds and hearts so that we may walk in purity and holiness. If we want more of God, we must then die unto the Self. Anointing is released through obedience, love, faith and the fear of the Lord. These qualities are only met within us when we allow the Holy Spirit to teach and guide us. The increase of the anointing and infilling of the Holy Spirit is therefore the degree to which our old man dies! If we then want to walk in God's holiness and glory, we need to walk in submission, obedience and faithfulness. It is that simple.

God is waiting for us to make up our minds so that He can move in us. He wants us to be vessels of honour through which His anointing can flow to touch a broken world. Indeed, we are called to aim and pursue godliness, for this defines our character to the glory of God.

We read in "1 Timothy 6: 11But as for you, O man of God, flee from all these things; aim at and pursue righteousness (right standing with God and true goodness), godliness (which is the loving fear of God and being Christlike), faith, love, steadfastness (patience), and gentleness of heart. 12Fight the good fight of the faith; lay hold of the eternal life to which you were summoned and [for which] you confessed the good confession [of faith] before many witnesses. 13In the presence of God, Who preserves alive all living things, and of Christ Jesus, Who in His testimony before Pontius Pilate made the good confession, I [solemnly] charge you 14To keep all His precepts unsullied and flawless, irreproachable, until the appearing of our Lord Jesus Christ (the Anointed One), 15Which [appearing] will be shown forth in His own proper time by the blessed, only Sovereign (Ruler), the King of kings and the Lord of lords, 16Who alone has immortality [in the sense of exemption from every kind of death] and lives in unapproachable light, Whom no man has ever seen or can see. Unto Him be honor and everlasting power and dominion. Amen (so be it) ... 20O Timothy, guard and keep the deposit entrusted [to you]! Turn away from the irreverent babble and godless chatter, with the vain and empty and worldly phrases, and the subtleties and the contradictions in what is falsely called knowledge and spiritual illumination. "

Final instructions and words of advice usually contain treasures of worth – such as the instruction given to Paul in his epistle to Timothy, the young disciple. Final instructions are like a condensed version of the teacher's wisdom and knowledge, and portray fundamental truths and treasures of spiritual values. When it comes to his final instructions, Paul charges Timothy to flee from all things that are not from God and to pursue and aim for righteousness (right standing with God and true goodness), godliness (which is the loving fear of God and being Christlike), faith, love, steadfastness (patience), and gentleness of heart.

Both the verbs flee and pursue speak of action and deliberate decision – they speak of an action that simply doesn't happen, but it is an action that needs to happen by the will and the conscious decision of the one initiating the action. We are not simply going to wake up one day and by mere chance walk in righteousness, godliness, love, gentleness and faith.

These virtues speak after all about the fruits of the Spirit – therefore the Spirit of God – which implies we need to take decisive and conscious action by moving closer to God by seeking Him and obeying Him. We need to actively and with purpose submit to His will and intent. To pursue implies a forward motion, but such a journey towards God comes not merely by remaining motionless. No, we need to want and desire to pursue all that is right. This implies taking action when it comes to the way we think, what we say, what we do and how we do it.

Paul also speaks about keeping all His precepts unsullied and flawless, irreproachable, until the appearance of our Lord Jesus Christ (the Anointed One). Again, this speaks of action for the word "keep" is also the word used to imply keeping guard. We have to be mindful, aware, and alert and to be constantly striving every day to walk in the ways of God and in the ways of godliness until the coming of Jesus.

Again, emphasis is placed here on the continuous journey of pursuing goodness and godliness, for we need to do so until a set period, which is when the Lord returns, therefore, it should be an effort on our part that should never fade in terms of our resolute passion in the pursuit of being children of the Lord.

1 Peter 5: 7 Cast all your anxiety on him because he cares for you. 8 Be alert and of sober mind. Your enemy the devil prowls around like a roaring lion looking for someone to devour. 9 Resist him, standing firm in the faith because you know that the family of believers throughout the world is undergoing the same kind of suffering." Again, as with Paul, Peter places emphasis on the ongoing and active process of being alert, being sober-minded, standing firm and resisting the ways of the world. How we need to come to that point of realisation that the Lord is looking at us to also play an active and certain role in our spiritual development – we simply cannot be passive and lethargic but we need to be active, bold and determined to make sure that what we say, do and think is to His glory.

We all experience external pressures that make us walk not according to the ways of the Lord, but for this reason, we need to be actively aware of such dangers and pitfalls and instead seek to earnestly walk in His Spirit so that we may walk in true love and hope. The world is full of supposed role models, but many of these role models are the celebrities of Hollywood, the sports stars, the musicians and fashion icons. Sadly, as the world follows these "idols" of flesh and blood, they also tend to get influenced by such celebrities' conduct and speech. But such conduct and speech is most of the time anything worth following, for it speaks not of purity, faith, love or hope. It speaks of the fruits of the flesh and not of the Spirit.

When Jesus said to His disciples that they are the salt of the earth and the light of the world (Matthew 5), He was challenging the Church to become the role models in society. A broken world should be able to look up at the children of God and draw their hope, inspiration and love from us, and not the fallen "idols" of little spiritual worth. We are here to be the solution and not the problem. We are here to be a bridge to God and not the chasm of despair.

And this was the same charge issued by Paul to Timothy, for the wise teacher urged and admonished the young preacher to be an example of conduct. And this was no light challenge – Paul was daring Timothy to be an example so that people would be changed by it! He was daring Timothy to walk in such a manner that when people look at him they will not stumble in their faith or be driven deeper into spiritual darkness, but they would be so convicted by Timothy's manner of conduct, speech, love and faith and purity that they would turn to God. What a challenge and what a charge! But it is the same challenge and charge laid down by Jesus.

The question remains if after all these years since the days of Paul if we are setting an example of conduct or have we become so intertwined with the world that our lives mimic the example set by the supposed role models of this world. How the Lord must be longing for His children to stand up and to be accounted for by shining their light into the darkness so that the world's eyes will turn away from the role models of little value and to Jesus. Hasn't the time come for the Church to realize that Jesus wasn't advising us to be the light and the salt, but He was admonishing us to walk in such conduct and purity so that the world would see Him in us and so be saved and healed?

But the charge given to Timothy is anything but an easy one. For we have to set an example in speech, conduct, love, faith and purity. And this must be done not only on Sundays, not only when we are in public, but also at home and behind closed doors. How the Church needs to realise that we are called to be a living example of God's love and faith.

Yet it remains true that many people are turning away from God because of the conduct they have witnessed among Christians. The world has seen Christians quarrelling, arguing, fighting, bickering, and acting violently with rage and hate. They have seen Christians not hold their tongue, they have seen Christians curse, they have seen Christians commit all kinds of vile acts, and they have seen Christians walk more in spiritual darkness than light.

This cannot be! James 4: What causes fights and quarrels among you? Don't they come from your desires that battle within you? 2 You desire but do not have, so you kill. You covet but you cannot get what you want, so you quarrel and fight. You do not have because you do not ask God. 3 When you ask, you do not receive, because you ask with wrong motives, that you may spend what you get on your pleasures." John 3:15 says, "15 Anyone who hates a brother or sister is a murderer, and you know that no murderer has eternal life residing in him.

Paul wrote many times about one's conduct, for example in "Colossians 3: 12Clothe yourselves therefore, as God's own chosen ones (His own picked representatives), [who are] purified and holy and well-beloved [by God Himself, by putting on behavior marked by] tenderhearted pity and mercy, kind feeling, a lowly opinion of yourselves, gentle ways, [and] patience [which is tireless and long-suffering, and has the power to endure whatever comes, with good temper]. 13Be gentle and forbearing with one another and, if one has a difference (a grievance or complaint) against another, readily pardoning each other; even as the Lord has [freely] forgiven you, so must you also [forgive]. 14And above all these [put on] love and enfold yourselves with the bond of perfectness [which binds everything together completely in ideal harmony]."

James also had the following to say regarding the tongue, which determines our speech: "James 3: 5 Even so the tongue is a little member, and it can boast of great things. See how much wood or how great a forest a tiny spark can set ablaze! 6And the tongue is a fire. [The tongue is a] world of wickedness set among our members, contaminating and depraving the whole body and setting on fire the wheel of birth (the cycle of man's nature), being itself ignited by hell (Gehenna). 7For every kind of beast and bird, of reptile and sea animal, can be tamed and has been tamed by human genius (nature). 8But the human tongue can be tamed by no man. It is a restless (undisciplined, irreconcilable) evil, full of deadly poison. 9With it we bless the Lord and Father, and with it we curse men who were made in God's likeness! 10Out of the same mouth come forth blessing and cursing. These things, my brethren, ought not to be so."

We have to realise that somewhere along the line, we have to decide if we are taking our relationship with God seriously or if we have just been fooling around and playing games. Somewhere along the line, we have to realise this is not some club we have joined or that it is about having a good time with God, but it is about His Name and Kingdom that we carry with us, and we have a responsibility and accountability through our conduct and speech for the world to see Jesus in us.

We are here as God's ambassadors. We are here as His ministers and representatives. We are here to uphold His Name. The time has surely come that we must repent for the way we have acted – many times rebellious and as naughty children – and take our faith in God seriously. It is time that His love in us begins to shine by the way we speak and act; otherwise, we deceive ourselves and this world by walking in darkness.

Ultimately, our conduct and the fruits we carry will be our testimony. To say one is a Christian these days means very little. The world scoffs at it for it has seen the fruits of Christianity, for we have failed to follow God in reverence and love. 2 Corinthians 3 says, "2 You yourselves are our letter, written on our hearts, known and read by everyone. 3 You show that you are a letter from Christ, the result of our ministry, written not with ink but with the Spirit of the living God, not on tablets of stone but on tablets of human hearts."

Indeed, we are letters written by the Spirit of God. When people "read" us, will they come to Jesus, or will they find tales and stories that drive them away from the throne of mercy? Let it be our prayer and our zealous endeavour to walk in such conduct and manner that glorifies God and brings Him praise and glory. After all, He deserves nothing less from His children whom He has saved and redeemed.

End-time prophets to arise

Prophetically, let us understand the Lord is busy with mighty work in this time and season of reordering and putting the true Bride of the Lord, thus the Church, into alignment with God's will. The prophetic plays a key role in this alignment, for those who walk in the true prophetic are called to declare the Word and Truth of God. But there is a very significant connection between the prophetic and the Holy Spirit that we need to assess and realise, for it is by the power of the Holy Spirit that the alignment and reordering will take place.

God is calling His prophets – the true servants and not those wandering by the counterfeit – to reassess, to realign and to make sure they are abiding and walking in God's order, His will and presence to speak by His voice. Such prophets will be raised more than ever during the end times. These will be the true prophets, not the ones who pretend to speak with the mouth of God. After all, there are so many prophets who speak out of the flesh, or the imagination or even worse, by a demonic spirit.

Genesis 1 Amplified Bible (AMP): 1 In the beginning God (Elohim) created [by forming from nothing] the heavens and the earth. 2 The earth was formless and void or a waste and emptiness, and darkness was upon the face of the deep [primaeval ocean that covered the unformed earth]. The Spirit of God was moving (hovering, brooding) over the face of the waters. 3 And God said, "Let there be light"; and there was light.

Significantly, the Holy Spirit was evident right at the beginning. Genesis 1 is a clear indication that the Spirit of the Lord does not simply move or act or work on His own accord without being given the 'green light' by the Father. Yes, God is the Trinity of the Father, Son and the Spirit, but all three work in unity. So here at the start of creation, the Spirit of the Lord HOVERED, meaning He was in a state of waiting, and creation only came to be in existence when the Lord (Father) spoke, and upon that command, the Spirit moved to activate the power in manifested creation.

Let us therefore understand that the Spirit of the Lord is the ACTIVATION OF POWER. What God speaks and wills, the Spirit of the Lord will activate in a manifestation of power. You see, the Spirit of the Lord was hovering. The Spirit of the Lord was WAITING for the command of the Father. Once God spoke, then the Spirit of the Lord moved, and there was an activation of power, which resulted in the creation of the earth as we know it. The Holy Spirit was only poured out at the time when it was so ordained by the Kingdom of Heaven, not merely by its own accord. God is a God of order, and the outpouring which sparked the birth of the Church was in accordance with God's will and at the right time for a specific time and season.

In the Trinity, there is perfect order to fulfil the perfect will of the Kingdom of Heaven. We need to note that the Spirit of the Lord was "hovering", and clearly the Spirit of the Lord was not acting according to his own purpose. So the Spirit of the Lord will activate through power what God speaks and desires. And this is all for a certain purpose, and what He has spoken shall be. "Isaiah 55:11 So is my word that goes out from my mouth: It will not return to me empty, but will accomplish what I desire and achieve the purpose for which I sent it."

You can thus call the Spirit's work as a process of regeneration. Another word for regeneration is "rebirth," from which we get the concept of being "born again." The classic proof text for this can be found in John's gospel: "I tell you the truth, no one can see the kingdom of God unless he is born again" (John 3:3).

We also need to understand that the Holy Spirit – who is God Himself as part of the Trinity - is the source of new life. So we see how right in the beginning, the world was dark and void of life. We read that the Holy Spirit hovered. Yes, He was first mentioned as part of the Trinity. Only when the Father spoke, "Let there be light", did the Holy Spirit move and bring about life. Yes, the Father spoke, and so the Spirit was activated to bring about life, and so the earth was rebirthed. If we are talking about the Holy Spirit being the conceiver of life, consider "Matthew 1:20 But while he thought on these things, behold, the angel of the Lord appeared unto him in a dream, saying, Joseph, thou son of David, fear not to take unto thee Mary thy wife: for that which is conceived in her is of the Holy Ghost."

Yes, the Lord Jesus was conceived and brought to life by the Spirit of the living Lord! Indeed, Jesus said He is the Life and He gives Life in abundance, but remember the Lord is ONE, and so Jesus, while on earth, was operating and functioning in the life-giving power of the Holy Spirit! After all, Jesus was baptised by the Holy Spirit.

Job 33: 4 The spirit of God hath made me, and the breath of the Almighty hath given me life.

The Holy Spirit is the Ruach – the very breath of life.

AS THE SPIRIT WAS PRESENT RIGHT AT THE BEGINNING TO BRING ORDER WHERE THERE WAS A DARK VOID, TO BRING SHAPE AND FORM TO WHAT WAS FORMLESS AND TO BRING SUBSTANCE TO WHAT WAS EMPTY, NOW MORE THAN EVER WE NEED THE SPIRIT OF THE LORD AGAIN TO BRING ALIGNMENT, ORDER AND LIFE BACK TO THE BRIDE

OF GOD. And as the Bride connects and walks in the glory and will of God once again, then the Bride will truly again be the light that shines in the darkness and be a carrier of His Spirit who brings meaning and hope to all. We have been called to be worshippers in Spirit and truth.

You see, the Spirit of the Lord activates the life-giving power so that we are reborn, rebirthed and rec-connected with divinity! We can see the powerful work of the Holy Spirit as the activator of life also in "Psalm 33:6 By the word of the Lord were the heavens made; and all the host of them by the breath of his mouth."

John 6:63 says in the Amplified that "it is the Spirit who gives life; the flesh conveys no benefit [it is of no account]. The words I have spoken to you are spirit and life [providing eternal life]." King James says it as follows: It is the spirit that quickeneth ...

We need the Spirit to quicken in the Bride of God more than ever, but there needs to be a connection between God and the prophetic. Why? The Spirit hovered and then moved right at the beginning, and the Spirit moved to bring about the conception of Jesus because it was the will of the Lord. Right at the beginning, GOD SPOKE, and there was an activation, and the Spirit moved and brought about the manifestation of God's complete and Sovereign Will.

And here we have to understand something important. THE HOLY SPIRIT WILL NOT MOVE OR BE ACTIVATED OR BRING ABOUT ANY MANIFESTATION WHEN COMMANDED OR SPOKEN TO BY THE VOICE OF MAN, BUT ONLY BY THE VOICE OF THE LORD. And so the Lord says more than ever we are finding in churches where so many who are prophesying and uttering prophetic words are speaking empty words, and there is no movement or activation of the Spirit, for they speak not by the voice of God. The Spirit of the Lord will not move or bring about God's will, alignment or order unless God has so spoken. And here is an important understanding – a prophet is supposed to speak by the voice of God and only by the voice of God, for then the Spirit will be active, and the authority will be active, and the faith will be activated.

We find that in the Scriptures, Jesus declares that His words are Spirit, and therefore life. Jesus, the Word made flesh, therefore speaks words which are Spirit and life, because on earth He was also baptised in the Spirit. Remember, the Holy Spirit dwelt within Jesus, for this happened on the day of the baptism. Yes, the Lord was conceived by the Spirit, but the Spirit only dwelt within Jesus at the start of His ministry. This was very important because the Spirit of the Lord needed to move and activate the ministry of Jesus. This was done when the Spirit connected with the Son so that what the Son speaks as God Himself, the Spirit can then move and activate what the Lord speaks. Jesus also said: "My teaching is not mine, but his who sent me" (John 7:16). This is the very essence of the prophetic – speaking only what God declares and speaks. So Jesus fulfils the very office of the prophet. Jesus also connected the prophetic with the Spirit, for it is absolutely vital and of critical importance to declare the truth of the Kingdom of Heaven.

The problem we are finding in churches is that so many prophetic utterances hold no life or power, for they are void of the Spirit of God, and it is spoken out of the flesh or the imagination of man. It is thus spoken not by the voice of the Father, and if so, cannot be spoken in the will, and according to the purpose of the Lord. So many are thus speaking according to the dictates of the flesh and not the Spirit (Romans 8).

Ezekiel 13 declares, "6 They have seen falsehood and lying divination, saying, 'The Lord says,' but the Lord has not sent them. Yet they hope and make men to hope for the confirmation of their word. 7 Did you not see (make up) a false vision and speak a lying divination when you said, 'The Lord declares,' but it is not I who have spoken?" Take note, God says, regarding the false prophets and those seeing false visions, it was not He who had spoken to them. Thus, they had spoken out of their own will and by their own imagination. We also read in the same chapter: "8 Therefore, thus says the Lord God, 'Because you have spoken empty and delusive words and have seen lies, therefore behold, I am against you," says the Lord God.

God wants to bring order and life back to the Bride of God, yet those servants called into the prophetic need to begin to speak with the voice of God, and not merely by their own delusions, ideas or opinions. It is time for them to stand up, wear the mantle of the prophetic and begin to declare the Lord's will and intent as He speaks through the Spirit. It is time to arise from the slumber, to come out of the caves and to lay down the self to the glory of the Lord. For then the Spirit shall move and manifest and activate the will of the Lord to bring about the order and alignment for the Church. Proverbs 18:21 declares, "Death and life are in the power of the tongue, and those who love it will eat its fruit."

Indeed, many are speaking foolishness and they are commanding and even ordering the Spirit, yet they speak not in the voice of the Lord, thus by His authority. Jesus spoke as someone with authority, and not as a teacher of the law (Matthew 7:29). Why? Because He spoke as the Lord, and He spoke only what He heard and received to speak. Jesus was the Son of God and God Himself, but He still only followed the purpose of the Father (which is clear in the Garden of Gethsemane).

The reality is we can only know the heart and mind and ways of the Lord through the inner working of the Spirit within us, and thus know His will and know His voice. More than ever we need those in the prophetic to reconnect with the Spirit, for this will lead us back to the voice and the will of the Lord. We do not just need the Presence of the Spirit in our lives; we need the Spirit within us, and we need the Spirit operating and functioning so that the Spirit can change us from the inside out so that we are more closely connected to God and His Kingdom.

If we do not know the voice of the Lord, then we will never be able to walk in God's truth. To have a voice means to have an opinion, and if you have an opinion, you have an influence, so there has always been a struggle from the beginning of time regarding what VOICE the world listens to.

What VOICE the world listens to will determine the influence exerted upon the actions, thoughts, and behaviour. Satan wants to influence people negatively, and the Lord wants to influence people positively so that they may shine His light in a dark world. Satan wants us to walk the wide road, and God wants us to follow the true and narrow path. We are influenced by the VOICE that we are listening to. The voice we are listening to, it will determine our influence in life.

It is time again that we will listen to the voice of God. It is time again for us to receive a true revelation of God. It is time for those called into the prophetic to make sure they are listening only to God's voice. It is time that we listen to the voice of God, and it is time that we thirst for a revelation of God. It is time that we return to God, because truly then will we know the voice of God. The greatest revelation we can receive is not a revelation from God, but a revelation about God and who God is. We need to know Him! Then only will the VOICE of God change us, and then only will the voice of God begin to mould us and influence us so that we can become more like God.

It is time that we return to God because we have been listening to the wrong voices for far too long. If we listen to the wrong voice, we will become confused, and we will be deceived because Satan has come to deceive and to lie and to steal and to destroy. Indeed,

God is raising prophets who listen only to God, and they shall speak as the Spirit moves!

God is also speaking about a process of separation – a separation of the false and the real, the holy and unholy, the godly and the ungodly and between the immoral and the moral. This is a time of the separation between God's Truth and the truth of man, between God's Kingdom and the kingdom of man and between God's ways and the ways of man. In this process of separation, God is also now separating the true and the false prophet. Yes, God will expose the false prophecies of self-indulgence, self-glorification, self-edification and self-exaltation. It shall crumble and be exposed for its wickedness, says the Lord.

It says in Ezekiel 2 (words of God to the prophet Ezekiel): He said, "Son of man, I am sending you to the Israelites, to a rebellious nation that has rebelled against me; they and their ancestors have been in revolt against me to this very day. 4 The people to whom I am sending you are obstinate and stubborn. Say to them, 'This is what the Sovereign Lord says.' 5 And whether they listen or fail to listen—for they are a rebellious people—they will know that a prophet has been among them. 6 And you, son of man, do not be afraid of them or their words. Do not be afraid, though briers and thorns are all around you and you live among scorpions. Do not be afraid of what they say or be terrified by them, though they are a rebellious people. 7 You must speak my words to them, whether they listen or fail to listen, for they are rebellious. 8 But you, son of man, listen to what I say to you. Do not rebel like those rebellious people; open your mouth and eat what I give you."

We need to understand God is saying clearly the true prophets will not be welcomed, for they bring correction, and they bring God's Truth where there is rebellion and where apostasy, idolatry, immorality and deception thrive. Yet God is saying clearly He is raising up this army of prophets! God is sending them to the rebellious house as He did in the days of Ezekiel, and take note, that the world cannot be rebellious if not under the covenant. We can only be rebellious to God if we are under His covenant – so the rebellious house is God's church on earth.

These prophets will speak as the Lord leads, and the Lord is saying to them Do not be afraid, do not be dismayed, do not be discouraged, but speak as I lead. Yes, the prophets will be mocked, ridiculed, persecuted, and even threatened, but ultimately it is not the prophet who is being mocked but God Himself!

And the Lord is saying He is sending the prophets in these days to lead people WITHIN THE REBELLIOUS HOUSE of bondage – out of rebellion and out of apostasy and out of religion and into the Promised Land of God's ordination and Kingdom! And look, says the Lord, the Lord raised Moses the prophet to lead the people by great signs and wonders, just as the signs and wonders were with the prophets Elijah, Daniel, Elisha and Ezekiel. By great signs and wonders, the earth shook, fire fell, and kingdoms KNEW God was real and alive. So it shall be again declared the Lord!

For the Lord says Jesus, the Son of God, and the greatest prophet of all, also came in the prophetic mantle to lead the people out of bondage AND SIGNS AND WONDERS FOLLOWED THIS EXODUS OUT OF SLAVERY! For the Lord says Behold, the true prophets will arise from the ashes and now, yes, now is the time they shall be known not just for their purity, and for speaking God's Truth, but great, yes GREAT, signs and wonders will accompany them like never before. For the rebellious house shall know a prophet is among them, says the Lord.

Behold, says God, My True Word shall be spoken to the rebellious house, and if they listen or if they shall not listen, they shall know by the prophet I am in the House. Reject the prophet says the Lord, then you shall reject My Word says the Lord. And so the Lord reminds us of "Matthew 23: 29 "Woe to you, teachers of the law and Pharisees, you hypocrites! You build tombs for the prophets and decorate the graves of the righteous. 30 And you say, 'If we had lived in the days of our ancestors, we would not have taken part with them in shedding the blood of the prophets.' 31 So you testify against yourselves that you are the descendants of those who murdered the prophets. 32 Go ahead, then, and complete what your ancestors started!"

For the Lord says a time will come when the true prophets will arise, but not always accepted, they will rise, but many will seek their downfall, and many will seek to see them destroyed, strewn and bloodied in the streets. For a murderous spirit is loose within the rebellious house, says the Lord, yes, a murderous spirit to destroy God's Truth and Kingdom. God shall arise in power and Glory to be the protector and deliverer, as He is the Deliverer of Israel!

End-time remnant walks in God's Glory and Presence

Years ago, I remember the Lord speaking clearly of how He will birth His Bride in the end times to walk in His Glory. I was made to understand that the Bride, the true remnant of believers, will not only endure troubling times, but will be able to thrive and prosper because of God's glory!

So we need to understand what God's glory to walk in it is! In verse 18 of Ezekiel 33 we read, "And he said, I beseech thee, shew me thy glory. 19And he said, I will make all my goodness pass before thee, and I will proclaim the name of the LORD before thee; and will be gracious to whom I will be gracious, and will shew mercy on whom I will shew mercy. 20And he said, Thou canst not see my face: for there shall no man see me, and live. 21And the LORD said, Behold, there is a place by me, and thou shalt stand upon a rock: 22And it shall come to pass, while my glory passeth by, that I will put thee in a clift of the rock, and will cover thee with my hand while I pass by: 23And I will take away mine hand, and thou shalt see my back parts: but my face shall not be seen."

What is God's glory that Moses so yearned for and sought? Is the Lord's glory the same as His presence? Is His glory the same as His Spirit? For the Lord is urging us to grasp and comprehend what is His glory, for if we do not understand His glory, how shall we understand what He has called us for, which is to become carriers of such glory? The urging of the Spirit – He the one who teaches us in all wisdom and knowledge and truth – is to take hold of the "reality" that we are called to give birth to His glory. This is in light of Him speaking about giving birth to the glory that is already inside of us. And by this birth, the earth will be covered by His glory. It is imperative to understand what His glory is. And yet, we don't quite yet understand what the glory of the Lord is. Some of us may equate it to power and others to holiness.

And yes, like Moses, we must every effort to walk in His glory to His glory. In the same chapter, we read, "11 So the Lord spoke to Moses face to face, as a man speaks to his friend. And he would return to the camp, but his servant Joshua the son of Nun, a young man, did not depart from the tabernacle." Do we hunger and yearn for God's presence as Joshua did? Do we truly yearn for God's glory in our lives? Joshua sought the Lord, earnestly seeking Him with all his strength, and eventually was chosen to lead the Israelites into the Promised Land. Are we not too quick to depart from God to seek the ways of the Lord? When we seek God with all our heart and mind and strength, we find the strength to overcome great challenges.

Ephesians 3:14–19 says, "For this reason I bow my knees to the Father of our Lord Jesus Christ, from whom the whole family in heaven and earth is named, that He would grant you, according to the riches of His glory, to be strengthened with might through His Spirit in the inner man, that Christ may dwell in your hearts through faith; that you, being rooted and grounded in love, may be able to comprehend with all the saints what is the width and length and depth and height— to know the love of Christ which passes knowledge; that you may be filled with all the fullness of God."

In the passage above we can see that it is according to the wealth of God's glory that we are strengthened with power through the Holy Spirit, to receive Christ living in our heart by faith, and so we become joined to the source of true love. We then go on to attain what all the saints have attained, that is knowing God through experiencing His love, so that we may be filled with all the fullness of God. For this reason, we need to walk in God's glory and give birth to such glory so that by the wealth of His glory we are strengthened through the Spirit who sanctifies us by truth.

In John 17 we read the following [Prayer of Jesus]: "22And the glory which thou gavest me I have given them; that they may be one, even as we are one: 23I in them, and thou in me, that they may be made perfect in one; and that the world may know that thou hast sent me, and hast loved them, as thou hast loved me. 24Father, I will that they also, whom thou hast given me, be with me where I am; that they may behold my glory, which thou hast given me: for thou lovedst me before the foundation of the world."

Quite amazingly, Jesus is here speaking about glory that the Father has given Him, and so He prays that we will also take hold of that glory when we are in Him. The Glory was given unto Jesus, He being the Son of Man was the first fruit and for Him and through Him all things are made (Colossians 1). The essence, substance, and weightiness of the Father's essence and nature was birthed into His Son, and just so when we are reborn [rebirthed] we find the glory dwells within by the work of the Spirit.

Colossians 1 says, "15He is the image of the invisible God, the firstborn over all creation. 16For by him all things were created: things in heaven and on earth, visible and invisible, whether thrones or powers or rulers or authorities; all things were created by him and for him. 17He is before all things, and in him all things hold together. 18And he is the head of the body, the church; he is the beginning and the firstborn from among the dead, so that in everything he might have the supremacy. 19For God was pleased to have all his fullness dwell in him, 20and through him to reconcile to himself all things, whether things on earth or things in heaven, by making peace through his blood, shed on the cross.

21Once you were alienated from God and were enemies in your minds because of[your evil behaviour. 22But now he has reconciled you by Christ's physical body through death to present you holy in his sight, without blemish and free from accusation—23if you continue in your faith, established and firm, not moved from the hope held out in the gospel. This is the gospel that you heard and that has been proclaimed to every creature under heaven, and of which I, Paul, have become a servant."

We read in 2 Corinthians 3 of the glory of the New Covenant: "7Now if the ministry that brought death, which was engraved in letters on stone, came with glory, so that the Israelites could not look steadily at the face of Moses because of its glory, fading though it was, 8will not the ministry of the Spirit be even more glorious? 9If the ministry that condemns men is glorious, how much more glorious is the ministry that brings righteousness! 10For what was glorious has no glory now in comparison with the surpassing glory. 11And if what was fading away came with glory, how much greater is the glory of that which lasts! 12Therefore, since we have such a hope, we are very bold. 13We are not like Moses, who would put a veil over his face to keep the Israelites from gazing at it while the radiance was fading away. 14But their minds were made dull, for to this day the same veil remains when the old covenant is read. It has not been removed, because only in Christ is it taken away. 15Even to this day when Moses is read, a veil covers their hearts. 16But whenever anyone turns to the Lord, the veil is taken away. 17Now the Lord is the Spirit, and where the Spirit of the Lord is, there is freedom. 18And we, who with unveiled faces all reflect the Lord's glory, are being transformed into his likeness with ever-increasing glory, which comes from the Lord, who is the Spirit."

It is, therefore, clear by Paul's writing that it is those who turn to Jesus and thus to the Spirit that they will begin to walk in Glory, which should be reflected in our walk. Yet, how often do we not miss verse 18, which speaks of an ever-increasing glory and a transformation – this applies a process of self-denial, a journey of sanctification, an abandonment unto God, and the continuous seeking after truth. This implies a process of turning away from those things that blind us spiritually, so that we may spiritually discern [see] and move in God's glory. It says in John 3 that only those who have been born of the Spirit will truly see the Kingdom of God. We cannot move in God's glory without moving beyond the Self, beyond the traditions and the customs of our way that veils us from His substance, weightiness and nature.

Yet, what is this glory that the Lord has placed in us and what does He want us to give birth? The original meaning of glory has to do with weightiness. The Hebrew word for "glory", which is Kabowd basically, means weight. In science, it would be the mass of an object of matter. It is the substance of a person or thing. For God, it is who He is, His character and power. We know that God is love, (1 John 4:16); love is God's character and power. God's glory manifests and reveals His love. The glory of God summarizes the seriousness, perfection, and infinite significance of all of the attributes of God. It sums up who He is, in the awesome brightness and weightiness of all His perfections.

The original meaning of the term glory was thus brightness, clearness, effulgence: from that it has come to signify honour, renown; and again, that which renders honourable, or demands honour, or renown, reverence, adoration, and worship—that which is worthy of confidence and trust. The glory of God is essential and declarative. By essential glory is meant that in Him which is glorious—that in his character which demands honour, worship, and adoration. His declarative glory is the showing forth, the revealing, the manifesting, the glory of his character—his essential glory—to his creatures: the laying open his glory to the apprehension of intelligence.

To understand more of God's glory, we have to look at God's reply when Moses asked for it. This was God's reply, "I will make all My goodness pass before you, and I will proclaim the name of the Lord before you. I will be gracious to whom I will be gracious, and I will have compassion on whom I will have compassion" (Exodus 33:19).

God told Moses to stand on a rock that was near Him. This symbolizes Jesus Christ, our rock. And the Lord said, "Here is a place by Me, and you shall stand on the rock. So it shall be, while My glory passes by, that I will put you in the cleft of the rock, and will cover you with My hand while I pass by. (Exodus 33:21–22). To stand upon the rock is symbolic of coming to Christ and putting your trust in Him, your weight upon Him. As God's glory passed by He put Moses in the cleft of the rock, symbolizing being in Christ. It is God the Father who positions you in Christ, adopting you as His child. This is the place where God's glory is revealed and received, the place we receive manifestations and revelations of the Father's love and power.

And the Lord passed before him and proclaimed, "The Lord, the Lord God, merciful and gracious, longsuffering, and abounding in goodness and truth" (Exodus 34:6). The word merciful is the Hebrew word rachum; it means to be full of compassion. This is the first word that God used to describe His glory. It reveals much about God's glory and character. It reveals the highest form of love, the kind of love God is. Rachum is only used about God. Because of the New Covenant, purchased by the blood of Jesus, we can now experience this holy love of God through the Holy Spirit (Romans 5:1-5). This love from God is fruit from the tree of life (Revelation 2:4-7).

The word gracious in Exodus 34:6 means to show favour, mercy, kindness, and forgiveness; longsuffering means to be patient; goodness means to show loving-kindness; truth means to be faithful and trustworthy. All of these characteristics are seen as characteristics of love in 1st Corinthians 13. They are also seen in the fruit of the Spirit mentioned in (Galatians 5:22). But the fruit of the Spirit is love, joy, peace, longsuffering, kindness, goodness, faithfulness. The word fruit in Galatians 5:22 is singular, there is only one fruit of the Spirit, which is love. All the other traits mentioned are characteristics of love. Likewise, in Exodus 34:6 the first thing that God reveals about His character is that He is rachum-"full of compassion". All of the other characteristics of Exodus 34:6 are contained in this compassionate love of God.

So what are we being told of Gods' glory? His glory is the weight and substance of the supreme God – this same God who is full of love, compassion, grace, mercy, kindness and power. This glory is the illumination of His very essence, made known to us by the Spirit so that we may know Him more. We are also called God's vessels of compassion – we who were created to receive the revelation of His glory. That He might make known the riches of His glory on the vessels of mercy (compassion), which He had prepared beforehand for glory, even us whom He called, not of the Jews only, but also of the Gentiles (Romans 9:23–24)

And this is what Moses sought - that God would reveal Himself to his mind so that he might know Him and so that he might have a clear and powerful apprehension of those things which constitute his glory. Moses was therefore making his desire known for more than he knew of God. He knew comparatively little of God. Something indeed he had known of Him, but he wished to know more - a desire to know that which makes God worthy of the homage and adoration of his creatures, and especially he desired to be so subdued by this knowledge and so subdued that his confidence might be perfect in Him so that he might never fail in his trust and leaning upon the Lord. God had called him to very arduous work, and he needed a very thorough acquaintance with Him.

What then does it mean to carry His glory? It places our focus on God and makes us God-conscious of His holiness, purity, of His character, nature and love. If we truly carry His glory, it will redefine the way we operate and function – for those who allow the Spirit to take them from glory to glory, mean certain abandonment unto God and alienation from the Self. Our motivations, intent and thoughts will be centred on His Will, His compassion, His love and his desire to see a lost world saved. It will place our hearts in alignment with His. We become God-conscious and not self-conscious in all that we do, say and think.

Alas, how we need to urgently recapture the centrality of glorifying God in our lives and work. Too much of what passes for evangelical Christianity is man-centred or even self-centred. God is reduced to a means to some other end, whether it be my self-fulfilment or the welfare of others. The results are disastrous for worship, discipleship, and witnesses. Worship either becomes tepid, or it becomes an experience we offer to people as a sort of consumer product rather than the adoration and consecration we offer to God.

Discipleship becomes a self-help program that leaves huge areas of life untouched, rather than a life-long love affair with God that lays every area of life on the altar to be consecrated to Him and to be conformed to His image. The witness becomes an invitation to sample a product rather than a royal summons to flee to a sovereign Savior. In effect, we reduce the Good News to mere good advice.

If the glory of God is our supreme passion, this will redefine both the goal of our task and how we pursue that task. The goal of our task is that the earth is filled with the knowledge of His glory as the waters cover the sea. Our passion is to see Him receive the glory that is due to His Name from every tribe, tongue, people and nation. Everything else is simply a means to that end. We are not seeking to add numbers that we can report to the organization; we are seeking to add worshippers to the choir of heaven, who will live every area of their lives to the praise of His glory. This focus invests a new, holy seriousness to discipleship and the life of the church. We are not content unless His glory is proclaimed, reflected, upheld and adored among the people to whom He has called us. The task is not about us, and it's not even ultimately about the nations. The focus is on Him.

A passion for the glory of God will also redefine how we pursue our tasks. If our supreme goal is to glorify Him, we will not be able to separate our personal lives from our work lives. The way we treat our families, the way we entertain ourselves, the way we spend our money, the way we relate to others, the way we treat our bodies, the hidden attitudes of our hearts, the time we spend nourishing our relationship with Him, cannot be compartmentalized away from our "work." It is our job to glorify Him in every area of life, not just through the tasks written on our job descriptions. Failure in the former will mean failure in the latter as well. We also cannot accept any means to the end that does not equally bring glory to God. This passion thus has a purifying effect, safeguarding us from the temptation to take shortcuts or utilize worldly means in the pursuit of our work.

Jesus has given us the same glory, the same love, which the Father gave Him. The glory of God and the Father's love is now within us because of the New Covenant. This glory unifies Christ body of believers and sanctifies us to be God's holy habitation. We glorify Him and we honour His Glory by walking in such glory.

We cannot add to His glory, for He is already perfectly and infinitely glorious. Rather, for us to glorify God means for us to ascribe the glory that is due to His Name in worship. It means that we acknowledge His glory by living as though His perfections are as serious and significant as they really are so that we reflect His glory through a pure mirror. It means that nothing horrifies us more than the thought of bringing dishonour to His glorious Name, and nothing delights us more than to feel His pleasure as we live to the praise of His glory. It also means that we declare His glory among the nations, inviting others to join us in our love affair with His glorious perfection. Glorifying God thus consumes and defines every aspect of our life and witness as well as our worship.

The Glory of the Lord was beautifully demonstrated in Matthew 17 when Jesus was transfigured into the fullness of His glory: "1 And after six days Jesus taketh Peter, James, and John his brother, and bringeth them up into an high mountain apart, 2And was transfigured before them: and his face did shine as the sun, and his raiment was white as the light. 3And, behold, there appeared unto them Moses and Elias talking with him. 4Then answered Peter, and said unto Jesus, Lord, it is good for us to be here: if thou wilt, let us make here three tabernacles; one for thee, and one for Moses, and one for Elias. 5While he yet spake, behold, a bright cloud overshadowed them: and behold a voice out of the cloud, which said, this is my beloved Son, in whom I am well pleased; hear ye him. 6And when the disciples heard it, they fell on their face, and were sore afraid. 7And Jesus came and touched them, and said, Arise, and be not afraid.

8And when they had lifted up their eyes, they saw no man, save Jesus only. 9And as they came down from the mountain, Jesus charged them, saying, Tell the vision to no man, until the Son of man be risen again from the dead."

When we look to Jesus the knowledge of the glory of God is revealed. For it is God who commanded light to shine out of darkness, who has shone in our hearts to give the light of the knowledge of the glory of God in the face of Jesus Christ (2

Corinthians 4:6). The signs, wonders, and miracles that Jesus did were manifestations of the glory of God, manifestations of His love and power. This beginning of signs Jesus did in Galilee, and manifested His glory; and His disciples believed in Him. (John 2:11)

We can now begin to comprehend what a tragedy it was when Ezekiel saw God's glory leave the temple! We read of this event in Ezekiel 10. The very weightiness and essence of the Lord that speaks of His presence, His love, His peace, His beauty and magnitude is leaving the land! Ezekiel must have been devastated. How else when you see the glory departing? We can only imagine what Ezekiel must be thinking – there goes God and no the land is void of the weightiness and fullness of His Presence. This is also what Moses realised when he cried out to the Lord that His glory must not depart from them, for he also knew that without God's presence there would surely be no love, hope and faith!

How we need to cry out and yearn and seek and pursue the Glory of the Lord as His Bride! How we must cry out for it, pray for it, seek it, and long for it, for it is a terrible prospect to be left without the Lord's Glory. There is indeed no joy, no love, no hope and no peace and no blessing without His Glory. How we need to crave for it, how we need to take hold of it and carry it so close to our hearts. To carry His glory is in the deep revelation and reality of walking in His love, compassion, truth, holiness and purity. When we walk in His glory, being god conscious and God centred, we give Him the praise and there the Kingdom will be manifested through the sons and daughters of the Living God! And where there is light, then darkness recedes. Where there is love, hatred disperses. Where there is forgiveness, bitterness and envy disintegrate. Can we see how, if we truly walk in His Glory, then the knowledge of His Glory – which is His love, compassion,

passion and hope – will touch every heart and every spirit in this world?

In Exodus 33 we read: "12 Then Moses said to the Lord, "See, You say to me, 'Bring up this people.' But You have not let me know whom You will send with me. Yet You have said, 'I know you by name, and you have also found grace in My sight.' 13 Now therefore, I pray, if I have found grace in Your sight, show me now Your way, that I may know You and that I may find grace in Your sight. And consider that this nation is Your people." 14 And He said, "My Presence will go with you, and I will give you rest." 15 Then he said to Him, "If Your Presence does not go with us, do not bring us up from here. 16 For how then will it be known that Your people and I have found grace in Your sight, except You go with us? So we shall be separate, Your people and I, from all the people who are upon the face of the earth." 17 So the Lord said to Moses, "I will also do this thing that you have spoken; for you have found grace in My sight, and I know you by name."

Moses said to God that they will not move or go from where they are unless the Presence of God is with them. He also made it clear that only with God's Presence will others know they are God's people. We also find that God said to Moses that His presence will be with them because Moses have found grace in the eyes of God and he is known by name. After all, they would speak face to face (Exodus 33:11).

In the days of Moses, the Presence was not yet indwelling in man, yet Moses understood the greatness of God's Presence. It says in "Deuteronomy 4:37: And because He loved your fathers, therefore He chose their descendants after them; and He brought you out of Egypt with His Presence, with His mighty power." The Presence of God is power and His glory. For it is God. It is the weightiness of His nature and existence.

Moses had an encounter with the Presence at the burning bush that empowered and strengthened him to fulfil God's mandate of leading the people out of bondage. Moses encountered God on Mount Sinai for 40 days to receive the Law. He encountered God's Presence when God's wrath manifested against those who chose to follow the golden calf. He saw God's glorious provision of the Presence with the manna in the wilderness, the water that gushed from a rock and how they enjoyed victory over their enemies. Yes, Moses knew about the Presence, for it says in Exodus 40:34 that "the cloud covered the tent of meeting, and the glory of the LORD filled the tabernacle." We also read in "Exodus 13:21: And the Lord went before them by day in a pillar of cloud to lead the way, and by night in a pillar of fire to give them light, so as to go by day and night."

The Presence did indeed not dwell with God's people internally and habitually in the days of Moses, for it was detached. It dwelt in the Holy of Holies of the Tabernacle. In Ezekiel 10 we read how the Glory of the Lord, thus the Presence, left the Temple because of the people's great idolatry. The Presence served the purpose of reminding the people that God is with them. It was their comfort, their hope, their strength and their joy.

Let us read what David writes of the Presence:

Psalm 9:3 When my enemies turn back, they shall fall and perish at Your presence (also Psalm 68:2).

Psalm 16:11 You will show me the path of life; in Your presence is fullness of joy.

Psalm 17:2 Let my vindication come from Your presence; let Your eyes look on the things that are upright.

Psalm 31:20 You shall hide them in the secret place of Your presence. From the plots of man; You shall keep them secretly in a pavilion from the strife of tongues.

Psalm 95:2 Let us come before His presence with thanksgiving; let us shout joyfully to Him with psalms.

Psalm 100:2 Serve the LORD with gladness; come before His presence with singing.

Psalm 140:13 Surely the righteous shall give thanks to Your name; the upright shall dwell in Your presence.

Glory to God! In His Presence, we find our strength, our vindication, our joy, our victory and our protection. Psalm 95:14 ties in with Hebrews 4 which reads: "Therefore, since we have a great high priest who has ascended into heaven, Jesus the Son of God, let us hold firmly to the faith we profess. 15 For we do not have a high priest who is unable to empathize with our weaknesses, but we have one who has been tempted in every way, just as we are—yet he did not sin. 16 Let us then approach God's throne of grace with confidence, so that we may receive mercy and find grace to help us in our time of need." Psalm 31:20 ties in with Psalm 91 which says: "He who dwells in the secret place of the Most High shall abide under the shadow of the Almighty. 2 I will say of the Lord, "He is my refuge and my fortress; My God, in Him I will trust." This speaks of being in the presence of The Presence, and here we are safe, for God is our refuge and our hope!

When Jesus came to the earth, the Presence as the Word that became flesh (John 1) was tangible and in the natural realm with the first disciples for 3½ years. No longer was the Presence detached. They were called to follow – meaning following the Presence – and wherever they went people knew them as the disciples of God because Jesus was with them. Thus as they followed then the Presence went before them and with them, just as the Presence went with Moses! The prophet understood they will only be known as God's people because of the Presence, and so the disciples would be known for being with the Presence and continuing to abide in the Presence through the baptism of the Holy Spirit.

In John 16 the Lord said: "7 Nevertheless I tell you the truth. It is to your advantage that I go away; for if I do not go away, the Helper will not come to you; but if I depart, I will send Him to you." Jesus knew the time was coming when He would physically be no longer present to be with His disciples. So He promised them another one will come – the Holy Spirit – to be ever present with believers. Glory to God.

And so, in Acts 1 we read: "4 And being assembled together with them, He commanded them not to depart from Jerusalem, but to wait for the Promise of the Father, "which," He said, "you have heard from Me; 5 for John truly baptized with water, but you shall be baptized with the Holy Spirit not many days from now." Just like Moses knew the people could not go ahead into the Promised Land without the presence of God, thus to be victorious and to walk in God's supreme will, just so Jesus told the disciples they could not be "witnesses to Me [Jesus] in Jerusalem, and all Judea and Samaria, and to the end of the earth" without the Presence of God. So He told them to wait because without the Presence of God the disciples would fail to fulfil the Great Commission. They needed the Presence to dwell with them habitually, to be comforted, to be protected, to be vindicated and to be strengthened!

The outpouring of the Spirit thus directly connects with Exodus 33! For God told Moses He would surely be with them – His very Presence – and He will give them rest. God upheld that promise by first sending Jesus – as the Presence of God manifested in flesh – and then through the outpouring of the Holy Spirit. Indeed, the disciples had to wait in the Upper Room because they like Moses could not go out in the streets to fulfil the Great Commission without God's Presence! God's Presence was with them in the form of the resurrected Lord, but God was not about to leave the Church without His Presence. God had spoken to Moses His Presence will go with His people and that Promise still stands and so the Spirit was poured out so that the Presence of God is always with us.

In Ezekiel 33 Moses also cried out to the Lord to show him His Glory. The Presence is for the purpose under the New Covenant not only to walk in the Presence but to know the Presence, thus abide in the Glory. For the Glory is the manifested reality of the greatness and goodness of God. In the Glory is life, and not just life, but resurrected life for the dead bones to come alive and for the spiritually poor and the lost to come home to an everlasting God of love! And so it says in "John 3: 3 Jesus answered and said to him, "Most assuredly, I say to you, unless one is born again, he cannot see the kingdom of God." When we are thus reborn, we abide in the Lord as worshippers in Spirit and truth, and we thus walk in the Presence, abide in the Presence and we can "see" (thus meaning comprehend, understand and bear witness) the manifested reality and glory of the Kingdom!

Just as the Presence as the Glory descended on the Tent of Meeting in the days of Moses, now by the Spirit of God and by the death and resurrection of Jesus (which tore the veil in two) the Glory descends and takes habitation of the believer who is now the temple of God! Now the Presence of the Glory of God is with the believer, to worship, to follow and to glorify God. Thus to be witnesses of His Glory to the ends of the earth.

At the burning bush, Moses encountered the Presence of the Shekinah fire. When we are filled by God's Spirit, we are filled by the Shekinah glory of God. For our God is an all-consuming fire (Hebrews 12:29), so He desires to consume us with His Presence. 1 Thessalonians 5:19 speaks about not quenching the Spirit. Some translations speak of not quenching the fire of the Spirit. The reality is when we do quench the Spirit, we are thus not yielding and submitting to the Presence of God!

And it is so easy to quench the Spirit when we walk after the flesh when we follow the ways of religion, or traditions or the world. It says in "1 Corinthians 1: 28 and the base things of the world and the things which are despised God has chosen, and the things which are not, to bring to nothing the things that are, 29 that no flesh should glory in His presence." Yes, we can only glory in His Presence when we yield and submit unto Him, laying down the work of the flesh, so that we can go from glory to glory.

For it says in "2 Corinthians 3:18: And we all, who with unveiled faces contemplate the Lord's glory, are being transformed into his image with ever-increasing glory, which comes from the Lord, who is the Spirit." Yes, God tore the veil in two at Cavalry so that we may walk in His Presence habitually, for God longs to tabernacle with us so that in His Presence we are transformed into His likeness as a new creation.

The concept of glory to glory connects also to Ezekiel 33, for it is written "16 for how then will it be known that Your people and I have found grace in Your sight, except You go with us? So we shall be separate, Your people and I, from all the people who are upon the face of the earth." What is the purpose of the Presence? Yes, for God's people to be known by separation from the world! The Presence, thus the indwelling presence of God, is to make God's people known for a people who walk in God's glory, His anointing, His image, and thus His holiness. For truly, what fellowship can light have with darkness (2 Corinthians 6:14).

At the burning bush (Exodus 3), Moses encountered the Presence of God. It says: "5 Then He said, "Do not draw near this place. Take your sandals off your feet, for the place where you stand is holy ground." God is holy. His Presence is Holy. It is written in "1 Peter 1: 16 for it is written: 'Be holy, because I am holy.'"

God's Presence is to produce a people separated from the world by walking in God's holiness. A people sold out and committed to His Kingdom. It says in "1 Peter 2: 4 Coming to Him as to a living stone, rejected indeed by men, but chosen by God and precious, 5 you also, as living stones, are being built up a spiritual house, a holy priesthood, to offer up spiritual sacrifices acceptable to God through Jesus Christ."

Thus, the Presence dwelling in the believer is for the purpose to produce holiness, and by such holiness, the world will know we are God's people and walk in His light, love and truth. It says in "John 15: 5 "I am the vine, you are the branches. He who abides in Me, and I in him, bears much fruit; for without Me you can do nothing." In Matthew 7 it says: "17 Even so, every good tree bears good fruit, but a bad tree bears bad fruit. 18 A good tree cannot bear bad fruit, nor can a bad tree bear good fruit. 19 Every tree that does not bear good fruit is cut down and thrown into the fire. 20 Therefore by their fruits you will know them." Thus, when we abide in God – thus the Presence – we will bear much fruit, and by such good fruit we shall be known. Yet if we fail to abide in God thus the Presence, or we fail to honour the Presence, our fruit will not honour God. Before the arrest of Jesus, we read in "John 18: 17 Then the servant girl who kept the door said to Peter, "You are not also one of this Man's disciples, are you?" The disciples were recognized and known for they were accompanied by the Presence, thus the Glory of God.

In Exodus 33 we read specifically how God said He will be with Moses because Moses had found grace with God. Moses understood the Law for God gave the Law unto the prophet on the mountain, but Moses found favour in the eyes of God not because of the Law but because of grace. This laid the platform for the coming of Jesus so that only by grace we can walk in the Presence of God and thus bear much fruit. The reality is, we can do nothing but nothing if God's presence is not with us. And it is by grace that we may walk in the Presence. It is by grace the Spirit was poured out. And we can rely on God's Presence for Jesus' sacrifice was all about grace and mercy, and by tearing the veil in two, and because of His sacrifice we are truly known by God if we yield and submit unto Him.

There is joy in His Presence. In His Presence, we shall overcome and walk in His Glory. For in His Presence we know the following is true: "Jude 24 Now to Him who is able to keep you from stumbling, and to present you faultless before the presence of His glory with exceeding joy."

In Mark 16 we read: "17 And these signs will follow those who believe: In My name they will cast out demons; they will speak with new tongues; 18 they will take up serpents; and if they drink anything deadly, it will by no means hurt them; they will lay hands on the sick, and they will recover." If we follow God and abide in the Lord through His Spirit, then it says signs and wonders will follow, and there will be great manifestations of God's authority. Why? Because for those who follow God, then the Presence goes with us as the Presence went with Moses! It says in "Acts 15: 14 And believers were increasingly added to the Lord, multitudes of both men and women, 15 so that they brought the sick out into the streets and laid them on beds and couches, that at least the shadow of Peter passing by might fall on some of them." Much has been talked about the shadow of Peter. Reality is very simple – Peter was filled with the Spirit of God, so it was the Presence of God that fell on some. And in God's Presence, there is healing, deliverance and power!

We do not need to pray anymore for God's presence to go with us, but rather to thank the Lord that His Presence is with us, just as we are healed and it is finished. May we truly yield to God to walk in His mighty Presence, for Ephesians 3 will become a manifested reality of how out of His glorious riches we will be strengthened with power through His Spirit in our inner being.

End-time servants of love and faith

2 Timothy 1:7 KJV: For God hath not given us the spirit of fear; but of power, and of love, and of a sound mind.

Fear breeds doubt, and doubt eventually nibbles and gnaws at our faith. Faith without action is dead, and so the devil seeks to disarm the Christian's faith through fear, anxiety and disobedience. The devil does not want Christians to walk in faith, certainty or hope, for then they are too focused on God and His promises. We are living in a world of incredible fear. It is the fear of the unknown, the uncertain, of violence, calamity, strife, chaos and confusion. We need to guard against fear in such end-times, lest we become discouraged and lose our faith in a great and mighty God.

If we want to guard against unhealthy fear and doubt, we need to grow into the fullness of God – thus a maturity of character – so that we stand firm in our hope and faith. This will lead to a Christian who is at peace and who lives with certainty, therefore leading a life in Spirit and Truth. Therefore, a restless and immature Christian remains fearful and can easily fall for the ways of the flesh and the world. Fear, uncertainty and doubt come when we do not walk constantly in a relationship with God, leading to a breakdown in communication. God's intention is not for us to walk in fear. And we are talking here about an unhealthy, uncomfortable and distressing fear. Fear is a key stronghold in many people's lives, even believers, so fear needs to be addressed.

Let us first assess what fear is on a psychological level. Let us understand fear is a chain reaction in the brain that starts with a stressful stimulus and ends with the release of chemicals that cause a racing heart, fast breathing and energised muscles, among other things, also known as the fight-or-flight response. The amygdala is linked to the parts of the brain that govern your senses, muscles and hormones – enabling your body to react quickly to the sight or sound of a threat.

Fear is thus a human emotion that is triggered by a perceived threat. The problem is, when people live in constant fear, whether from physical dangers in their environment or threats they perceive, they can become incapacitated. And this is what the devil wants. He wants us to live in such fear that we become incapacitated, constantly in flight or fight mode. Fear can lead us to hide, to run away, or to freeze in our tracks. Fear can be uncomfortable and crippling.

Fear is an inherently unpleasant experience that can range from mild to paralysing—from anticipating the results of a medical checkup, to hearing news of a deadly terrorist attack. Horrifying events can leave a permanent mark on your brain circuitry, which may require professional help. However, chronic stress, the low-intensity variety of fear expressed as free-floating anxiety, constant worry, and daily insecurity, can quietly but seriously harm your physical and mental health over time.

There is the opinion that fear is not all bad, for it is hardwired in our brains. This is because neuroscientists have identified distinct networks that run from the depths of the limbic system all the way to the prefrontal cortex and back. When these networks are electrically or chemically stimulated, they produce fear, even in the absence of a fearful stimulus. Feeling fear is seen as neither abnormal nor a sign of weakness: The capacity to be afraid is part of normal brain function.

Being fearless doesn't mean eliminating fear, which, according to one's brain, is impossible. Being fearless means knowing how to leverage fear. Fear is regarded as part instinct, part learned, part taught. Some fears are instinctive: Pain, for example, causes fear instinctively because of its implications for survival. Other fears are learned: We learn to be afraid of certain people, places, or situations because of negative associations and past experiences. A near-drowning incident, for example, may cause fear each time you get close to a body of water. Other fears are taught: Cultural norms often dictate whether something should be feared or not.

Fear is also partly imagined, and so it can arise in the absence of something scary. At the end of the day, fear can be seen as a collection of sensations and perceptions that tell us that something is threatening. What you may find threatening may not be what your friend, sibling, or partner finds threatening. The true inherent danger of fear is its ability to play with our emotions and challenge our perceptions.

Whatever level of fear one is experiencing, it is never a pleasant emotion. Fear is not comforting, nurturing, relaxing, or reassuring. What we all can agree on when it comes to fear is that it is distressing. It's uncomfortable, and most of the time we're in a state of fear, we're simply seeking to navigate our way back out again. Fear can lead to feelings of apprehension or dread, powerlessness, despair or hopelessness.

Now, let us return to what Paul writes, for he labels fear as something spiritual. He calls this a 'spirit of fear'. So we need to realise that the devil comes with a spiritual attack in our lives, so that we, on a psychological and physical level, may be subjected to fear. He harasses us with this spirit, so that our fear levels are accelerated, be it fears that we have learned, or been taught, or that are instinctive. The devil wants us to become paralysed by fear in this world,

The devil wants the Christian to walk in fear, for fear does cripple us. Remember, fear is the opposite of faith. And yes, there are many things one can fear, such as fearing death, fearing the unknown, fearing loneliness, fearing being ridiculed or mocked or simply the fear that comes from real physical and even spiritual dangers. Consider phobias, which are a manifestation of fear. Phobias are reckoned to be the most common mental disorders in the US. Approximately 10 per cent of people in America have specific phobias, 7.1 per cent experience social phobias, and 0.9 per cent have agoraphobia. These range from fears of spiders to heights to speaking in public.

A phobia is an overwhelming, irrational, and persistent fear that leads to avoiding the object or situation. It can be a fear of a specific thing or of a social setting. Phobias fall into a class of mental disorders known as anxiety disorders. This class also includes generalised anxiety disorder, panic disorder, post-traumatic stress disorder and obsessive-compulsive disorder.

Anxiety disorders generally are coupled with fear, which goes hand in hand with emotional and spiritual trauma. Consider the symptoms of phobia: Dizziness, trembling and increased heart rate; breathlessness; nausea; a sense of unreality; fear of dying; preoccupation with the fear object. In some cases, these symptoms can escalate into a full-scale anxiety attack.

It is important to note that Paul placed extra emphasis on fear, for we need to guard our gates from fear to enter. As mentioned, fear is not all bad, but what happens when it is something more, when it is an emotion we feel simply getting into our car, leaving our house or being in a crowd? Are these feelings of fear normal? The answer to that is no. This kind of fear is tormenting, and it does not come from our loving God.

God does not want us to walk in any kind of anxiety. He does not want us to be subjected to phobias, trauma resulting from fear or from disorders or from going through life afraid and afraid of something that will trigger the fear. The spirit of fear can take on many forms, but its intentions are clear, no matter what kind of spirit of fear it may be. It intends to keep you from fulfilling the destiny that God has for your life; from living a joyful, spirit-led existence where you give to others out of the overflow of love in your life. It will keep you awake with nightmares. It will keep you from leaving your home or overcoming past emotional and physical wounds. Unhealthy fear paralyses, immobilises, and causes stress, anxiety and worry. It takes us down a road of not trusting in the Lord and where we abandon our hope in God.

So how do we stand guard over this gate? Consider the following Scripture: There is no fear in love; but perfect love casteth out fear: because fear hath torment. He that feareth is not made perfect in love. 1 John 4:18, KJV

What exactly is perfect love? Of course, we all know it to be Jesus, the one who died on the cross to set us free from these spirits, but it is also Him moving through us in love with other people. For instance, if you are selfish and indulge your carnal flesh with things such as lying, cheating, stealing, gossiping, and being manipulative, you will also reap what you sow in fear. Sin, any kind of sin, attracts demonic spirits, and the spirit of fear is usually the first one through the door. That is why Paul tells us not to be anxious for anything. Anxiety is a form of fear.

Philippians 4:6-8: Do not be anxious about anything, but in everything, by prayer and petition, with thanksgiving, present your requests to God. And the peace of God, which transcends all understanding, will guard your hearts and your minds in Christ Jesus. Finally, brothers, whatever is true, whatever is noble, whatever is right, whatever is pure, whatever is lovely, whatever is admirable—if anything is excellent or praiseworthy—think about such things.

Fear robs us of our peace. It steals our joy. Unholy and unhealthy fear is one of the key attacks against believers these days.

After all, we live in a world of great fear. We fear what will happen to our families, we fear for our lives, for our wellbeing, and we fear the uncertainty of life. Yet, then the Lord speaks and says that perfect love drives out fear. And this is where we have to pause and consider what the Lord is saying – PERFECT LOVE drives out fear. So where there is perfect love, then we shall not walk in fear. Perfect love breeds faith. Faith breeds Trust and faith in God. He is truly our Good Shepherd (John 10, Psalm 23).

Now, what is PERFECT LOVE? 1 John 4: 7 Dear friends, let us love one another, for love comes from God. Everyone who loves has been born of God and knows God. 8 Whoever does not love does not know God, because God is love. 9 This is how God showed his love among us: He sent his one and only Son into the world that we might live through him. 10 This is love: not that we loved God, but that he loved us and sent his Son as an atoning sacrifice for our sins. 11 Dear friends, since God so loved us, we also ought to love one another. 12 No one has ever seen God; but if we love one another, God lives in us and his love is made complete in us. 13 This is how we know that we live in him and he in us: He has given us of his Spirit. 14 And we have seen and testify that the Father has sent his Son to be the Savior of the world. 15 If anyone acknowledges that Jesus is the Son of God, God lives in them and they in God. 16 And so we know and rely on the love God has for us. God is love. Whoever lives in love lives in God, and God in them. 17 This is how love is made complete among us so that we will have confidence on the day of judgment: In this world, we are like Jesus. 18 There is no fear in love. But perfect love drives out fear, because fear has to do with punishment. The one who fears is not made perfect in love. 19 We love because he first loved us. 20 Whoever claims to love God yet hates a brother or sister is a liar. For whoever does not love their brother and sister, whom they have seen, cannot love God, whom they have not seen. 21 And he has given us this command: Anyone who loves God must also love their brother and sister.

Firstly, we need to understand PERFECT LOVE rests with God, for God loves unconditionally, demonstrated by Him sending His Son to die for our trespasses. We can therefore only love the way God loves us when we abide in Him; therefore, abide in PERFECT LOVE.

In our own strength, we cannot love perfectly, for true love comes from God, who is love. True love, by definition, is that God first loved us. It is the same with our moral development. We cannot bear the fruit of the Spirit of Galatians 5 by our own strength; this is why it is called the fruits of the SPIRT (capital S), not the fruit of our own spirit (therefore our own strength). We can only become more pure and holy and love more when we abide and rest in the Lord who IS pure, holy, and who IS love.

Then we read the following: 13 This is how we know that we live in him and he in us: He has given us of his Spirit. 14 And we have seen and testify that the Father has sent his Son to be the Savior of the world. 15 If anyone acknowledges that Jesus is the Son of God, God lives in them and they in God. 16 And so we know and rely on the love God has for us. God is love. Whoever lives in love lives in God, and God in them. 17 This is how love is made complete among us so that we will have confidence on the day of judgment: In this world, we are like Jesus.

We can love perfectly and abide in perfect love when we abide and rest in the one who is perfect – Jesus. And we are called to walk by the Spirit so that we can truly become more like our Lord (more in character, in virtue and love) for the Spirit of the Lord leads us in all truth (John 16) and the Spirit of the Lord leads us to become morally virtuous according to Galatians 5.

So how do we abide in perfect love? We do so when we abide in the Lord, and we do so in the Spirit, for as we read in Romans

8, if anyone does not have the Spirit of Christ, they do not belong to Christ. This is again why John 3 is so important: 3 Jesus replied, "Very truly I tell you, no one can see the kingdom of God unless they are born again." 4 "How can someone be born when they are old?" Nicodemus asked. "Surely they cannot enter a second time into their mother's womb to be born!" 5 Jesus answered, "Very truly I tell you, no one can enter the kingdom of God unless they are born of water and the Spirit. 6 Flesh gives birth to flesh, but the Spirit[b] gives birth to spirit. 7 You should not be surprised at my saying, 'You must be born again.'

So, to walk in PERFECT LOVE requires resting, abiding by the Spirit of the Lord in the Presence of the Lord. John 15: 5 "I am the vine; you are the branches. If you remain in me and I in you, you will bear much fruit; apart from me you can do nothing. 6 If you do not remain in me, you are like a branch that is thrown away and withers; such branches are picked up, thrown into the fire and burned. 7 If you remain in me and my words remain in you, ask whatever you wish, and it will be done for you. 8 This is to my Father's glory, that you bear much fruit, showing yourselves to be my disciples. 9 "As the Father has loved me, so have I loved you. Now remain in my love. 10 If you keep my commands, you will remain in my love, just as I have kept my Father's commands and remain in his love. 11 I have told you this so that my joy may be in you and that your joy may be complete. 12 My command is this: Love each other as I have loved you. 13 Greater love has no one than this: to lay down one's life for one's friends. 14 You are my friends if you do what I command. 15 I no longer call you servants, because a servant does not know his master's business. Instead, I have called you friends, for everything that I learned from my Father I have made known to you. 16 You did not choose me, but I chose you and appointed you so that you might go and bear fruit—fruit that will last—and so that whatever you ask in my name the Father will give you. 17 This is my command: Love each other.

So John 15, Romans 8 and Galatians 5 all speak of love, of being IN Christ and belonging to our Lord. Why? So that as we submit to the Lord and obey Him in love, we can walk in perfect love for He is LOVE. And why the necessity to walk in perfect love? Because in love there is no fear! Can we, therefore, see why the Lord deems it so important that we abide in Him, and that we know that He is Love? We shall then avoid the dangers and pitfalls of walking in fear that comes with walking in the flesh and not the Spirit!

So again, let us return to 1 John 4, which speaks about how there is no fear in love and that perfect love drives out fear. Indeed, there is no fear in love because love is found in God, so when we love, we know God, and when we know the Lord, we shall not fear punishment or the uncertainty of life. We shall not fear the terrors.

For this reason, Moses wrote in "Psalm 91: 1 Whoever dwells in the shelter of the Most High will rest in the shadow of the Almighty. 2 I will say of the Lord, "He is my refuge and my fortress, my God, in whom I trust." 3 Surely he will save you from the fowler's snare and from the deadly pestilence. 4 He will cover you with his feathers, and under his wings you will find refuge; his faithfulness will be your shield and rampart. 5 You will not fear the terror of night, nor the arrow that flies by day, 6 nor the pestilence that stalks in the darkness, nor the plague that destroys at midday. 9 If you say, "The Lord is my refuge," and you make the Most High your dwelling, 10 no harm will overtake you, no disaster will come near your tent. 11 For he will command his angels concerning you to guard you in all your ways; 12 they will lift you up in their hands, so that you will not strike your foot against a stone. 13 You will tread on the lion and the cobra; you will trample the great lion and the serpent. 14 "Because he loves me," says the Lord, "I will rescue him; I will protect him, for he acknowledges my name. 15 He will call on me, and I will answer him; I will be with him in trouble, I will deliver him and honor him. 16 With long life I will satisfy him and show him my salvation."

Also, take what John writes, "the one who fears is not made perfect in love." Wow! What a statement. He, therefore, is saying we shall succumb to fear when love is not perfected in love, which happens when we are not fully and utterly submitted to the Lord and abiding in His Glory and Majesty. How can we truly fear if we know the Lord?

After all, the Scriptures speak about how we are more than conquerors (Romans 8:37) and if He is for us, who can be against us? It also says in "Romans 8: 35 Who shall separate us from the love of Christ? Shall trouble or hardship or persecution or famine or nakedness or danger or sword? 36 As it is written: "For your sake we face death all day long; we are considered as sheep to be slaughtered." 37 No, in all these things we are more than conquerors through him who loved us. 38 For I am convinced that neither death nor life, neither angels nor demons, neither the present nor the future, nor any powers, 39 neither height nor depth, nor anything else in all creation, will be able to separate us from the love of God that is in Christ Jesus our Lord."

And also "Isaiah 8: 11 This is what the Lord says to me with his strong hand upon me, warning me not to follow the way of this people: 12 "Do not call conspiracy everything this people calls a conspiracy; do not fear what they fear, and do not dread it. 13 The Lord Almighty is the one you are to regard as holy, he is the one you are to fear, he is the one you are to dread. Indeed, we are more than conquerors, and we do not have to fear this world because he first loved us! Praise the Lord! Yet, if we are truly made perfect in love, as John reminds us, we will love our brothers and sisters (in the Body of Christ as well). For it is written: For whoever does not love their brother and sister, whom they have seen, cannot love God, whom they have not seen. 21 And he has given us this command: Anyone who loves God must also love their brother and sister."

So if we fear, we know not love. We cannot know love if we do not know God. If we know the Lord, we shall walk in love, in faith and in hope. For we are called not to fear this world but to fear the Lord, for to fear the Lord is the beginning of wisdom (Job 28:28).

And so we are ultimately reminded of the Good Shepherd and His love in John 10: The Good Shepherd and His Sheep: 1 "Very truly I tell you Pharisees, anyone who does not enter the sheep pen by the gate, but climbs in by some other way, is a thief and a robber. 2 The one who enters by the gate is the shepherd of the sheep. 3 The gatekeeper opens the gate for him, and the sheep listen to his voice. He calls his own sheep by name and leads them out. 4 When he has brought out all his own, he goes on ahead of them, and his sheep follow him because they know his voice. 5 But they will never follow a stranger; in fact, they will run away from him because they do not recognize a stranger's voice." 6 Jesus used this figure of speech, but the Pharisees did not understand what he was telling them. 7 Therefore Jesus said again, "Very truly I tell you, I am the gate for the sheep. 8 All who have come before me are thieves and robbers, but the sheep have not listened to them. 9 I am the gate; whoever enters through me will be saved. They will come in and go out, and find pasture. 10 The thief comes only to steal and kill and destroy; I have come that they may have life, and have it to the full. 11 "I am the good shepherd. The good shepherd lays down his life for the sheep. 12 The hired hand is not the shepherd and does not own the sheep. So when he sees the wolf coming, he abandons the sheep and runs away. Then the wolf attacks the flock and scatters it. 13 The man runs away because he is a hired hand and cares nothing for the sheep. 14 "I am the good shepherd; I know my sheep and my sheep know me— 15 just as the Father knows me and I know the Father—and I lay down my life for the sheep.

The Lord is calling us to a life of no fear but a life of love and of faith. Indeed, the Lord has not given us a spirit of fear but of power, love and self-discipline (1 Timothy 1:7). We walk by power when we truly are perfect by love by walking by the Spirit, and the Spirit teaches us self-discipline and how to become more like Jesus who IS love.

And when we walk by love, it means we abide in the Lord, and when we abide in Him, we trust and have faith in His perfect and complete plan. For this reason, the Lord said in Matthew 6: 25 "Therefore I say to you, do not worry about your life, what you will eat or what you will drink; nor about your body, what you will put on. Isn't life more than food and the body more than clothing? 26 Look at the birds of the air, for they neither sow nor reap nor gather into barns; yet your heavenly Father feeds them. Are you not of more value than they? 27 Which of you by worrying can add one cubit to his stature? 28 "So why do you worry about clothing? Consider the lilies of the field, how they grow: they neither toil nor spin; 29 and yet I say to you that even Solomon in all his glory was not arrayed like one of these. 30 Now if God so clothes the grass of the field, which today is, and tomorrow is thrown into the oven, will He not much more clothe you, O you of little faith? 31 "Therefore do not worry, saying, 'What shall we eat?' or 'What shall we drink?' or 'What shall we wear?' 32 For after all these things the Gentiles seek. For your heavenly Father knows that you need all these things. 33 But seek first the kingdom of God and His righteousness, and all these things shall be added to you. 34 Therefore do not worry about tomorrow, for tomorrow will worry about its own things. Sufficient for the day is its own trouble.

The opposite of trusting God is to worry, and worry is a form of stress, fear and anxiety! So the Lord gives us a commandment not to worry, thus do not be anxious and do not be full of fear. After all, God shall take care of us and God is with us. There is no need to fear in this world and we must guard against fear. The Lord God is our protector, our provider, our refuge, our hope, our shield, our salvation and our strength. Psalm 23 verse says Yea, though I walk through the valley of the shadow of death, I will fear no evil; For You are with me; Your rod and Your staff, they comfort me. Our Lord protects us from the snare of the fowler, and His eye is upon the righteous (Psalm 34:15). Why then be fearful? We are called to walk in His Presence and not be caught up in a flight or fight mode.

In 2 Timothy 4:7, Paul writes, "I have fought the good fight, I have finished the race, I have kept the faith." The apostle wrote these words near the end of his life. Take note, he has 1) fought the good fight, 2) finished the race, and 3) kept the faith. We need to, therefore, keep fighting for the Gospel, making sure we finish the race in respect to our salvation, and thirdly, we need to keep believing in Christ, in His Word and His Truth.

In his letter to Timothy, Paul is not commending himself for having run the full distance; rather, he is simply describing what the grace of God had enabled him to do. In the book of Acts, Paul says these powerful words: "I consider my life worth nothing to me, if only I may finish the race and complete the task the Lord Jesus has given me—the task of testifying to the gospel of God's grace" (Acts 20:24).

Paul is telling Timothy that he had put every effort into the work of proclaiming the gospel of salvation to all. He had completed the course set before him; he had left nothing undone. He was ready to cross the finish line into heaven. In a race, only one runner wins. However, in the Christian "race," everyone who pays the price of vigilant training for the cause of Christ can win. We are not competing against one another, as in athletic games, but against the struggles, physical and spiritual, that stand in the way of our reaching the prize (Philippians 3:14). In 1 Timothy 6:12, he also wrote, "Fight the good fight of the faith. Take hold of the eternal life to which you were called when you made your good confession in the presence of many witnesses."

Oh yes, we must thus put in every effort to run the race, fight the good fight and not relent in our duty of fulfilling the Great Commission! This is especially true in the end times. We must continue to abide in God, love Him, fear Him and obey the Lord to fulfil our duties as ministers of the Gospel. Paul exhorts us to "run in such a way as to get the prize," and to do this, we must set aside anything that might hinder us from living and teaching the gospel of Christ. The writer of Hebrews echoes the words of Paul: "Lay aside every weight, and the sin which so easily ensnares us, and let us run with endurance the race that is set before us, looking unto Jesus, the author and finisher of our faith" (Hebrews 12:1-2).

And the reward for standing our ground and running the race? It says also in "2 Timothy 4: 8 Now there is in store for me the crown of righteousness, which the Lord, the righteous Judge, will award to me on that day—and not only to me, but also to all who have longed for his appearing." Glory to God. Our reward is eternal joy with God, a blissful existence with majesty and a divine union with our Lord. In James 1, we read, "2 Consider it pure joy, my brothers and sisters, whenever you face trials of many kinds, 3 because you know that the testing of your faith produces perseverance. 4 Let perseverance finish its work so that you may be mature and complete, not lacking anything."

Paul knew all about trials and testing of the faith, but he persevered (ran the race). His life speaks of maturity, not lacking anything, and bearing fruit to the glory of God because even in the suffering and troubled times, Paul found his strength and joy in God. 'Not to lack' doesn't always speak about being prosperous in wealth, but it speaks of inner joy and peace that surpasses all understanding (Philippians 4:6). Jesus spoke of not lacking in Matthew 6, yet we were reminded of first seeking God's will, Kingdom and righteousness above all else. After all, Romans 14:17 says, "For the kingdom of God is not a matter of eating and drinking, but of righteousness, peace and joy in the Holy Spirit."

Paul writes in "Philippians 4: 4 Rejoice in the Lord always. I will say it again: Rejoice! 5 Let your gentleness be evident to all. The Lord is near. 6 Do not be anxious about anything, but in every situation, by prayer and petition, with thanksgiving, present your requests to God. 7 And the peace of God, which transcends all understanding, will guard your hearts and your minds in Christ Jesus."

Hebrews 12 holds a very powerful truth. It says in verse 2 (New King James Version), "looking unto Jesus, the author and finisher of our faith, who for the joy that was set before Him endured the cross, despising the shame, and has sat down at the right hand of the throne of God."

The word author in Greek is Archegos, which speaks of the chief leader, thus one who takes the lead in anything. The word finisher in Greek is Teleiotes, which speaks of a perfector, thus referring to Christ who has in His own person raised faith to its perfection and so set before us the highest example of faith. Hebrews 12 thus tells us that we must allow God as the author of our lives to write our story and to complete it. This calls to persistently place our faith in God. We must allow God to write every chapter and sentence of our life, and in doing so, bring to perfection His will, His purpose and His plan in our lives. We need to trust God by always looking at Him, for only God can write the best story for our lives!

And oh yes, how we need to accept, surrender and yield to the story that God wants to write! We need to keep faith in terrible times. And this is a living story. A story to glorify God. A story of hope, blessing, salvation and redemption. Jeremiah 29:11 says, "For I know the plans I have for you," declares the Lord, "plans to prosper you and not to harm you, plans to give you hope and a future." This has always been God's intention. He is not a cruel God. He is a loving and good Father! So God wants to complete the story for our lives. It is a story that points to Jesus. Paul writes in "2 Corinthians 3: 2 You are our epistle written in our hearts, known and read by all men; 3 clearly you are an epistle of Christ, ministered by us, written not with ink but by the Spirit of the living God, not on tablets of stone but on tablets of flesh, that is, of the heart." Indeed, God's story for our lives is ingrained in our souls and in our spirits for all men to see. God's story is always about God. It is about His love and beauty. His story should be the light that shines in our lives for all to witness.

God is calling for a people in the end-time to cultivate an unshakable faith. The truth is, when we have an unshakable faith in an almighty God, then we will have unshakable peace! It is a peace that surpasses all understanding. Colossians 3:15 states: "Let the peace of Christ rule in your hearts". This means God must have complete control and dominion over your life. This is very important.

The Word of God also states we walk by faith and not by sight. It is well known that what we see or hear determines our reality, and it determines our emotional reaction. But God is calling for faith in a mighty God that surpasses what we see or hear in the natural, and then walk by the supernatural reality and truth of God. So, what rules your heart today? Do you walk by the faith of Hebrews 11? Do we walk by faith where we trust in the impossible and know we serve a God of the impossible? For God is truly in control of our very being, we shall not fear, and we shall walk by unshakable peace!

Philippians 4:7 states, "and the peace of God, which transcends all understanding, will guard your hearts and your minds in Christ Jesus". So if we let God rule and have dominion, as we walk by unshakable faith and trust, then our minds and hearts will be guarded against all fear, trouble and anxiety! And we shall know peace, thus Shalom, and we shall be whole and at rest. May we walk in God's unshakable peace with unshakable faith!

Glory to God, there is no reason to fear, there is no reason to be anxious, for the Lord is indeed the Lord of the battle. And how the Lord reminds us He is the only and true master of any battle, no matter what kind of battle, no matter what kind of struggle we face, no matter the obstacles hindering us or the circumstances that threaten to surround us. We may face the battles of the mind, or the battles of the physical, or the battles of the spiritual, but the battle that wages is never greater or distant from the hand of God. Indeed, is the hand of the Lord too short to save or deliver? Isaiah 59 says, "1 Surely the arm of the LORD is not too short to save, nor his ear too dull to hear."

There are countless tales of how the battle belongs to God and how we do not have to fear, so take heart, be full of joy, for God is with us. He slays the mighty, He brings low the lofty, and He brings kings to their knees and shakes empires until it is mere dust. What a God we serve. So love Him and keep the faith!

Prophetic word on faith

Praise the Lord! Indeed, all praise belongs to God! He is Mighty! He is Glorious! For hear the Lord, believers of the Most High! It is time to step out in faith, says the Lord. Step out like never before. Step out into the unknown. Step away from your comfort zone! Step away from your worry and anguish! Step in line with the steps of Jesus. Nothing is impossible for our God. Do you believe?

It is time, says the Lord. It is time. Just believe, just believe. Let not this world hold you back. Let not fear hold you back. Let not what you see hold you back. Let not what you hear hold you back. Look only at Jesus! Hear Him! Listen to Him! For He is Mighty to Deliver and Mighty to Save and Mighty to Heal. For we no longer truly BELIEVE this is the Mighty Lord who still heals, who still delivers, who still prospers, for He still makes a way. Just believe, just believe. Sing Hallelujah. Sing to the Lamb that was slain and the One who has the power to open the seals in heaven.

It is time to believe in the IMPOSSIBLE. Believe in the Glory. Believe God will sustain. Believe God will part the way. Believe. Just believe, cries the Lord! Oh child of God, it is not a mustard seed but small, so the Lord asks not of the impossible, but just the simple cry of obedience, of faithfulness, and to know He is the Lord of Love and Mercy. Just believe, for the Lord who shook Egypt and Babylon, who has shaken the hearts of man and the ground we walk on, surely this Great I Am shall be with His children. Just believe!

Nothing says the Lord is impossible to Him. Nothing but nothing can defeat Him. Nothing is greater than Him. Nothing is more powerful than Him. Nothing is more awesome than Him. Just believe! Oh, believers, it is time to step out in faith. It is time to believe in the Glory that will shake the heavens and the earth. For the Lord is moved by the righteous who move in faith!

Do we believe He not only heals but also keeps us healthy? Do we believe He is the Lord who will guard us against all sickness, dread diseases and injuries? Do we believe He is the same God who spoke through Moses in Exodus 15: 26: "If you diligently heed the voice of the LORD your God and do what is right in His sight, give ear to His commandments and keep all His statutes, I will put none of the diseases on you which I have brought on the Egyptians. For I am the LORD who heals you."

Just believe, for it says in Luke 1:37: "For with God nothing will be impossible." Is anything too hard for me, says the Lord? So why fear? Has the Blood of the Lord lost its power? Its value? Its hope? Is Jesus not the same as ever and tomorrow? Is He the Lion of Judah? Is He not the Balm of Gilead? Glory to God.

For yes, all praise belongs to Him. All the praise. All the glory. He is the Mighty One. He is the I Am. No man shall stand against Him. No man shall defeat Him. No spiritual force can destroy Him. For those who stand with Him stand in the might of our God who still saves, still heals and still delivers!

Today, the Lord asks us as His children: Do we believe? Did He not say in John 11: "Did I not say to you that if you would believe you would see the glory of God?" Glory to God! It is time to step out of faith. Believe and trust not in this world, but have faith in the Almighty! Seek Him! Have faith for He shall make a way! Let not your heart be troubled, and let not your knees buckle. For He shall carry you. For He shall strengthen you to run and to walk in His might and glory. For He shall be your refuge and High Tower. Why fear?

Come, come all, and bow before Majesty. Bow before the Great I Am. He washes away all sins. Break all yokes. Destroys all bondages. Not even the gates of hell shall prevail against the steadfast believer! Let us sing the Song of Moses: "The LORD is my strength and song, And He has become my salvation; He is my God, and I will praise Him; My father's God, and I will exalt Him. The LORD is a man of war; The LORD is His name."

End-time rooted in Christ

Matthew 7: 4 Therefore whoever hears these sayings of Mine, and does them, I will liken him to a wise man who built his house on the rock: 25 and the rain descended, the floods came, and the winds blew and beat on that house; and it did not fall, for it was founded on the rock. 26 "But everyone who hears these sayings of Mine, and does not do them, will be like a foolish man who built his house on the sand: 27 and the rain descended, the floods came, and the winds blew and beat on that house; and it fell. And great was its fall."

The end times will be marked by great calamity, uncertainty, fears, violence, lawlessness and deception. It is time when the devil is brainwashing people to believe all kinds of lies. We can only survive such times, meaning overcoming, when our entire lives are built upon the Rock of Christ. Two thousand years ago, a man set foot on our planet who claimed to be from a place beyond space and time. Although he had no credentials or political backing, his life and words changed our world. His name is Jesus Christ. Hundreds of years before Jesus was born, Old Testament prophets from Moses to Zechariah foretold of a coming Messiah. This Messiah, or Christ, was to pay the penalty for man's sin and be a light to the world. And, according to the prophet Isaiah, he would be God in human form. (Isaiah 9:6)

Matthew 21 speaks of Jesus being the capstone or the cornerstone. This implies that without such a stone, the entire building cannot stand. It says in "Ephesians 2: 19 Now, therefore, you are no longer strangers and foreigners, but fellow citizens with the saints and members of the household of God, 20 having been built on the foundation of the apostles and prophets, Jesus Christ Himself being the chief cornerstone, 21 in whom the whole building, being fitted together, grows into a holy temple in the Lord, 22 in whom you also are being built together for a dwelling place of God in the Spirit."

Jesus is the Rock, whereupon the believer stands and is built as the church. If we fail to stand upon this rock, we shall experience that our entire life will collapse.

If we build our foundation upon the true Rock of Jesus, and by doing so, walk in God's just and right ways to His Glory and for His Glory, so that the oppressed, downtrodden, abused, enslaved and mistreated may be set free by His love. There is one Truth, and Jesus is the Truth, and He is the Way and Life. There are no variations, differing opinions, or interpretations of the Truth. Jesus is the TRUTH. And all fullness – meaning all truth – is fulfilled in Him. The Law is fulfilled in Him. Jesus prayed in John 17:17 that we must be sanctified by the Word, which means we can only become holy and set apart when we apply the Word of God, which is the Truth. Jesus is also the Word that became Flesh. There are no shades to the truth, only the truth. We are called to worship in Spirit and Truth.

If we walk not in the Truth, where is the Spirit then in our life? If we walk in our truth, then this speaks of a lack of submission to God's will and ways. This then implies rebellion, and rebellion is like the sin of witchcraft. Jesus is the TRUTH, and He came to teach and show us all TRUTH, not part of it, not a portion, but all of it. When we follow God completely and wholeheartedly, then we follow God and His Truth. The answer to everything is Jesus, the Son of the Living God. His pure love for us and our pure love for Him is all that is important, and it is all that matters. For millennia, the world has been led away from Jesus by following many different other voices, so many different paths, so many false ways, and so many false shepherds. Jesus is the only Voice that we must listen to, He is the only Way, He is the only Shepherd, and He is the only answer and the only way to the throne room of God the Father.

It should be noted that when the Lord teaches about the house built upon a rock, we have to take note that the house is not immune to any storm, wind or rain. Yes, even this house is vulnerable to the elements. The only difference between the house built on the rock and the house built on sand is that one will completely collapse. There is the notion that disciples will be spared from trials and tribulations. Consider Paul, who endured multiple hardships (2 Corinthians 11), but he endured until the end because his life was built upon the rock of Jesus. Too often, disciples want the simple life, but we are called to be a light in the darkness (therefore, we are surrounded by darkness), to be the salt when the world has chosen wickedness and to endure in times of persecution.

Disciples of the Lord are not immune to this world. They are not immune to its storms. The disciples in the boat realised this reality when the storm waged around them, and so in fear cried out to Jesus to help them. And with one word, the Master had calmed the waves. Yes, we are not immune to the ups and downs. Jesus may have died for our trespasses and secured our healing, but the reality is that believers are not gods or super-humans, merely vessels of flesh and blood trying to be worthy vessels of His majesty. King Solomon understood the truth that the sun shines on both the wicked and the good when writing Ecclesiastes. Many times it seems God does not care or has abandoned us when the storm hits and when the wind blows, but eventually, those who remain in the

Lord will remain standing while those who continue in their evil ways will be toppled.

This is the crux of David's message in "Psalm 1: Blessed is the man who walks not in the counsel of the ungodly, Nor stands in the path of sinners, Nor sits in the seat of the scornful; 2 But his delight is in the law of the Lord, and in His law, he meditates day and night. 3 He shall be like a tree planted by the rivers of water, That brings forth its fruit in its season, whose leaf also shall not wither; And whatever he does shall prosper."

Psalm 1 speaks of a tree that is planted, which speaks of a system of being rooted, which is the same as being grounded on the Rock. A tree will not topple when the roots are healthy and strong, meaning we as His disciples will endure the rain and the wind, but we shall not topple if we are grounded and rooted in His Presence. After all, we shall be known for our roots, meaning those who truly serve the Lord are those who obey Him and have submitted to His ways, truth and life. Such disciples walk in the Spirit (Romans 8, Galatians 5), thus manifesting the fruits of the Spirit, and they avoid evil and walking in the carnal nature of the flesh. Those who are grounded in Jesus truly find they are a new creation by His strength and might.

The Lord calls us to walk in His ways and in His Truth and in His Life, which means following Jesus, who is the Truth, Way and Life. David, the author of this psalm, reminds us that if we indeed walk in the ways of our Lord, then we will be fruitful and we will prosper. If we thus remain in Jesus (John 15), meaning grounded and rooted, we will bear much fruit and will grow in strength and maturity and in spiritual fortitude. It says in "3 John: 2 Beloved, I pray that you may prosper in every way and [that your body] may keep well, even as [I know] your soul keeps well and prospers."

John writes how he longs for believers to prosper in soul, body, and then ultimately in spirit. To prosper should be seen in the light of following Jesus and should be first regarded as a matter of the spiritual, then the natural. Jesus reminds us of this in Matthew 5 when He preaches about first seeking the kingdom of the Lord and His righteousness before the rest [material] will be added.

Thus, we are reminded in Psalm 1 and John 15 that if we abide and follow Jesus then we truly prosper first in spirit and then we will also grow in soul and body [natural, material]. To be planted by the streams is a reference to abiding in Jesus. John 7 says, "37 On the last and greatest day of the festival, Jesus stood and said in a loud voice, "Let anyone who is thirsty come to me and drink. 38 Whoever believes in me, as Scripture has said, rivers of living water will flow from within them." 39 By this he meant the Spirit, whom those who believed in him were later to receive. Up to that time the Spirit had not been given, since Jesus had not yet been glorified."

Jesus was speaking here about the great work of the Holy Spirit within a believer. But we have to remember God is one – even though expressed differently through the work of the Father, Son and Holy Spirit. Jesus said He needed to leave this earth so that the Comforter [Holy Spirit] may come and dwell within man. Thus, John 7 reminds us that if we truly follow The Triune God [who is ONE] by following the Spirit, abiding in Jesus and worshipping the Father, then living waters will truly flow out of us. And such living waters imply the life, light and love of the Lord. It implies healing [prosperity], it implies glory, and it implies eternal hope that flows within us.

And this is what it means according to Psalm 1 to be planted by the river – it means planted in the Lord [who is the giver of the waters of life] so that we may be nourished by Him for us to grow, prosper and mature spiritually and then in the body and the soul. Nothing can grow without water, and just so we cannot grow without the indwelling presence of God [The Holy Spirit]. We cannot grow spiritually unless the Spirit of the Lord dwells within and changes us.

We read in "Revelation 21: 6 And He said to me, "It is done! I am the Alpha and the Omega, the Beginning and the End. I will give of the fountain of the water of life freely to him who thirsts. 7 He who overcomes shall inherit all things, and I will be his God and he shall be My son. 8 But the cowardly, unbelieving, abominable, murderers, sexually immoral, sorcerers, idolaters, and all liars shall have their part in the lake which burns with fire and brimstone, which is the second death." Indeed, when we abide in the Lord, there is abundance, hope and joy!

We see in the Old Testament how the nation of Israel was often referred to as being 'nourished' by God's Presence [Water]. God provided water out of a rock when they entered the wilderness, and so the Lord provides spiritual and physical nourishment and sustenance to those who seek and serve Him, no matter their circumstances. But we also see how once Israel turned away from Him, that 'water' turned dry.

In John 17, we are reminded we are not of the world but in the world. It means while we are not immune to the storms of the world as we are IN this world, we find our strength, help, and deliverance come not from the world but God. So the house in Matthew 7 is a house that remains in the world, but it shall not be toppled because it is built upon a rock that is not of this world! Now, also understand the wonderful truth of "Hebrews 6:20: This hope we have as an anchor of the soul, both sure and steadfast, and which enters the Presence behind the veil, here the forerunner has entered for us, even Jesus, having become High Priest forever according to the order of Melchizedek."

Praise God! Jesus, the Lamb who was slain before the foundation of the world and who has paid the price for our sins and who has conquered death, is indeed forever the ANCHOR of our soul and the hope of our glory (Colossians 1:27). He is the one who has made a way for us to be in a relationship with divinity, and to become sons and daughters of the eternal King. He is forever our hope, for He shall forever endure and He shall forever sit on the throne!

Of this eternal King, it is also written in "Hebrews 4: 14-16: Seeing then that we have a great High Priest who has passed through the heavens, Jesus the Son of God, let us hold fast our confession. We do not have a High Priest who cannot sympathise with our weaknesses but be in all points tempted as we are, yet without sin. Let us, therefore, come boldly to the throne of grace, that we may obtain mercy and find grace to help in time of need." We are called to hold onto Jesus, who is our anchor and our hope in times of storms, trials and tribulations. And we can trust Him, and have faith in His ways, because we have a High Priest who can sympathise with our weaknesses, and who was in all points tempted as we are, yet without sin. Glory to God!

It should be noted that hundreds of years ago, an anchor was a large rock or a stone. So when we read of Jesus being the anchor 2000 years ago, we think of an anchor as being a stone, just as Jesus is our Rock and the Capstone of the Kingdom on earth. He is the Stone according to the prophet Daniel that will eventually smash all kingdoms apart. The beauty of an anchor is that a sailor on a ship does not have to worry about the anchor doing its job. An anchor will do what an anchor has been designed to do. A sailor will not now and then jump in the water to check on the anchor. The sailor can therefore rest in the knowledge that the anchor will keep the ship secure and safe when the storms come. This is how it is with Jesus being our anchor. We can rest in the truth that He will keep us safe, secure and rooted no matter how circumstances and situations. We do not have to question Him and wonder if He will keep us anchored. He is God. We just need to trust and have faith in Him.

We can also apply the image of a ship to the image of the house. Just like a house being vulnerable to the elements, any ship is vulnerable to storms. Yet, the ship will remain grounded and will survive a shipwreck because of the anchor. Let us hold onto the anchor of Jesus! But it is also important to be reminded of John 15 when Jesus said that we need to abide in Him so that we may abide in Him. An anchor can only do its work if it remains fastened to the ship or boat. Jesus can only be our Lord, King, Master and Saviour when we are built upon Him so that we are anchored by His Almighty Glory.

Matthew 7 also reminds us that it is wise when you not only know the teachings and commands of the Lord but also follow them. This calls for obedience and faithfulness. In churches across the world, the importance of obedience unto the Lord has been watered down by erroneous teaching on hyper-grace, the exaggerated yet also false emphasis on legalism and the complete dismissal of God's law and order. For the Lord Himself said those who love Him will obey Him (John 14:23).

It is wise to hold onto Jesus no matter what life throws at us. It is wise to trust in Him and not this world. Paul reminds us in 1 Corinthians 1 that the Lord brings low the wisdom of the world, yet those who are truly wise will place their hope and faith in the cross. Indeed, if we wish to survive this world and its storms, we need to be wise by staying faithful to the Lord and building our lives upon His wisdom, teachings and commandments. If we obey Him, we shall remain grounded and anchored, even when it seems everything around us falls apart.

We after all walk by faith and not by sight (2 Corinthians 5:7). We are called to completely surrender unto Him for then, as Psalms 91, states we shall find our rest under the shadow of His wing.

For those who walk by Spirit and Truth, shall know the truth of Psalm 37 when David wrote: "The Lord knows the days of the upright, And their inheritance shall be forever. 19 They shall not be ashamed in the evil time, and in the days of famine, they shall be satisfied. 20 But the wicked shall perish; And the enemies of the Lord, like the splendor of the meadows, shall vanish. Into smoke they shall vanish away. "

Indeed, let us be wise and not foolish, for indeed we live in foolish times, by building upon the rock of Jesus and trusting our ways to Him. Only the foolish abandon the ways of God and seek their path and truth. For indeed, it does rain on the righteous and the unrighteous, but our Lord returns soon, and I will want to be found on the Rock that never moves, and I shall strive to be found by His side when my name is called at the separation of the sheep and the goats.

A time like this of many storms – natural and supernatural - calls for wisdom and not for foolishness, otherwise, we shall drown in the flood of iniquity, darkness and chaos. And for those who walk in the Lord's wisdom, as mentioned in Matthew 7, will truly walk in authority, for such wisdom is not based on religion but a true and personal relationship with our Lord Jesus.

The growth of the tree is also like the metamorphosis of a caterpillar. The caterpillar is doomed to a life on the ground if it is freed from its struggle inside a cocoon prematurely. The struggle in the cocoon is what gives the future butterfly the wing power to fly. Just so, our spiritual growth towards maturity calls for constant refinement, purification, dying to the self (mortification) and abandonment unto God as we lay down the old man. This process is called working out our salvation with fear and trembling. This is not an easy process, and it is one of constant struggle and wrestling with oneself and with God, but with determination and dedication, as we deny the Self we then become rooted in God, and we break free from the old man once and for all at the right time to walk in the liberty of the Spirit. For the spiritually mature, Isaiah 40 becomes a reality: 31 But those who wait on the Lord shall renew their strength; they shall mount up with wings like eagles, they shall run and not be weary, they shall walk and not faint.

The principle of growth we also find in "Mark 4: The Parable of the Growing Seed: 26 And He said, "The kingdom of God is as if a man should scatter seed on the ground, 27 and should sleep by night and rise by day, and the seed should sprout and grow, he himself does not know how. 28 For the earth yields crops by itself: first the blade, then the head, after that the full grain in the head."

In 2 Peter 1, Peter reminds us that as we grow into spiritual maturity, we "will be neither barren nor unfruitful in the knowledge of our Lord Jesus Christ". And in this knowledge of the Lord, we continue in our growth into maturity. The author of the Book of Hebrews also wrote on the "Peril of Not Progressing" in chapter 6: "1 Therefore, leaving the discussion of the elementary principles of Christ, let us go on to perfection, not laying again the foundation of repentance from dead works and of faith toward God, 2 of the doctrine of baptisms, of laying on of hands, of resurrection of the dead, and of eternal judgment. 3 And this we will do if God permits. 4 For it is impossible for those who were once enlightened, and have tasted the heavenly gift, and have become partakers of the Holy Spirit, 5 and have tasted the good word of God and the powers of the age to come, 6 if they fall away, to renew them again to repentance, since they crucify again for themselves the Son of God, and put Him to an open shame."

Take note, the author, most likely Luke, calls the believers to GO ON to perfection, not laying again the foundation which should have been laid in the first years of our spiritual growth. Indeed, a time should arrive when the believer is strong in the foundation of faith, can now grow, can expand and can be of service to the Kingdom to the Glory of God. Let us then make sure we grow spiritually into mature through our primary fellowship with God, as we become worshippers in spirit and truth. For we shall walk as children of the Living Lord, not going astray, not being deceived, but being led by the Spirit in wisdom, knowledge, counsel, understanding and power.

Just as we are called to be rooted in Christ to bear fruit to the glory of God, just so we must uproot all and everything that stands against God's Kingdom and God's truth and ways. Therefore, uproot what prevents us from carrying the fruits of God.

To Jeremiah, it was said in chapter 1: "See, I have appointed you this day over the nations and over the kingdoms, To uproot and break down, To destroy and to overthrow, To build and to plant." This reminds of "2 Corinthians 10: 4 The weapons of our warfare are not physical [weapons of flesh and blood]. Our weapons are divinely powerful for the destruction of fortresses. 5 We are destroying sophisticated arguments and every exalted and proud thing that sets itself up against the [true] knowledge of God, and we are taking every thought and purpose captive to the obedience of Christ, 6 being ready to punish every act of disobedience, when your own obedience [as a church] is complete."

A life dedicated to God is a call to uproot what is unholy, immoral, unjust and untrue in our lives. It is a call to cast down those things and words and ideas and doctrines that have set themselves up against the Kingdom of God. It is a call to identify all that is false, treacherous, divisive and idolatrous that prevents us from carrying fruit to the glory of God.

Let us be reminded that our lives are caught up in the war between the Kingdom of Light and the kingdom of darkness. Warfare implies strategy, and it implies a certain plan of action to defeat the enemy. Our strategy as the children of God is to lead people to the Lord, to the cross and to the Covenant. The devil wants this world to bow before all kinds of false altars, idols, gods, lies and wickedness. Throughout the Old Testament, we see this constant struggle between the Kingdom of Light and the kingdom of darkness playing out, as God's servants erected altars in honour of the true King while the worshippers of the 'false gods' also erected their altars and idols. There are also at times instances when altars are broken down as a declaration of war.

It says in "1 Corinthians 3: 12 But if anyone builds on the foundation with gold, silver, precious stones, wood, hay, straw, 13 each one's work will be clearly shown [for what it is]; for the day [of judgment] will disclose it, because it is to be revealed with fire, and the fire will test the quality and character and worth of each person's work. 14 If any person's work which he has built [on this foundation, that is, any outcome of his effort] remains [and survives this test], he will receive a reward. 15 But if any person's work is burned up [by the test], he will suffer the loss [of his reward]; yet he himself will be saved, but only as [one who has barely escaped] through fire."

Galatians 6:7 (Amplified Bible) says: "Do not be deceived and deluded and misled; God will not allow Himself to be sneered at (scorned, disdained, or mocked by mere pretensions or professions, or by His precepts being set aside.) [He inevitably deludes himself who attempts to delude God.] For whatever a man sows that and that only is what he will reap."

2 Chronicles 33: 10 The LORD spoke to Manasseh and his people, but they paid no attention. 11 So the LORD brought against them the army commanders of the king of Assyria, who took Manasseh prisoner, put a hook in his nose, bound him with bronze shackles and took him to Babylon. 12 In his distress he sought the favor of the LORD his God and humbled himself greatly before the God of his ancestors. 13 And when he prayed to him, the LORD was moved by his entreaty and listened to his

plea; so he brought him back to Jerusalem and to his kingdom. Then Manasseh knew that the LORD is God." We read in the chronicles that Manasseh was a man who "did evil in the eyes of the Lord, following the detestable practices of the nations the Lord had driven out before the Israelites." We, therefore, find a king who was following in the ways of darkness and corruption. He was thus spiritually alienated from God, paying no attention to the Lord.

Manasseh's rebellion against the Lord came to a grinding halt when the Lord brought Assyria to his doorstep. And in that moment of distress, Manasseh cried out to God, and his pride was brought low and the Lord showed him favour. We find here a fulfilment of the Scriptures of Matthew 23:12 which says "For those who exalt themselves will be humbled, and those who humble themselves will be exalted". Indeed, Manasseh humbled himself and so the Lord exalted him by bringing him back to Jerusalem.

We read an astonishingly beautiful yet powerful word of testimony – "Then Manasseh knew that the LORD is God." Manasseh, who had defied God, who had resisted His reign, who had provoked God, and who was saturated with spiritual darkness, came to a point in his life where he could testify and declare who God is, thus who the Great I AM is. What a turnaround! What a spiritual rebirth!

And why did this happen? From his days of terror and anxiety until the days of his spiritual awakening, Manasseh endured a spiritual realisation. His prayers were answered, for he humbled himself. Manasseh had a true meeting with God. And in that encounter between God and man, Manasseh realised without a doubt who God is and who he is. Manasseh may have been king, but God is the King of kings and the Lord of lords. And how else for Manasseh not to bow down before God after receiving such a revelation – how else for Manasseh to forego his wayward ways and seek and pursue the Lord for he had a deep and profound understanding of who God is!

And what is the outcome of this realisation? "14 Afterward he rebuilt the outer wall of the City of David, west of the Gihon spring in the valley, as far as the entrance of the Fish Gate and encircling the hill of Ophel; he also made it much higher. He stationed military commanders in all the fortified cities in Judah. 15 He got rid of the foreign gods and removed the image from the temple of the LORD, as well as all the altars he had built on the temple hill and in Jerusalem; and he threw them out of the city. 16 Then he restored the altar of the LORD and sacrificed fellowship offerings and thank offerings on it, and told Judah to serve the LORD, the God of Israel." Manasseh now sought to serve the Lord; all because he came at a point in his life that he knew who the Great I AM is!

We can only truly abide in God to bear fruit when we come to a point of deep repentance, of seeking the Lord, of seeking His Truth, His Kingdom and Way. One of the greatest reformations is found in 2 Kings 22 and 23 during Josiah's reign. Revival and restoration were sparked because the Lord's house was rebuilt, the law was discovered, judges were called to confirm the truth and the law, there was then repentance among the entire nation, then the covenant was renewed, and then the idols and false altars were destroyed, and then God returned in His glory. It is about the Covenant with God, walking again in His Truth, His Way and Spirit. But it is also about destroying everything, firstly in our own lives, which are not from God (uprooting and breaking the false altars) and then being true watchmen to cry out against the false altars amid the Church.

In 2 Kings 11, we read of how a young Joash came to sit on the throne and the fall of the wicked Athaliah, Queen of Judah. Before Joash took the throne, the priest Jehoiada made a covenant between the Lord, the king, and the people, that they would be the Lord's people (verse 17). We also read "18 Then all the people of the land went to the house of Baal and tore it down. They utterly smashed his altar and his images to pieces, and they put Mattan the priest of Baal to death in front of the altars."

As with Josiah, we find Jehoiada taking the same course of action – the utter destruction of the false altars and the destruction of all things that stood against God. Therefore, the action was taken against the open rebellion, apostasy and the schemes of the devil. Yes, in the days of Josiah and Jehoiada, all things unholy were smashed and destroyed.

We also need to destroy every unholy stronghold and every idol and every false altar if we wish to truly see God's face. We need to take a stand against all things – word or deed or action or structure – firstly in our own lives and corporally in our midst if we wish to truly walk in God's glory again. Such action follows restoring the altar, which means recommitting to the Lord, to His Covenant and His Truth.

We also read of such a decree against in 2 Chronicles 29 when Hezekiah succeeded Ahaz in Judah. He also reconfirmed the Covenant with the Lord and called for the consecrating of the priests and the house of the Lord. We then read from verse 15, "They gathered their brothers (fellow Levites) together, consecrated themselves, and went in to cleanse the house of the Lord, as the king had commanded by the words of the Lord. 16 The priests went into the inner part of the house of the Lord to cleanse it, and every unclean thing they found in the temple of the Lord they brought out to the courtyard of the Lord's house. Then the Levites received it to take out to the Kidron Valley [for disposal]. 17 Now they began the consecration on the first [day] of the first month, and on the eighth day of the month they came to the porch of the Lord. Then for eight days they consecrated the house of the

Lord, and on the sixteenth day of the first month they finished. 18 Then they went inside to King Hezekiah and said, "We have cleansed the entire house (temple) of the Lord, the altar of burnt offering with all of its utensils, and the table of showbread with all its utensils."

Hezekiah restored Temple worship, and then we read in verse 27 that he gave the order to offer the burnt offering on the altar (therefore, the restoration of the altar). And when the burnt offering began, the song to the Lord also began with the trumpets accompanied by the instruments of David, king of Israel. "28 The entire congregation worshiped, the singers also sang, and the trumpets sounded; all this continued until the burnt offering was finished.29 When the burnt offerings were completed, the king and all who were present with him bowed down and worshiped [God]. 30 Also King Hezekiah and the officials ordered the Levites to exclaim praises to the Lord with the words of David and of Asaph the seer. And they exclaimed praises with joy, and bowed down and worshiped."

Note how the people BOWED DOWN and worshipped. True worship is one of love and devotion, but also submission and sacrifice to the true King. As with Josiah and Jehoiada, Hezekiah focused on cleansing and consecrating God's Temple, on the Covenant, on worship, and on uprooting everything evil and unholy. Just so, we need to first restore the altar within ourselves, for we are the temple of the Lord. We need to first make sure we are consecrated and cleansed. Secondly, we need to corporately make sure the Church of the Lord (His Bride) is consecrated and cleansed once again from all defilement, impurities, idolatry and uncleanliness. Ephesians 5: 26 so that He might sanctify the church, having cleansed her by the washing of water with the word [of God], 27 so that [in turn] He might present the church to Himself in glorious splendor, without spot or wrinkle or any such thing; but that she would be holy [set apart for God] and blameless.

It is time again for all that offends God to be uprooted. It is time again for true and real repentance in our hearts and in gatherings where the believers meet. Let our repentance be a fulfilment of "Joel 2: 17 Let the priests, those who serve the LORD, weep from the vestibule all the way back to the altar. Let them say, "Have pity, O LORD, on your people; please do not turn over your inheritance to be mocked, to become a proverb among the nations. Why should it be said among the peoples, "Where is their God?"

In Joel 2, we find the priests weeping from one end of the temple to the other, pleading with the Lord to spare the people of Judah during a time of distress. This is just a way of emphasising the weeping in the temple. May there be such corporate weeping and repentance once again! It is time for us to repent and be converted into a praying priesthood that will destroy and uproot the false idols and altars. It is time to travail for the lost who are on the highway to hell! It is time for us to weep between the porch and the altar!

We need a revival of holiness, a revival of character, and a revival of people who are utterly selfless and prepared to lay their lives on the altar for God. Lord, send the fire because we need another Pentecost! For then we shall remain standing in the end times of great dangers and depravity!

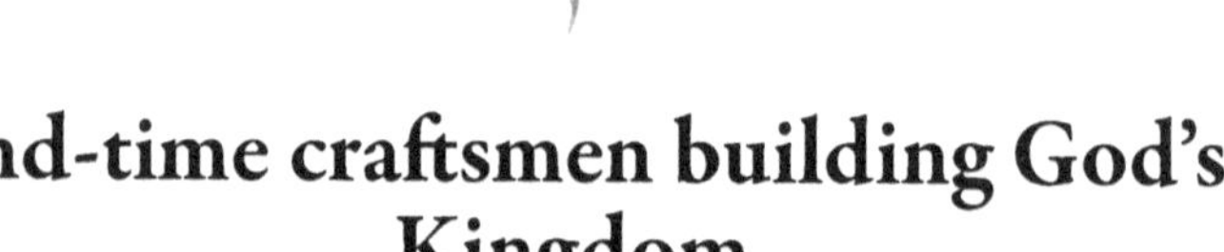

End-time craftsmen building God's Kingdom

A craftsman is defined as a worker skilled in a particular craft. A craft is any kind of activity involving skills in making things by hand. It is your skill (s). Consider that every person on earth is a craftsman in some way or another – either we are building God's Kingdom or we are working on building the kingdom of darkness (even the agnostics and atheists are fuelling the devil's agenda).

In the Old Testament, we read how God called certain craftsmen to build first the tabernacle in the time of Moses and then the temple in the time of Solomon. We read in "Exodus 35: 30 And Moses said to the children of Israel, "See, the Lord has called by name Bezalel the son of Uri, the son of Hur, of the tribe of Judah; 31 and He has filled him with the Spirit of God, in wisdom and understanding, in knowledge and all manner of workmanship, 32 to design artistic works, to work in gold and silver and bronze, 33 in cutting jewels for setting, in carving wood, and to work in all manner of artistic workmanship.", 34 "And He has put in his heart the ability to teach, in him and Aholiab the son of Ahisamach, of the tribe of Dan. 35 He has filled them with skill to do all manner of work of the engraver and the designer and the tapestry maker, in blue, purple, and scarlet thread, and fine linen, and of the weaver—those who do every work and those who design artistic works." And chapter 34, "1And Bezalel and Aholiab, and every gifted artisan in whom the Lord has put wisdom and understanding, to know how to do all manner of work for the service of the sanctuary, shall do according to all that the Lord has commanded."

In 1 Kings 7, we read, "13 Now King Solomon sent and brought Huram from Tyre. 14 He was the son of a widow from the tribe of Naphtali, and his father was a man of Tyre, a bronze worker; he was filled with wisdom, understanding and skill in working with all kinds of bronze work. So he came to King Solomon and did all his work."

We also read of the craftsman in "2 Chronicles 34: "1 Josiah was eight years old when he became king, and he reigned thirty-one years in Jerusalem. 2 And he did what was right in the sight of the Lord, and walked in the ways of his father David; he did not turn aside to the right hand or to the left. 8 In the eighteenth year of his reign, when he had purged the land and the temple, he sent Shaphan the son of Azaliah, Maaseiah the governor of the city, and Joah the son of Joahaz the recorder, to repair the house of the Lord his God. 9 When they came to Hilkiah the high priest, they delivered the money that was brought into the house of God, which the Levites who kept the doors had gathered from the hand of Manasseh and Ephraim, from all the remnant of Israel, from all Judah and Benjamin, and which they had brought back to Jerusalem. 10 Then they put it in the hand of the foremen who had the oversight of the house of the Lord; and they gave it to the workmen who worked in the house of the Lord, to repair and restore the house. 11 They gave it to the craftsmen and builders to buy hewn stone and timber for beams, and to floor the houses which the kings of Judah had destroyed."

We need to realise we are called to be craftsmen in God's Kingdom. God has empowered His children with skills, talents, abilities and spiritual gifts to build His Kingdom. None of us is worthless or useless, for we have all been created by God for a purpose. 1 Corinthians 12 says, "4 There are different kinds of gifts, but the same Spirit distributes them. 5 There are different kinds of service, but the same Lord. 6 There are different kinds of working, but in all of them and in everyone it is the same God at work. 12 Just as a body, though one, has many parts, but all its many parts form one body, so it is with Christ. 13 For we were all baptized by one Spirit so as to form one body—whether Jews or Gentiles, slave or free—and we were all given the one Spirit to drink. 14 Even so the body is not made up of one part but of many." At the end of times, God is calling His children to be true to their "craft", therefore, their abilities and talents as led by the Spirit of God. They must be true to their calling and mandate.

In Acts 6 we read, "1 Now in those days, when the number of the disciples was multiplying, there arose a complaint against the Hebrews by the Hellenists, because their widows were neglected in the daily distribution. 2 Then the twelve summoned the multitude of the disciples and said, "It is not desirable that we should leave the word of God and serve tables. 3 Therefore, brethren, seek out from among you seven men of good reputation, full of the Holy Spirit and wisdom, whom we may appoint over this business; 4 but we will give ourselves continually to prayer and to the ministry of the word." 5 And the saying pleased the whole multitude. And they chose Stephen, a man full of faith and the Holy Spirit."

Stephen was called to be a craftsman of serving tables! But he did so willingly, and because he stayed true to God and the craft he was appointed to oversee, we read: "8 Now Stephen, a man full of God's grace and power, performed great wonders and signs among the people. 9 Opposition arose, however, from members of the Synagogue of the Freedmen (as it was called)—Jews of Cyrene and Alexandria as well as the provinces of Cilicia and Asia—who began to argue with Stephen. 10 But they could not stand up against the wisdom the Spirit gave him as he spoke."

We read in Acts 7 how Stephen testified to God's greatness and goodness. "54 When the members of the Sanhedrin heard this, they were furious and gnashed their teeth at him. 55 But Stephen, full of the Holy Spirit, looked up to heaven and saw the glory of God, and Jesus standing at the right hand of God. 56 "Look," he said, "I see heaven open and the Son of Man standing at the right hand of God." What a testimony! Because of Stephen's faithfulness to God, he was used powerfully as a servant in his own unique way to glorify God.

Take note that Stephen was full of the Spirit of God. He was willing to play His part in expanding God's Kingdom, even if it meant attending tables. In Exodus 35, we read how Bezalel was filled with the Spirit of God, in wisdom and understanding. It doesn't matter what craft (s) we are called to be faithful to; we remain disciples of God, and we must labour in God's Kingdom in the excellence of the Spirit of God. We are called to expand God's Kingdom in these end times, and we must do so led by the Spirit of God in all wisdom and understanding.

The reality is, we can either labour for God or labour for the world. It says in "Deuteronomy 27:15 Cursed is the one who makes a carved or molded image, an abomination to the Lord, the work of the hands of the craftsman, and sets it up in secret.' "And all the people shall answer and say, 'Amen!'" Also, read Isaiah 44 about the foolishness of idolatry and the rebellion of crafting idols. Yes, so many people are busy 'crafting' the devil's kingdom through their rebellion and foolishness!

In 2 Kings 24, we read, "14 Also he carried into captivity all Jerusalem: all the captains and all the mighty men of valor, ten thousand captives, and all the craftsmen and smiths. None remained except the poorest people of the land. 16 All the valiant men, seven thousand, and craftsmen and smiths, one thousand, all who were strong and fit for war, these the king of Babylon brought captive to Babylon." Why was the craftsman carried away? Because then they cannot build, construct, or design. They had taken away the power of restoration! Still today, the devil is targeting the children of God to make sure that they do not live out their true potential in Christ! The devil is keeping the children of God distracted and occupied with worldly or selfish agendas. This is a strategy so that we fail in our endeavours to build the Kingdom of God!

2 Timothy 3 speaks of the end times, where people become lovers of the Self. This is the agenda of the devil, so that people focus on themselves instead of the greater and eternal picture. This is especially true in the churches, where believers are "crafting" their own kingdoms (working on their careers, for example) instead of building the Kingdom of God. Israel was equally guilty of such a selfish attitude after the exile, for they were so busy living for themselves that God's House (His Temple) remained in ruins. We read in "Haggai 1: 4 "Is it a time for you yourselves to be living in your paneled houses, while this house remains a ruin?" 5 Now this is what the Lord Almighty says: "Give careful thought to your ways. 6 You have planted much, but harvested little. You eat, but never have enough. You drink, but never have your fill. You put on clothes, but are not warm. You earn wages, only to put them in a purse with holes in it."

There is a blessing when we truly craft God's Kingdom. The end-time crafters will not be preoccupied with their kingdoms, needs or wants. They will be focused on God's Kingdom, and they will be sold out to glorify God in their God-given talents, abilities and skills. It is the message of Matthew 6:33 of first seeking God's Kingdom. His Kingdom is our highest priority. As a craftsman, we must lend our time, abilities and skills to help TOGETHER accomplish God's work on earth.

Revelation 18 says, "21 Then a mighty angel took up a stone like a great millstone and threw it into the sea, saying, "Thus with violence the great city Babylon shall be thrown down, and shall not be found anymore. 22 The sound of harpists, musicians, flutists, and trumpeters shall not be heard in you anymore. No craftsman of any craft shall be found in you anymore, and the sound of a millstone shall not be heard in you anymore." Take note, no "craftsman" was left behind. Again, Babylon will no longer be rebuilt or restored. No one will be able to craft to build the kingdom of darkness. It is done so that the eternal light may shine so bright.

2 Corinthians 11 again reminds us that many are working for another purpose or agenda, even in the church: "13 For such people are false apostles, deceitful workers, masquerading as apostles of Christ. 14 And no wonder, for Satan himself masquerades as an angel of light. 15 It is not surprising, then, if his servants also masquerade as servants of righteousness. Their end will be what their actions deserve." We must be aware of the craftsman who sows destruction in and outside the church. We need to become aware of those who seek to destroy and deceive, for their work shall account for nothing in the eyes of God.

God is the Creator and the Craftsman of all! It says in "Proverbs 8: 30 Then I was beside Him as a master craftsman; and I was daily His delight, Rejoicing always before Him, 31 Rejoicing in His inhabited world, and my delight was with the sons of men." As children of God, we are all workers (craftsmen) in His Kingdom. 2 Timothy 2 says, "15 Do your best to present yourself to God as one approved, a worker who does not need to be ashamed and who correctly handles the word of truth." What are we constructing? What are we doing with our God-given talents and abilities? We are called to yield to God as our Master Craftsman so that we may craft His Kingdom. This is especially true in such diabolical end times of strife, error and wickedness.

In Matthew 9:37, we read, "Then he said to his disciples, 'The harvest is plentiful but the workers are few." Jesus used a farming analogy to talk about how there are many people out there to be cared for and brought to God, but few people willing to go out there and do the work. Yes, many children are crafting their own kingdoms, not using their talents and spiritual gifts to build the Kingdom of God! This is indeed sad. This is also partly because we have failed to fulfil the Great Commission, therefore, making true disciples who will be able to serve God's glory and expand the Kingdom on earth. God is calling for an end-time remnant who will make disciples, who will lead people to Christ to be empowered in their craft (s) by the power of the Holy Spirit to build the Kingdom.

Yes, we are all called to be workers in God's House. Our work is to build the Kingdom of God in the hearts of man by declaring the Gospel and fulfilling Matthew 28. Romans 16:3 says, "Greet Priscilla and Aquila, my co-workers in Christ Jesus," while we read in "1 Corinthians 3:9 For we are co-workers in God's service; you are God's field, God's building."

In Zachariah 1 we read, "18 Then I raised my eyes and looked, and there were four horns. 19 And I said to the angel who talked with me, "What are these?" So he answered me, "These are the horns that have scattered Judah, Israel, and Jerusalem." 20 Then the Lord showed me four craftsmen. 21 And I said, "What are these coming to do?" So he said, "These are the horns that scattered Judah, so that no one could lift up his head; but the craftsmen are coming to terrify them, to cast out the horns of the nations that lifted up their horn against the land of Judah to scatter it."

If we study the prophecies and visions of Daniel, the four "powers" who had such an impact on Israel and the world were the Babylonians, Persians, Greeks and Romans. God spoke about four craftsmen, therefore, skilled in certain abilities, to bring down these powers. We know, for example, Cyrus the Persians defeated the Babylonians, while Alexander the Great of Greece defeated the Persians. Many people were involved in the demise of the Greek and Roman Empires, but clearly, God had certain individuals in mind. Just so, in these last days, God's craftsman will prove to be a huge challenge to the kingdom of darkness, for they shall shine the light of Christ and share the Gospel they leading many to Christ, therefore, out of captivity and slavery into freedom (for Christ has come to set the captives free).

In Daniel 2, we read, "31 "Your Majesty looked, and there before you stood a large statue—an enormous, dazzling statue, awesome in appearance. 32 The head of the statue was made of pure gold, its chest and arms of silver, its belly and thighs of bronze, 33 its legs of iron, its feet partly of iron and partly of baked clay. 34 While you were watching, a rock was cut out, but not by human hands. It struck the statue on its feet of iron and clay and smashed them. 35 Then the iron, the clay, the bronze, the silver and the gold were all broken to pieces and became like chaff on a threshing floor in the summer. The wind swept them away without leaving a trace. But the rock that struck the statue became a huge mountain and filled the whole earth." This was the vision of the four "powers", and how the Kingdom of God (the Rock) destroys them. Indeed, we are called to craft God's Kingdom, for this Rock shall stand forever and will bring all things evil and wicked to its knees. Yes, even the end of days Babylonian system of power shall fall!

End-time craftsman have been empowered by the Spirit and Word of God to tear down strongholds and darkness and to plan the kingdom of light into the hearts of man. Paul wrote of such spiritual warfare in 2 Corinthians 10 and Ephesians 6. As children of God, we need to be wise and listen to God in these last days. We must not be foolish. 1 Corinthians 3:19 warns, "For the wisdom of this world is foolishness with God. For it is written, "He catches the wise in their own craftiness." 2 Corinthians 4 says, "2 But we have renounced the hidden things of shame, not walking in craftiness nor handling the word of God deceitfully, but by manifestation of the truth commending ourselves to every man's conscience in the sight of God."

We need to work to God's glory and stay on track regarding our calling and mandate. We must yield and submit to God, lest we are also deceived. Ephesians 4:14 says, "that we should no longer be children, tossed to and fro and carried about with every wind of doctrine, by the trickery of men, in the cunning craftiness of deceitful plotting,"

A disciple of God must cultivate a spirit of excellence. Thus the quality of being outstanding in our craft (s). But such a spirit of excellence is not as a result of man's sole endeavour, neither does it mean a pursuit of lofty education or wealth, but it simply means a life which is dedicated to the pursuit of serving and following an excellent God.

Exodus 15:7: And in the greatness of Your excellence You have overthrown those who rose against You; You sent forth Your wrath; It consumed them like stubble" and also "Psalm 68:34: Ascribe strength to God; His excellence is over Israel, and His strength is in the clouds." There are many ways to describe God and the goodness of God, but one of them is that we serve an excellent God. He is outstanding in all He does, for just look at creation. He has made man excellent in the way we function, think and feel. The excellence of God is all around us. And as we have been made in His image, we are surely called to pursue such excellence, which comes as a result of a life being led by the Spirit of the living God. In all things that we do as disciples, be it our conduct, be it in our daily actions, it must be excellent in the sense that it glorifies God and brings Him praise and worship.

We are reminded in 2 Corinthians 5:20 that we are Christ's ambassadors on earth. We thus represent His Kingdom. We are called to craft to His Glory, and we must do so in excellence! We represent His excellence on earth. We are called to be carriers of His Presence, thus carriers of His excellence. The world must see Christ in us, thus see we serve an excellent God who is outstanding in His grace, mercy and goodness.

We must be a workman (craftsmen) of excellence approved by God in our actions, how we carry ourselves and how we represent the Kingdom. It says in "Romans 14:17 For the kingdom of God is not a matter of eating and drinking, but of righteousness, peace and joy in the Holy Spirit." A workman in pursuit of God's excellence is in pursuit of the Kingdom (Matthew 6:33), and such a kingdom is not focused on the tangible, but on God's values of righteousness and peace. It is centred on a life led and driven and guided by the excellence of the Spirit of the Lord.

Jesus says in John 15:19, "You are not of the world, but I chose you out of the world." Titus 2:13-14 expands on that thought, saying, "Christ Jesus, who gave Himself for us to redeem us from every lawless deed, and to purify for Himself a people for His own possession, zealous for good deeds." Thus, 1 Peter 2:9 reminds us, "you are a chosen race, a royal priesthood, a HOLY NATION, a people for God's own possession." The concept that we are God's own possession should make us reflect on the fact that living under the New Covenant, we are the temple of God (1 Corinthians 3:16-17). We must therefore pursue excellence.

If we desire God's presence in our lives, we must practice moral excellence. For it says in James 4:8, "Draw near to God and He will draw near to you. Cleanse your hands, you sinners; and purify your hearts, you double-minded." We can only be useful to God in furthering His cause as we practice moral excellence. Jesus teaches in Matthew 5:13-14, 16, "You are the salt of the earth; but if the salt has become tasteless, how can it be made salty again? It is no longer good for anything, except to be thrown out and trampled underfoot by men....You are the light of the world.

A city set on a hill cannot be hidden; Let your light shine before men in such a way that they may see your good works, and glorify your Father who is in heaven." And, finally, in Philippians 2:15-16, we read, "prove yourselves to be blameless and innocent, children of God above reproach in the midst of a crooked and perverse generation, among whom you appear as lights in the world, holding fast the word of life."

The Apostle Paul commands us in Romans 12:2, "do not be conformed to this world, but be transformed by the renewing of your mind, so that you may prove what the will of God is, that which is good and acceptable and perfect." A life of excellence needs to be pursued and cultivated, thus a daily action of intent just as we need to renew our minds. It also says in Proverbs 4:23, "Above all else, guard your heart, for it is the well-spring of life." We need to guard our hearts and minds against pollution so that we walk in excellence. It also says in "Philippians 4:8: Finally, brethren, whatever things are true, whatever things are noble, whatever things are just, whatever things are pure, whatever things are lovely, whatever things are of good report, if there is any virtue and if there is anything praiseworthy—meditate on these things."

You see, it doesn't matter what we are called to do (craft), it must be done in excellence. Of Daniel we read in "Daniel 6: 3 Then this Daniel distinguished himself above the governors and satraps, because an excellent spirit was in him; and the king gave thought to setting him over the whole realm." If we seek and serve God, and we pursue excellence, we shall surely be distinguished and find favour with God and man.

Excellence comes from a life in the Spirit and seeking God's wisdom and truth. It says in "Ecclesiastes 7:12: For wisdom is a defense as money is a defense, but the excellence of knowledge is that wisdom gives life to those who have it." We also read of the value of wisdom in "Proverbs 2: My son, if you receive my words, and treasure my commands within you, 2 So that you incline your ear to wisdom, and apply your heart to understanding; 3 Yes, if you cry out for discernment, and lift up your voice for understanding, 4 If you seek her as silver, and search for her as for hidden treasures; 5 Then you will understand the fear of the Lord, and find the knowledge of God. 6 For the Lord gives wisdom; from His mouth come knowledge and understanding; 7 He stores up sound wisdom for the upright; He is a shield to those who walk uprightly; 8 He guards the paths of justice, and preserves the way of His saints. 9 Then you will understand righteousness and justice, equity and every good path."

Excellence thus comes from following God, and God's ways and His wisdom. Paul writes in "1 Corinthians 2:1: And I, brethren, when I came to you, did not come with excellence of speech or of wisdom, declaring to you the testimony of God." It is not about how great we sound or our levels or education or our intelligence, but it is all about a life dedicated to God, following the Spirit of God and a life of sanctification and obedience. For in God is the Truth and the Life to bring forth excellence.

We are thus called to first seek the Kingdom, for then we seek excellence. It is written in "2 Corinthians 4: 5 For we do not preach ourselves, but Christ Jesus the Lord, and ourselves your bondservants for Jesus' sake. 6 For it is the God who commanded the light to shine out of darkness, who has shone in our hearts to give the light of the knowledge of the glory of God in the face of Jesus Christ. 7 But we have this treasure in earthen vessels, that the excellence of the power may be of God and not of us. 8 We are hard-pressed on every side, yet not crushed; we are perplexed, but not in despair; 9 persecuted, but not forsaken; struck down, but not destroyed— 10 always carrying about in the body the dying of the Lord Jesus, that the life of Jesus also may be manifested in our body."

We have indeed been called to lead a life of excellence in the power of God, but it shall be the excellence of the power of God and not of man. It is the excellence of a workman approved by God. It is the power on High by the infilling of the Holy Spirit. It is the power to love, to forgive, to be morally excellent, and to seek righteousness and truth. It says in "Philippians 3:8: Yet indeed I also count all things loss for the excellence of the knowledge of Christ Jesus my Lord, for whom I have suffered the loss of all things, and count them as rubbish, that I may gain Christ." A pursuit of excellence is a pursuit of Jesus, in whom we find all the treasures of wisdom (Colossians 2:3).

We are called to pursue excellence in faith. James 2:14 says, "What does it profit, my brethren, if someone says he has faith but does not have works?" Excellent faith produces excellent works to the glory of God. Thus, works of servanthood and stewardship. It also says in 'Matthew 17:20: So Jesus said to them, "Because of your unbelief; for assuredly, I say to you, if you have faith as a mustard seed, you will say to this mountain, 'Move from here to there,' and it will move; and nothing will be impossible for you.' Excellent faith produces excellence in boldness to pursue and declare the Kingdom of God. Hebrews 11 is the great chapter on faith, for excellent faith produces excellence in resilience, in overcoming, in victory, and in trusting God daily for provision. Excellence in faith simply produces excellence in trust and hope.

We are called to pursue excellence in love. It says in "1 John 2: 15 Do not love the world or the things in the world. If anyone loves the world, the love of the Father is not in him. 16 For all that is in the world—the lust of the flesh, the lust of the eyes, and the pride of life—is not of the Father but is of the world. 17 And the world is passing away, and the lust of it; but he who does the will of God abides forever." And excellence in love produces an excellence in holiness and sanctification. It also says in the same chapter "9 he who says he is in the light, and hates his brother, is in darkness until now. 10 He who loves his brother abides in the light, and there is no cause for stumbling in him. 11 But he who hates his brother is in darkness and walks in darkness, and does not know where he is going, because the darkness has blinded his eyes." Excellence love produces excellent light, and by light, we shall no longer walk in darkness but in the illumination of truth and the liberty of the Spirit.

Ultimately, what we craft shall stand and be proven by God when it is done in the Spirit of excellence. Of this truth we read in "1 Corinthians 3: 10 By the grace God has given me, I laid a foundation as a wise builder, and someone else is building on it. But each one should build with care. 11 For no one can lay any foundation other than the one already laid, which is Jesus Christ. 12 If anyone builds on this foundation using gold, silver, costly stones, wood, hay or straw, 13 their work will be shown for what it is, because the Day will bring it to light. It will be revealed with fire, and the fire will test the quality of each person's work. 14 If what has been built survives, the builder will receive a reward. 15 If it is burned up, the builder will suffer loss but yet will be saved—even though only as one escaping through the flames."

Let us pursue excellence as craftsmen, therefore, as disciples of God. Let us be virtuous and morally excellent as we are led by the dictates of the Spirit (Romans 8). As worshippers in Spirit and truth, we shall glorify God, and may the world see His excellence shine brightly for all to see. May we build His excellent Kingdom in these end times of darkness and moral corruption, for then the light of His glory shall lead many home.

Walking in the place of God's purpose

Throughout Scripture, God not only works through people, but He also works through places, movements, journeys, seasons, and divine positioning. The Bible repeatedly reveals that geographical alignment can play a major role in spiritual identity, destiny, covenant, preparation, protection, and calling.

This is why the end-time remnant needs to remain in the will of God, so that we may be positioned to bring in the harvest in the end-time revival. God's will unlocks strategy, His power and authority. When we are properly aligned, we grow in our identity, purpose and active participation.

Alignment does not mean God is limited by geography, nor that holiness is attached to special locations in a mystical sense. God is sovereign everywhere. Yet Scripture clearly shows that there are moments when obedience to God requires movement — leaving one place and going to another — because certain assignments, encounters, growth, and covenant purposes unfold only in the place where God directs.

The journeys of Abraham and Jacob especially reveal this principle. One of the first major patterns in Scripture is this: God often reveals destiny progressively through movement and obedience. Abraham was not shown the entire plan immediately. He was first called to leave. God said to Abraham: "Go from your country, your people and your father's household to the land I will show you." Notice the command came before the full revelation, movement preceded manifestation, and obedience preceded inheritance. Abraham's destiny was connected to geographical obedience.

Had Abraham refused to move, he would not have entered covenant land, his descendants would not have inherited the promise, and the unfolding of redemptive history would have looked entirely different. This reveals a profound spiritual principle: Sometimes remaining where God has told you to leave delays what God intends to establish.

God uses places to shape people. Certain locations in Scripture became wildernesses of testing, mountains of revelation, deserts of purification, valleys of humility, and territories of inheritance. The issue was never the soil itself. The issue was what God intended to accomplish there.

Israel could not become a covenant people while remaining in Egypt. David could not become king while remaining only a shepherd in Bethlehem. The disciples could not fulfil their mission while remaining hidden behind locked doors. Movement became part of transformation.

Jacob's life is one of the clearest biblical examples showing how God uses journeys and locations to shape identity and destiny. Jacob's life can almost be mapped through spiritual geography. Each location represented transition, confrontation, revelation, transformation, or covenant advancement.

Jacob begins in the household of Isaac, but after deception and conflict with Esau, he is forced to leave. At first glance, this appears merely circumstantial. But spiritually, God was repositioning Jacob. Jacob could not remain who he was and become who God intended. The journey itself became part of the transformation. Many times, believers resist movement because familiarity feels safe, comfort feels secure, and the known feels controllable. But destiny often requires separation from what is familiar. God frequently disrupts comfort to establish a calling.

One of the most powerful moments in Jacob's journey occurs at Bethel. Jacob sleeps with a stone for a pillow and receives a heavenly vision: a ladder reaching heaven, angels ascending and descending, and God reaffirming covenant promises. Before this moment, Jacob was running. After this moment, Jacob became marked by encounter. Bethel became a place of revelation, divine alignment, covenant confirmation, and spiritual awakening. Jacob even declares, "Surely the Lord is in this place." This reveals an important truth: Sometimes God brings us into specific seasons and places because He intends to reveal Himself there in a deeper way.

Certain revelations in Jacob's life came only because he journeyed. Had he remained stationary, Bethel would never have happened. Jacob's years in Haran under Laban were difficult. He endured labor, deception, waiting, frustration, and endurance. Yet Haran became God's workshop. The deceiver himself was now being confronted and refined. Not every divinely appointed place feels pleasant. Some places are assigned for character formation, humility, endurance, wisdom, and purification.

Modern culture often assumes: "If it is difficult, it cannot be God." But Scripture repeatedly shows the opposite. God often sends His people into uncomfortable places to prepare them for greater responsibility. Moses had the wilderness. Joseph had prison. David had caves. Jacob had Haran. Geographical alignment is not always about comfort. It is about divine purpose.

Eventually God tells Jacob: "Return to the land of your fathers." Why? Because covenant destiny was tied to alignment with God's purposes. Jacob could not remain indefinitely in Haran. The season had changed. What was once preparation could become limitation if he stayed too long. This is another vital principle: Staying in a former season after God has called you onward can hinder destiny. Many believers understand entering seasons, but struggle to discern when God is calling them out of those seasons.

Before meeting Esau again, Jacob wrestles with God at Peniel. There Jacob is broken, renamed, and transformed. Jacob becomes Israel. This encounter happens in transit. He is between places, between identities, and between seasons. God often transforms people in transitional places. Peniel teaches that geographical movement can coincide with spiritual transformation. Jacob crossed over physically, but also spiritually.

His journey and its signifance can be summed as follows:

<u>Beersheba — The Beginning</u>

Jacob begins in the land of his father Isaac in Beersheba. After receiving Isaac's blessing and deceiving Esau, he is forced to flee because Esau seeks to kill him. Spiritual significance: separation from the old season, beginning of transformation, and departure into destiny.

<u>Bethel — The Place of Encounter</u>

On the journey northward, Jacob stops at Bethel and dreams of a ladder reaching heaven with angels ascending and descending. God confirms the covenant promises to him there. Spiritual significance: divine revelation, covenant confirmation, and awakening to God's presence. Jacob declares "Surely the Lord is in this place."

<u>Haran — The Place of Formation</u>

Jacob arrives in Haran, the land of his relatives, where he lives under Laban. Here he marries Leah and Rachel. He works many years, gains wealth, experiences deception, and grows spiritually. Spiritual significance: character refinement, humility and endurance, and preparation for leadership.

<u>Leaving Haran — Obedience to Return</u>

God tells Jacob to return to the land of his fathers. Jacob departs with his family and possessions, though tensions arise with

Laban during the departure. Spiritual significance: transition into a new season, obedience to God's direction, and leaving behind preparation for fulfilment.

<u>Mahanaim — Divine Protection</u>

As Jacob journeys homeward, angels of God meet him at Mahanaim. Spiritual significance: assurance of heavenly protection, and encouragement before confrontation.

<u>Peniel (Penuel) — The Place of Wrestling</u>

Before meeting Esau, Jacob wrestles through the night with a divine being. There his hip is touched, his name changes from Jacob to Israel, and he is transformed. Spiritual significance: breaking of self-reliance, identity transformation, and spiritual surrender and victory.

<u>Reunion with Esau</u>

Jacob meets Esau in fear, yet reconciliation unexpectedly takes place peacefully. Spiritual significance: restoration, God's faithfulness, and victory over past fear.

<u>Succoth and Shechem — Settling in the Land</u>

Jacob temporarily settles in Succoth and later near Shechem. Important events unfold there involving his family and covenant identity. Spiritual significance: transition and testing, challenges within covenant life.

<u>Return to Bethel — Renewal</u>

God calls Jacob back to Bethel. There, Jacob removes idols from his household, builds an altar, and renews covenant worship. Spiritual significance: spiritual cleansing, renewal of consecration, and returning to the first encounter.

<u>Bethlehem (Ephrath) — Sorrow and Legacy</u>

Rachel dies while giving birth to Benjamin near Bethlehem. Spiritual significance: pain amid promise, covenant legacy continuing through suffering.

<u>Hebron — Return to Isaac</u>

Jacob eventually returns to Hebron, where Isaac is living. Spiritual significance: restoration to covenant family, completion of a major journey cycle

<u>Egypt — Preservation and Fulfilment</u>

Late in life, famine drives Jacob and his family into Egypt through Joseph's provision. Jacob blesses his sons there before dying. Spiritual significance: preservation during famine, preparation for the future nation of Israel, and transition into the next stage of redemptive history. His geographical journey mirrored his spiritual journey from Jacob the deceiver to Israel the covenant patriarch.

This principle of geographical importance still matters today, though it must be approached with wisdom and balance. Not every move is divinely orchestrated. Not every city change is prophetic. Not every relocation is a spiritual destiny. However, Scripture does show that God may direct believers geographically for purposes such as assignments, ministry, preparation, protection, relationships, growth, provision, or calling.

Sometimes God calls people out of spiritually destructive environments, away from compromise, into places of preparation, or toward divinely appointed opportunities. The key issue is not wanderlust or emotional impulse. The key issue is obedience.

There are moments in Scripture where people remained where they should have moved. Lot pitched his tent toward Sodom before eventually living within it. Jonah fled from the direction God commanded. Elimelech left Bethlehem during famine and entered Moab, where tragedy followed. Again, this does not mean every hardship results from being in the wrong location. But Scripture does show that disobedient positioning can bring spiritual consequences. Location matters when God has specifically spoken.

Balance is, however, essential. Some people become obsessed with special locations, prophetic lands, or mystical ideas about geography. But the ultimate goal is not a place. The ultimate goal is obedience to God. The Promised Land itself meant nothing without a covenant relationship. A believer can be geographically "correct" yet spiritually rebellious. True alignment begins with surrender, obedience, holiness, and intimacy with God. Geography only matters insofar as it relates to God's will and assignment.

Even Jesus walked in divine timing and positioning. He travelled intentionally to Galilee, Samaria, Jerusalem, wilderness places, mountains of prayer, and ultimately toward the cross. At one point, Scripture says: "He needed to go through Samaria." Why? Because a divine encounter awaited there. The woman at the well was part of a prophetic appointment tied to location and timing. God orchestrates places as well as people.

How can believers discern geographical alignment? Not merely through emotions, restlessness, ambition, or fantasy. But through prayer, wisdom, counsel, Scripture, peace from God, spiritual fruit, and clarity of calling. Sometimes God says, "Go." Sometimes God says, "Stay." Both require obedience. The issue is not movement itself. The issue is alignment with God's purposes.

Jacob's journeys reveal that destiny is often unfolded progressively through movement, testing, encounter, and obedience. Bethel, Haran, Peniel, and the return to the covenant land were not random locations. They were stages in God's shaping of Jacob into Israel. Likewise, believers today must understand that God guides, God positions, God redirects, and God aligns His people according to His purposes. Sometimes, the next stage of spiritual growth, calling, healing, preparation, or breakthrough is connected to obedience in movement.

The question is not merely: "Where do I want to be?" But rather: "Lord, where are You calling me to stand?" For there is great power in being positioned where God desires, walking in alignment with His will, under His direction, and within the unfolding path of His divine purpose.

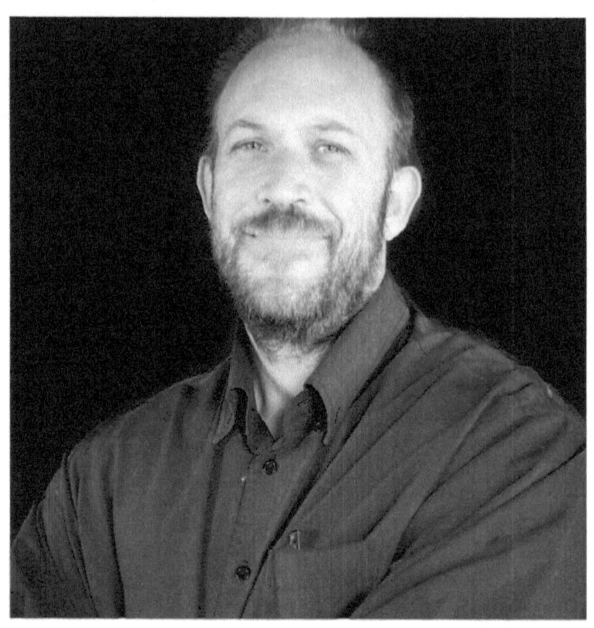

About the Author

Ps Riaan Engelbrecht is the founder of Avishua Ministries, the vice-president of Lighthouse Ministries International and the station manager of Lighthouse Radio. His ministry deals primarily with the prophetic, but he also has a passion to teach the Truth of the Lord Jesus and His Kingdom for only the Truth of the Lord sets us free (John 8:32). He is also a qualified and seasoned journalist.

Read more at https://avishuaministries.wixsite.com/avishua.